The Science of Speaking

Nick & Melissa Enge

Copyright © 2018
by Nick & Melissa Enge

ISBN-10: 0998688509
ISBN-13: 978-0998688503

First Edition

scienceofspeaking.com
twitter.com/scienceofspeak
facebook.com/scienceofspeak

Cioppino Press
Austin, TX

Contents

I	**Introduction**	
1	All the World's a Stage	1
II	**Nervousness**	**7**
2	Nervousness	9
III	**Delivery**	**27**
3	The Body	31
4	The Voice	43
5	The Face	49
IV	**Organization**	**55**
6	The Gift	59
7	The Box	67
8	The Bow	75
V	**Visual Aids**	**87**
9	Pick	93

	10	Optimize	101
	11	Present	123
VI		**Pitching**	**131**
	12	Ask, Audience, and Angle	135
	13	Push and Pull	147
	14	Expertise and Efficiency	159
VII		**Technical Communication**	**169**
	15	Excite	175
	16	Enlighten	183
VIII		**Conclusion**	**195**
	26	The Science of Speaking Cheat Sheet	197
	27	Epilogue	199
		References	201
		Acknowledgments	233
		Index	237

Part I

Introduction

Chapter 1

All the World's a Stage

> And all the men and women merely players;
> They have their exits and their entrances,
> And one man in his time plays many parts.
> — Jacques, *As You Like It*, William Shakespeare[1]

Four hundred years later, we still know this to be true. In a classic study, researchers found that we spend up to 80% of our waking hours engaged in communication—with two-thirds of that in the form of speaking.[2]

Of course, communication is not only common: it's essential. In a recent survey, engineering alumni were asked to list the most important factors contributing to success in their careers. The #2 response was communication skills, second only to work ethic.[3] In fact, the engineers rated communication skills as even more important than their actual engineering skills, which came in at #4. In a similar survey of business management recruiters, communication skills were rated as the #1 attribute they look for in business school graduates, more important than "leadership potential," "strategic thinking," and even "willingness to relocate to the required job location."[4] Regardless of the field you're in, it's clear that communication skills will be key to your success.

A Toolbox, Not a Rulebook

Our goal in writing this book is to help you succeed by showing you how you can communicate more effectively. While our main focus will be on public speaking—which research has identified as being particularly important—many of its lessons can also be applied more broadly.[5]

What differentiates this book from hundreds of others on communication is its focus on the *science* of speaking. Rather than simply presenting our opinions, we have scoured the literature for actual scientific research so we can base our recommendations on evidence, instead of our own personal preferences. Where there are gaps in the research (which we hope will be filled soon![†]), we have drawn our advice from over forty years of experience with both stage performance and technical presenting and nearly a decade of teaching public speaking in academia and industry.

One of the most important lessons we've learned from teaching public speaking is that there isn't only one way to speak well. Every speaker develops their own style of speaking, and that's a good thing: it would be terribly boring if we all spoke exactly the same way. So while this book presents *a* scientific view of speaking, we make no claim that it presents the *only* way to speak well. It's meant to open your mind to new possibilities, not to close it by telling you there's only one way to do things. There isn't only one way: never has been, never will be. The purpose of this book is to give you a toolbox, not a rulebook—to inspire you, not to limit you.

What You Will Learn

As you will learn in Chapter 7, your audience will find it easier to understand and remember your speech when you give them a roadmap of what you're going to say. Applying this advice to *The Science of Speaking*, here is what you can expect to learn:

[†] This book will periodically be updated as the science evolves. In the meantime, you can follow new developments at scienceofspeaking.com/blog.

Part II: Nervousness

Part II (Chapter 2, p. 9) is about **nervousness**. Recognizing that everyone gets nervous about giving speeches, we'll give you some easy, evidence-based techniques you can use to reduce your anxiety and feel more confident about your speaking.

Part III: Delivery

Part III is about delivery, the physical aspect of speaking. In Chapter 3 (p. 31), we'll take a look at **the body**, including stance (how to stand and where to put your hands), gestures (how to move your hands in order to punctuate your speech), movement (essentially, gestures you make with your feet), and attire (which can have a major impact on how your audience views you). In Chapter 4 (p. 43), we'll turn to **the voice** and explore how you can speak even more effectively by paying attention to volume, velocity, and variation. Finally, in Chapter 5 (p. 49), we'll focus on **the face**, including the importance of connecting with your audience through eye contact and conveying emotion through appropriate facial expressions.

Part IV: Organization

Part IV is about organizing your presentation, which can be thought of as a gift in a box with a bow. In Chapter 6 (p. 59), we'll look at **the gift**, which is the main takeaway of your talk. We'll also explore the iceberg model of brainstorming and see how you can distill your ideas into several well-defined points that work together to support your main message. In Chapter 7 (p. 67), we'll move on to **the box**, which is the logical structure and flow of your talk. Finally, in Chapter 8 (p. 75), we'll discuss **the bow**, which includes embellishments to make your talk even more memorable, like an unique, engaging hook and a strong finale.

Part V: Visual Aids

Part V is about visual aids. In Chapter 9 (p. 93), you will learn how to **pick** your visual aids by considering some of the different types you can use, including slides, drawings, props and demos, audio and video, audience involvement, and even dance and imagination. In Chapter 10 (p. 101), you will learn how to **optimize** your visual aids by considering the best ways to convey ideas visually. In Chapter 11 (p. 123), you will learn how to effectively **present** using visuals. By applying the tips in these three chapters, you can ensure that your visual aids will POP!

Part VI: Pitching

Part VI is about pitching, also known as persuasive speaking. In Chapter 12 (p. 135), you will learn how to successfully pitch your ideas by presenting a clear **ask** to a particular **audience** while approaching them with a personalized **angle**. In Chapter 13 (p. 147), you will learn the importance of simultaneously **pushing** your audience away from the status quo while **pulling** them toward your proposed solution. In Chapter 14 (p. 159), you will learn the importance of presenting your **expertise** and pitching with **efficiency**.

Part VII: Technical Communication

Part VII is about technical communication—effectively conveying complex technical ideas to a general audience. In Chapter 15 (p. 175), you will learn how you can **excite** your audience by making your topic relevant, arousing curiosity, showing your enthusiasm, involving the audience, and presenting something they'll always remember. In Chapter 16 (p. 183), you will learn how you can **enlighten** your audience by acting as a tour guide through the foreign land of your topic—translating the language, drawing a map, showing the highlights, and making it an experience.

Although there are good reasons why we have organized these ideas this way—it's also how we organize our classes and workshops—each chapter is relatively self-contained, so if you want to jump around, you're welcome to do so. This book is your resource, so feel free to use it as you see fit!

Part II

Nervousness

Chapter 2

Nervousness

Ten minutes from now, you will be required to give a speech. Standing before a panel of three judges, you will have five minutes to present yourself as the perfect candidate for your dream job. Your speech will also be video-recorded and evaluated by experts trained in verbal and nonverbal communication.

What are you waiting for? The clock is ticking!

If the very thought of giving a speech has you shaking in your boots, don't worry: everyone gets nervous about speaking in public. (And you don't really have to give a speech...yet.)

Even people who perform every day still regularly experience stage fright. Best-selling tenor Andrea Bocelli says, "Stage fright is my worst problem."[1] Billionaire CEO Richard Branson reports, "My shyness and stutter have never disappeared completely. I am still always nervous before going onstage."[2] Even the great Roman orator Cicero suffered from stage fright, writing, "I turn pale at the outset of a speech and quake in every limb and in all my soul."[3]

In fact, this feeling of stage fright is so universal that when psychologists need a way to induce stress in research participants, they simply ask them to give a speech, using a variation of the prompt at the top of this page! In the lab, researchers have found this prompt to be an extremely reliable way of inducing stress, causing participants' heart rates and stress levels to shoot up.[4]

Unfortunately, while this reliably stressed-out response to public speaking is useful for psychologists studying stress, it's not so useful for you as a speaker. Fortunately, these psychologists have published the results of their studies, which reveal a variety of different techniques you can use to alleviate the stress of speaking. In this chapter, we'll show you how you can apply these techniques to feel more confident about your future presentations.

Preparation

"We need to talk."

We've all experienced the complete and utter dread that inevitably results from these four simple words. "What do we need to talk about? How did I screw up? Are we going to break up?"

Similar feelings of dread often bubble up when we are told we need to *give* a talk. "What am I going to talk about? What if I screw up? Are they going to laugh at me?"

The psychology behind these reactions is simple: uncertainty amplifies emotion.[5] The more unknowns there are surrounding your speech, the more nervous you will feel about it. Conversely, the fewer unknowns there are, the less nervous you will feel. In fact, a recent study found a direct (negative) correlation between preparation and nervousness: the more prepared you are, the less nervous you will feel.[6]

Therefore, instead of waiting until the last minute to work on your speech, start early, then practice, practice, practice. In addition to practicing your speech by yourself, practice at least once in front of a test audience, if you can. A recent study found that when you practice in front of an audience, your speech performance improves even more than when you practice alone. In fact, the bigger the rehearsal audience, the greater the improvement.[7] Another study found that receiving positive feedback on your speech from a test audience can also significantly reduce your anxiety.[8]

Social Support

On that note, while speech anxiety can often feel like something we must suffer through alone, research has shown that this isn't quite true: our friends and family can help us through it. In one recent study involving the stress-inducing speaking task at the beginning of this chapter, half of the participants struggled through it alone, while the other half were accompanied by their best friend. The friend was instructed to "offer both instrumental and emotional support" and "be as helpful as possible" while the participant was preparing their speech. While all of the participants were stressed by giving a speech, the participants who were supported by a friend were significantly less stressed.[9]

This suggests that another effective way you can decrease your speech anxiety is to lean on your friends and family for support. Whether it's in the form of listening to your speech and providing feedback, or listening to you talk about your nerves and telling you it's all going to be okay, social support can help you feel significantly less nervous about your speech.[†]

While our friends and family can't always be there when we're feeling stressed, a recent study suggested that we may be able to recreate at least some of their power ourselves. When participants who were assigned to complete a new exercise regimen told themselves "you can do it," they reported more positive attitudes toward exercising and expressed greater intentions to exercise in the coming week than those who told themselves "I can do it." As for why this might be, the researchers speculated that "second-person self-talk may have this beneficial effect because it cues memories of receiving support and encouragement from others."[11]

[†] Other studies have shown that receiving physical support—for example, by holding hands or getting a shoulder massage—can also significantly reduce your speaking anxiety.[10]

Visualization

How nervous you feel before a speech is largely a result of how you view yourself and the task of speaking. When people with high speaking anxiety are asked to draw pictures of themselves speaking, they produce more negative and less vivid images than people with lower anxiety do.[12] They also experience more negative thoughts and fewer positive thoughts before, during, and after speaking.[13] On the other hand, speakers who maintain a positive attitude toward speaking report less anxiety.[14]

This suggests that if anxious speakers can learn to generate images of themselves that are more positive and more vivid, they may begin to feel less nervous. In fact, this is exactly what studies have found: visualizing yourself giving a successful speech can significantly reduce your speaking anxiety.[15]

You can follow a script (guided visualization[†]) or invent your own—both techniques can be effective.[16] Visualization is also a technique that can be used at any time: it is effective regardless of whether it is practiced a day, or even a week, before your speech.[17] In addition, the effects of visualization are long-lived: in one study, speakers who practiced visualization not only reported an immediate reduction in speaking anxiety but also less anxiety when tested again four and eight months later.[18]

Beyond reducing speaking anxiety, visualization can also improve speech performance. In one study, students who had visualized giving a successful speech displayed less rigidity and inhibition during their actual speech. As a result, they were rated by the audience as significantly more natural and less nervous.[19]

Relaxation

Before Nick started teaching, he performed in many plays and musicals. Shortly before every performance, he would put on his

---

[†] If you're interested in trying guided visualization, you can find a script at scienceofspeaking.com/visualization.

headphones and listen to the same song, "Wonder" by Butterfly Jones, from the soundtrack of one of his favorite shows. Listening to this song never failed to put him in a state of deep relaxation, soothing the stage fright that always comes with performing.

Around the same time, two Australian psychologists were working on a similar idea, using music to treat speaking anxiety. In their study, students were asked to prepare an impromptu speech about a technical topic related to their field of study and were told they would be video-taped and evaluated by a panel of judges.

In the control group, students were simply left to prepare their speeches. Unsurprisingly, these students were stressed: their heart rate, blood pressure, and anxiety levels shot up. In the treatment group, students were also left to prepare their speeches, but this time, Pachelbel's *Canon in D Major* was playing on repeat. Amazingly, despite receiving the same stressful assignment, students in this group experienced little to no increase in heart rate, blood pressure, and anxiety. For many students, there was actually a decrease in these measures.[20] Apparently, when relaxing music is added, preparing a technical speech can be a stress reliever!

Psychologists have also investigated a variety of other techniques for relaxing nervous speakers, including progressive tensing and relaxing of muscles,[21] heart rate biofeedback,[22] and self-administered hand massage,[23] all of which have shown promise. And a recent study confirmed what we all already knew: watching cat videos can help us relax.[24] Whatever method works best for you, finding a way to relax before your speech can make you feel significantly less nervous about it.

Meditation

The power of breath to foster relaxation is one of the timeless treasures of human wisdom, known and practiced for thousands of years. By closing your eyes and focusing on your breath, you can find a greater sense of peace and relaxation.[25]

A particularly useful form of this practice is Martin Boroson's "one-moment meditation," which he describes in his book of the same name.[26] While many meditation practices begin with a short session (say, 5 minutes) with the goal of working your way up to longer and longer sessions, one-moment meditation flips this idea on its head. Instead, you start with 1 minute, then work your way *down* to shorter and shorter sessions. In the end, the goal is to find the same sense of peace in one moment as you might find in a longer session of meditation.

To practice one-moment meditation, find a comfortable position, set a timer for one minute, then close your eyes and focus on your breathing. Whenever you find your mind wandering, simply guide it back to your breath. Even after just one minute of breathing, it's possible to feel significantly more relaxed.

With practice, you can learn to find this same sense of peace in a single breath—with your eyes open.[†] You can use this idea of a single, centering breath to great effect before, and even during, your speech. Take a breath right before you go onstage and another right before you start speaking. Then take one again whenever you pause or whenever you are feeling particularly stressed. As simple as this practice is, it can be surprisingly effective!

Power Posing

What if we told you there was a simple technique that could decrease your speaking anxiety with even less effort than breathing? Here it is: shortly before you go on stage, adopt an open and expansive posture, what Harvard psychologist Amy Cuddy calls a "power pose." Popular power poses include the "Wonder Woman," standing tall with your hands on your hips, or the "casual executive," sitting with your feet up on the table and your hands clasped behind your head. As silly as this may seem, studies have shown that power posing can actually make you feel more powerful.[‡]

[†] Keep in mind that this practice doesn't need to be perfect to be useful, it just needs to make you feel a little better than you did before!

[‡] If you don't have an opportunity to physically power pose, studies have found that thinking about a time you felt powerful can have a similar effect.[27]

Of course, we're not suggesting you adopt a full-on Wonder Woman stance *while* giving your speech (as we'll see in the next chapter, that has negative effects). But before your speech, power posing can be an easy way to pump yourself up in private.[†]

Skills Training

Although many believe public speaking ability is a natural gift that you either possess from birth or not, it's actually a skill that can be honed by anyone.[31] Before going on to give what many consider to be the greatest speech of the 20th century, Martin Luther King, Jr. received a "C" in Public Speaking at Crozer Theological Seminary![32]

By picking up this book, you have already taken a giant leap forward in reducing your speaking anxiety. In addition to teaching you a variety of anxiety-reducing techniques, later chapters of this book will teach you how to hone your public speaking skills. Studies have shown that after receiving training in speech delivery and organization, people experience significantly less speaking anxiety.[33] In addition, when they go on to give a speech in front of an audience, they are perceived as less nervous thanks to their improved speaking techniques.[34]

Taking a public speaking class is also a great way to conquer your fears. Although it can initially be scary for an anxious speaker, studies have shown that graduates of a public speaking class are significantly more confident about their speaking abilities.[35] Furthermore, simply having a greater number of speeches under your

---

[†] As you may have heard, power posing is currently the subject of controversy after the validity of the original study was called into question. In addition to the fact that a larger study failed to replicate the claim that power posing increases testosterone and decreases cortisol, one of the authors of the original study has disowned it, citing flawed methodology.[28] As a result, we've taken a conservative approach to power posing, presenting only the finding that has been independently replicated, i.e., that it can make you feel more powerful. (And as Amy Cuddy notes in her response to the controversy, this result has been confirmed many times.[29]) The reason we're including a section about power posing at all is that many of our students have told us it helps them. And when dealing with public speaking anxiety, anything that helps is truly appreciated![30]

belt can help reduce your anxiety, so whenever you are offered the chance to speak, take it![†]

Myth-Busting

For particularly severe cases of speaking anxiety, psychologists employ a technique they call "rational emotive therapy," which basically boils down to a kind of myth-busting.[37] Psychologists identify the irrational thoughts at the root of a speaker's anxiety and work with the speaker to replace these thoughts with more rational ones. While not all anxious speakers require rational emotive therapy, it's still useful to address some of the mistaken beliefs at the root of speaking anxiety. Below, you'll find some of the most pervasive myths we've encountered and responses we've found helpful for conquering them.

Myth #1: Nervousness is a bad thing

"I don't want to feel nervous! I shouldn't feel nervous! Why does this always happen to me?!" One of the worst things about stage fright is how easily it can spiral out of control. Rather than accepting that nervousness is natural—which it is—we freak out about the fact that we're nervous, which only makes it worse.

As an actor who experienced quite a bit of stage fright, Nick was so interested in this process that he wrote his senior thesis in high school about it. His conclusion? An adaptation of Roosevelt's "the only thing we have to fear is fear itself."[38] The biggest problem is not that we're nervous, it's that we believe being nervous is a bad thing. It doesn't have to be this way!

In order to positively reframe your nervousness, pretend you have a speech to give, but the audience is a group of rocks rather than people. Would you be nervous for this speech? Probably not—the rocks probably don't care much about what you have to say—not to mention they probably don't even have ears to hear it!

[†] What have you got to lose? Studies have shown that in the long term, you're more likely to regret things you didn't do than things you did![36]

In any case, they certainly aren't going to judge your performance! Overall, nothing is really at stake here.

So how is this different from reality? Your audience. Unlike rocks, people have opinions, and naturally, you want people to like you. You feel nervous because you care about the audience's reaction to your speech. Which means nervousness is actually a good thing! If you weren't nervous (like in the rocks scenario), it might be an indication that you don't really care about the presentation.

Gregg Allman of The Allman Brothers Band notes that stage fright is important in this way because it helps us avoid the apathy of overconfidence. "If I went out there thinkin', 'Eh, we'll go slaughter 'em,'" he says, "I'm positive something would go seriously wrong."[39] Caring deeply about our performance gives us the motivation to do our best. Fleetwood Mac's Stevie Nicks takes this idea even further, musing, "If you have stage fright, it never goes away. But then I wonder: is the key to that magical performance because of the fear?"[40]

While it may be hard to believe, it's possible, like Allman and Nicks, to view nervousness as a good thing. Speech coach Elayne Snyder calls this "positive nervousness," defining it as "a zesty, enthusiastic, lively feeling with a slight edge to it … It's still nervousness, but it feels different. You're no longer victimized by it; instead, you're vitalized by it."[41] Similarly, you can reconceptualize stage fright as "stage excitement," or "stage enthusiasm," a feeling of alertness and readiness to perform.[42]

A recent study at Harvard Business School suggested that this method of dealing with speaking anxiety may be even more beneficial than strategies designed to help you calm down. Before giving a speech, participants were asked to say either "I am calm" or "I am excited." Speakers who told themselves they were excited were rated as significantly more confident, more competent, and more persuasive by their audiences than speakers who told themselves they were calm. While they didn't feel any less nervous, "excited" speakers performed better.[43]

In addition, simply believing nervousness is a good thing can, by itself, improve your performance. In another Harvard study, randomly selected students taking a Graduate Record Examination (GRE) practice test were told not to worry if they felt anxious while taking the test because there is research that suggests people who feel anxious during a test might actually perform better.

Students who had been given this pep-talk performed significantly better on the test compared to students who hadn't, even after accounting for SAT scores, GPA, prior coursework, and time spent studying. Several months later, these students also performed significantly better on the actual GRE![44] So while it often feels like we'd be better off without our nerves, in actuality, it can pay to embrace them.

Myth #2: It needs to be perfect

Every speech you give is a work in progress. No matter how much you practice, nothing is ever going to be perfectly the way you want it to be. And that's okay! [Insert pause for our Stanford students to gasp.] It's okay, we've been there too: we know how it feels to be a perfectionist.[†] But once you've given as many presentation as we have, you realize that no presentation is ever going to be perfect, and that's fine. As Dale Carnegie once put it, "There are always three speeches for every one you actually gave. The one you practiced, the one you gave, and the one you wish you gave."[45]

[†] This is why only two of the four books Nick has written have ever been seen by anyone else! Maybe someday he'll take his own advice and publish the rest.

As you give more talks, you will also come to realize that the audience's perception of your speech is usually much different—and often much better—than your own. As they only see the speech you gave, they have no idea that it's not what you hoped for. They simply appreciate that they got to hear it.

Myth #3: They're out to get you

Nervous speakers often believe the audience is out to get them, looking for every chance to criticize them. But as we saw in the last myth, this simply isn't true: your audience is often much less critical of you than you are of yourself.

Take a moment and ask yourself why the audience showed up to your talk. Most likely, they showed up because they were interested in your presentation. They took time out of their busy lives to learn something from you. While this may initially sound daunting, it's far less scary than thinking they showed up to critique you! And to be honest, an interested audience isn't something to fear. Instead, think of it this way: "A lot of people showed up today. I must have done a good job advertising my talk! Now it's time to speak about something I love with an audience that feels the same way!" Any reframing you can do along these lines will not only ease your anxiety—it will also be much closer to reality.

In addition, during any talk, if you look out at the audience, you'll always find a few people who seem particularly interested in what you're saying—nodding along, smiling, or giving other positive signals. Whenever you're feeling nervous, make eye contact with one of them for a few seconds. Their friendly demeanor and attentiveness will help assure you that you're doing alright and counteract any frazzled feelings you may have.†

Finally, recognize that while facial expressions are often a good indicator of a person's feelings, they are by no means perfect. Sometimes you will find that the audience member with the dourest face

---

† It can also be fun to "pay it forward" in this way, choosing to be this engaged audience member for other speakers.[46]

during your presentation will be the first person to come up to you afterwards and gush about how much they enjoyed it.[†]

Myth #4: They can see you sweat

On the first day of the public speaking classes at Stanford, after our students gave their first impromptu speech, we always asked them how they felt, and pretty much everyone admitted they were terrified. But then we asked their peers how the speaker looked, and in most cases, they didn't see any signs of nervousness at all.

This difference in perception can be attributed to a psychological bias called the "spotlight effect," which causes us to believe that other people are paying more attention to us than they actually are. For example, in a recent study, participants were asked to wear a potentially embarrassing t-shirt, then estimate how many of their classmates had noticed it. While fewer than 25% of their classmates actually noticed, the participants believed that almost 50% had. In another experiment, less than 10% of their classmates noticed their attire, while again, participants believed that nearly 50% had! In an experiment in which participants were asked how their classmates would rate their performance in a discussion, participants believed that their performance stood out much more than it actually did (in both a positive and negative direction).[48]

Obviously, the spotlight effect can be a major contributor to speech anxiety. And in fact, a variety of studies have confirmed that the more self-focused we are, the more anxiety (and other negative emotions) we feel.[49] So what can we do to overcome it?

First, simply realize that the spotlight effect exists, and this means you are going to be much more critical of yourself than your audience will be. Don't worry so much about what they think of you because they're not thinking about you as much as you think. (After all, they mostly have their own spotlights on themselves.)

[†] Some people, including Nick, are afflicted with "resting bitch face," which means their neutral expression shows physical markers of contempt, even when they're not feeling any contempt.[47] So if he looks like he has contempt for your speech, don't worry: it's far more likely he's just concentrating.

An even better way to overcome the spotlight effect is to consciously shift the spotlight off of yourself and onto something else—for example, to focus on why you're giving the speech or what you want the audience to take away from it. As the research on self-focus has shown, when you shift the heat of spotlight off yourself, you'll begin to feel much better.

Finally, recognize that even if all of the audience's spotlights were actually on you, most signs of nervousness are actually invisible. Although it may be hard to believe, you have already have ample anecdotal evidence to this effect. Think back on a recent presentation you attended. Did the speaker appear nervous to you? Probably not. But as we've established time and again throughout this chapter, practically every speaker is nervous. So if they didn't look nervous, you probably don't either!

Although it's easy to dismiss as a worn cliché, "fake it 'till you make it" is actually a powerful sentiment, and it's absolutely true in the context of speaking: if you fake confidence, your audience will see you as confident and respond as such. This response in turn will help you gain real confidence. It's a win-win cycle! If you're wondering how to fake confidence, the delivery techniques in the next chapter will help.

Myth #5: Nervousness is constant

While it's true that nervousness never goes away, this is a statement that applies to a lifetime. On shorter time scales, studies have shown that anxiety levels actually vary quite a lot, with different levels of nervousness occurring at different stages in the speech-making process. This led us to wonder what a chart of nervousness over time would look like. In other words, can we plot a "nerve curve"? By combining the data from several recent studies we can! In each of these studies, researchers measured the anxiety levels at different stages in the speaking process.[50] Here's what it looks like when we plot the data chronologically:

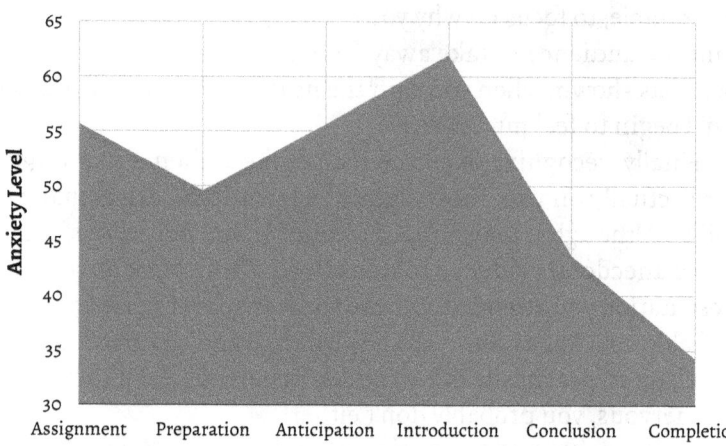

The Nerve Curve

Nervousness begins when you find out that you need to give a speech (labeled "Assignment" above). From there, it decreases slightly as you prepare your speech ("Preparation"). But as the speech approaches, nervousness increases again ("Anticipation"), up to the moment when you begin your speech, when nervousness is at an all-time high ("Introduction").

As you continue speaking, however, nervousness begins to fade, steadily decreasing from the beginning of your speech to the end ("Conclusion"). After your speech is finally over, nervousness falls to an all-time low ("Completion").

There are several lessons we can take from this data. First, the beginning of your speech is the worst part—once you get past that, it's all downhill from there. This suggests that one good way of managing your nerves is to really focus on preparing your introduction so you can totally nail your opening lines. Once you get through this particularly well-prepared portion of your speech, you'll already be feeling much better.

In addition, the closer to the beginning of your speech you get, the more nervous you are going to feel, so the closer to the beginning of your speech you can practice the techniques you learned in this chapter, the better.

Finally, although it usually doesn't feel this way to the speaker—who often feels like they're the only person in the world who gets nervous—nervousness really is a universal phenomenon, well-defined enough that we can plot a curve of it! While this may not make your nervousness go away entirely, perhaps it will help a little bit to know we're all in this together.

Ritual

In a recent study, participants were asked to engage in an anxiety-inducing task: singing a song in front of a stranger. Before singing the song, some participants were asked to conduct a ritual: they drew a picture of their feelings, sprinkled salt on it, and counted to five before crumpling up the paper and throwing it in the trash.

As silly as this ritual sounds, the participants who engaged in it reported significantly less anxiety about singing and had lower heart rates than those who didn't! And that's not all: the ritual made them perform better too!

Interestingly, it didn't matter what the ritual was—an alternative ritual that involved writing down a sequence of numbers was also effective. What did matter, however, was that is was called a "ritual." When the ritual was called what it really was—"a few random behaviors"—the benefit disappeared completely.

As the authors of the study concluded, "although some may dismiss rituals as irrational, those who enact rituals may well outperform the skeptics who forgo them." So whether it's salting your feelings, writing down numbers, or maybe even a practice that has additional anxiety-reducing effects (like those we've described in detail above), engaging in a ritual before your speech (and explicitly identifying it as such!) can be another effective method for overcoming your nerves.[51]

The Button

Throughout this chapter, we've given you a wide variety of techniques for managing nervousness. And when you put them into practice, each of these techniques can be quite effective. But what if, in addition to these techniques being effective, simply knowing they exist also had an effect?

While we know this may sound a bit out there, in *Option B: Facing Adversity, Building Resilience, and Finding Joy*, Sheryl Sandberg and Adam Grant cite the results of several studies to this effect:

> In classic experiments on stress, people performed tasks that required concentration, like solving puzzles, while being blasted at random intervals with uncomfortably loud sounds. They started sweating and their heart rates and blood pressure climbed. ... Searching for a way to reduce anxiety, researchers gave some of the participants an escape. If the noise became too unpleasant, they could press a button and make it stop. Sure enough, the button allowed them to stay calmer, make fewer mistakes, and show less irritation. That's not surprising. But here's what is: none of the participants actually pressed the button. Stopping the noise didn't make the difference ...knowing they could stop the noise did. The button gave them a sense of control and allowed them to endure the stress.[52]

Based on our own experience, and that of our students, it's clear that having a toolbox of strategies for nervousness can—even without using them—help to mitigate nervousness in a similar way. In other words, knowing that you have the power to control your nerves can, by itself, go a long way toward soothing them.[53]

Conclusion

Nervousness is a natural part of public speaking, and every speaker must find ways to overcome it. Fortunately, research has identified many effective ways to do this, including:

- **Preparation**: Reduce uncertainty as much as you can by giving yourself ample time to practice.

- **Social Support**: Don't be afraid to lean on friends and family for support in the time leading up to your presentation.

- **Visualization**: Visualize yourself giving a successful speech with as many positive, vivid details as you can.

- **Relaxation**: Find ways to relax before your speech, including listening to your favorite music.

- **Meditation**: Practice "one-moment meditation" to find peace and relaxation in a single breath. Do this before you speak and whenever you need to regain your center.

- **Power Posing**: Adopt an open and expansive posture before your speech (in private) in order to feel more powerful.

- **Skills Training**: Read this book. Take a class. Improving your public speaking skills and putting them into practice can greatly reduce your anxiety over time.

- **Myth-Busting**: Realize that nervousness is actually be a good thing. Remember that your speech doesn't need to be perfect, the audience wants you to succeed, you can look confident even when you don't feel it, and nervousness varies as a function of time.

- **Ritual**: Whatever you choose to do as a pre-presentation warm-up, you can increase its effects by calling it a "ritual."

- **The Button**: Recognize that you now have many techniques for fighting nervousness and that even without doing anything, this knowledge can help you.

Part III

Delivery

Introduction

In the next three chapters, we'll explore some easy ways you can improve your speaking by paying attention to your physical, vocal, and emotional delivery as they are conveyed by your body, voice, and face.

But first, let's check in and see how you're doing. To do so, you'll need a video of yourself speaking. If you have a video of a recent presentation, great! If not, it's easy to make one right now: simply give a short impromptu speech and record yourself. If you need a topic, try this: "If you had a superpower, what would it be, and how would you use it?"

Take a moment to do this now.

Now that you have a video of yourself speaking, it's time to watch it. [Insert pause for everyone to gasp.] Yes, we know it's awkward and uncomfortable. Even we don't enjoy watching ourselves speak. But it's a great way to see how you're doing and what you'd like to improve next time.[†] We'll watch the video several times, each time focusing on different aspects of your delivery.

The first time through, just watch the video as you'd watch any presentation, taking in the whole picture. Is there anything that stands out to you as something you did well or something you'd like to change? Write it down, so you can refer to it later.

Now let's watch the video again, but this time, *without the sound*. This will allow you to focus on your physical and emotional

---

[†] Interestingly, although it can be quite uncomfortable in the moment, several studies have found that watching videos of yourself is actually another effective way to reduce your speaking anxiety![1]

delivery—your stance, gestures, movement, eye contact, facial expressions, and attire—without being distracted by what you're saying. Again, write down what you did well and anything you'd like to change.

Let's watch the video one last time. This time, turn the sound back on, but *close your eyes* so you can focus entirely on your verbal delivery—the quality of your voice and the words you're saying. What did you like, and what might you change?

Now that you have a baseline for your delivery, let's learn a bit more about how you can improve each aspect and make your future speeches even better!

Chapter 3

The Body

Picture this: the speaker gets ready to start their presentation, but even before they begin speaking, their hands start shaking. To calm them, the speaker tries to flatten them against their sides, but this only serves to rustle the keys in their pocket. As if that weren't bad enough, the speaker begins to shuffle their feet, then starts kicking the air with one foot and then the other.

While it may be hard to believe, this was how the nervous energy of a Stanford football player presented itself during his first speech in our public speaking class. Understandably, the audience was distracted by these physical tics, and as a result, they didn't remember much of his speech. As the quarter progressed, however, this student got better and better at controlling his nerves and projecting a calm and confident presence. In his final speech, a story about growing up in the country, he captivated everyone, with one student reporting that they felt like they were "transported to his living room, and we were all chatting by a warm fire."

How did he do this? How can *you* do this? By focusing on your physical delivery—your stance, gestures, movement, and attire.

Stance

Standing still is hard for many people, and constantly shifting weight from one foot to the other is one of the most common mistakes novice speakers make. Their nervous energy has to go somewhere, so these speakers sway back and forth, like palm trees in the breeze. Unfortunately, this communicates their nervousness to the audience. But with a little practice, it's easy to fix.

While speaking, you want to maintain a stance that is solid and still, with your feet about shoulder width apart. Remember to keep your knees relaxed though, as locking your knees can inhibit blood flow, which, combined with the emotional stress of speaking, can lead to fainting![1]

In addition, you want your stance to appear self-confident. While maintaining a full-on power pose while speaking would look a little ridiculous, the same basic principles apply. In addition to making you look and feel more confident, studies have shown that speaking with an open body position will make your audience more likely to agree with you.[2]

Now we get to the fun question: "What should I do with my hands?" It's one of the most common questions we get as presentation coaches, and one that has many different answers, depending on whom you ask. Given the importance of this question, and the surprising lack of research on it, in 2016 we conducted an informal survey at Stanford to gather some preliminary data. On the first day of class, before teaching anything, we asked 98 incoming public speaking students to choose words to describe five of the most common resting hand positions: Crossed Arms, Fig Leaf, Hands on Hips, Hands at Sides, and Peace Offering, which were illustrated simultaneously by a male and female model. Words that could be used to describe the positions were: aggressive, defensive, nervous, relaxed, friendly, and confident.

The results of this survey are presented below. As you might expect, Crossed Arms and Fig Leaf were rated the most negatively, with Crossed Arms coming off as aggressive and defensive and Fig Leaf being perceived as defensive and nervous. Hands on Hips split the middle, simultaneously projecting confidence but also coming off as the most aggressive.

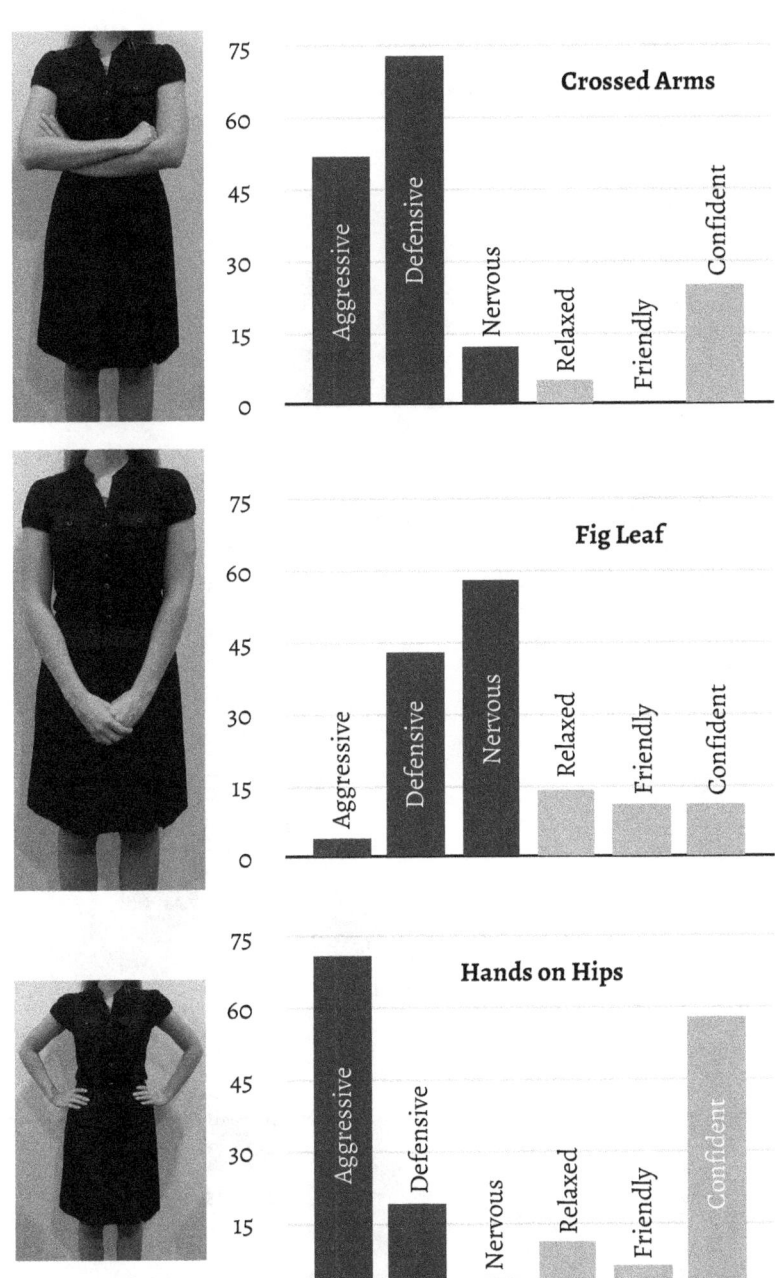

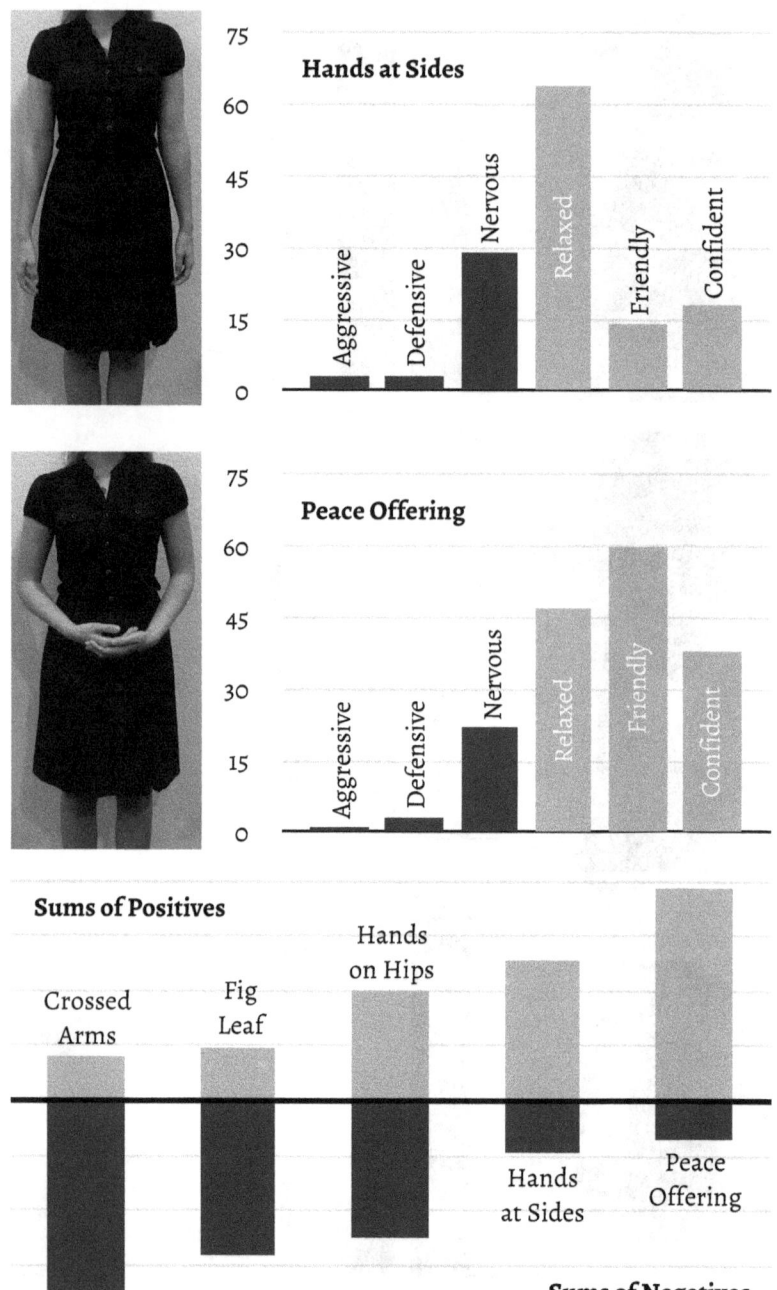

Hands at Sides and Peace Offering, however, both performed well, with Hands at Sides appearing the most relaxed and Peace Offering providing a good mix of relaxed, friendly, and confident.

In the end, this data shows that what you should do with your hands depends on what you want to project. If you want to look relaxed, go for Hands at Sides. If you want friendly and confident, use the Peace Offering. If the task at hand calls for aggressive and confident, by all means, go for Hands on Hips.[†]

Regardless of what position you choose to speak from, it's important to remember not to fidget. With Hands at Sides, presenters often play with their clothing, while in the Peace Offering, they often wring their hands. Unsurprisingly, studies have shown that these nervous tics result in lower ratings of speaker effectiveness.[3] Wherever you choose to put your hands, keep them still until you're ready to gesture.

Gestures

Gestures are essential to human communication. Without any formal training, people of all ages and cultures spontaneously gesture when they speak.[4] Babies begin gesturing before they can talk, and even people who are born blind and have never seen a gesture spontaneously move their hands when they speak.[5]

In addition to being an inevitable part of any speech, gesturing while speaking has many benefits, both for you and your audience. For you as a speaker, studies have found that speaking with gestures places less demand on working memory than speaking without gestures, meaning that gesturing can actually help you remember what you want to say during your speech![6]

In addition to helping you remember what you want to say, gestures can also help your audience remember what you said. Research has shown that gesturing while speaking increases your audience's comprehension of your speech and results in higher

---

[†] While probably not appropriate for any full speech, Hands on Hips and Crossed Arms can be effective gestures within a speech!

rates of learning.[7] Gestures do this by capturing and maintaining your listeners' attention, providing additional support for your verbal message, and grounding your words in the physical world.[8]

In one particularly dramatic demonstration of the power of gestures, researchers found that simply accompanying a piece of information with a descriptive gesture made it more than five times as likely to be remembered a week later![9]

Beyond facilitating your audience's understanding and memory, gestures can also make you a more dynamic and popular speaker. On TED.com, home of videos from the popular TED conferences, the popularity of a talk is correlated with the number of gestures it contains, with the most popular talks containing almost twice as many gestures as less popular talks.[†]

In the same study, ratings of charisma, credibility, and intelligence were found to be the same regardless of whether or not the speakers were on mute.[11] Of course, this doesn't mean that the words you say don't matter—conveying a particular verbal message is the whole reason you're giving a speech—but it does suggest that nonverbals often matter far more than we think.[‡]

Of course, this isn't to say that you can simply flail your arms around and automatically reap the benefits of gesturing. It's not just *that* you gesture, but also *how* you gesture, that matters. In particular, your gestures should always be visible and purposeful.

For example, many well-intentioned speakers illustrate a list by counting on their fingers, but this is often difficult for the audience to see, especially in a big room. Instead, ensure that everyone in your audience can see by moving your whole arm from right to left, or top to bottom, instead of just your fingers or hand. Imagine you have a personal bubble surrounding you: your gestures should be big enough to break out of this bubble.

[†] Another study found that gesturing is also correlated with ratings of social skill and hireability in interviews![10]

[‡] A classic example of this is the first televised U.S. presidential debate, between Vice President Richard Nixon and Senator John F. Kennedy in September 1960. Americans who listened to the debate on the radio thought Nixon was the clear winner. But Americans who watched the debate saw Kennedy as the clear winner. Four days after winning the election by a narrow margin, Kennedy reported, "It was the TV more than anything else that turned the tide."[12]

In addition, make sure your gestures actually serve a purpose. Small, ambiguous gestures down by your sides ("penguin gestures") or in front of your torso ("T-rex arms") add nothing to your speech: they only make you look fidgety and nervous.

While there are nearly an infinite number of gestures you can use, it's helpful to consider three of their most common functions. For example, gestures can be used to:

- **Direct**: One of the most common kinds of gestures is that which directs the audience's attention. This can either be physical—pointing to a particular data point on a graph—or metaphorical—emphasizing something you're saying. As we'll see a bit later, movement attracts attention, so gestures can be an effective way of highlighting key points.

- **Demonstrate**: Another useful kind of gesture is that which demonstrates something by acting it out with your hands. For example, try acting out "talking on the phone" or "drinking a cup of tea." In improv, we call this using "space objects."

- **Draw**: In addition to using your hands to demonstrate, you can also simply use them to draw a picture in space. For example, you could use your hands to illustrate relationships or processes by drawing them out in front of the audience. (You might even draw out the outline of your speech by physically laying out your points in space.)

When visually describing things in front of the audience, you want to make sure that it makes sense from their perspective. For example, when illustrating a chronological sequence, many novice speakers gesture from their left to their right, which initially makes sense, because that's the way they read. To the audience, however, this appears backwards:

.this like is right your to left your from Gesturing

To clarify things from the audience's perspective, be sure to gesture the way they read, i.e., from your right to your left.[†]

[†] Of course, if you're speaking to an audience that is used to reading right to left, as is the case in Arabic, you can adjust this advice accordingly.

In addition, be aware that gestures that seem universal to American speakers—a thumbs up, an OK sign, or two raised fingers to indicate the number two—don't always have the same meaning around the world. In many places, a thumbs up means "up yours." In others, an OK sign refers to one or more delicate orifices. In the British Commonwealth, holding up your first two fingers with the back of your hand facing the audience is similar to giving your listeners the finger.[13] Therefore, when presenting in a foreign country, it's a good idea to study up on the local gestures to avoid unintentionally insulting your audience.† Roger Axtell's *Gestures: The Do's and Taboos of Body Language Around the World* and Romana Lefevre's *Rude Hand Gestures of the World* are great resources.

Movement

Movement is like a gesture you perform with your feet. This means everything you've learned about gestures also applies to movement, with one exception: while every speech should incorporate gestures, not every speech requires movement.

Sometimes movement, or the lack thereof, is defined by the situation: Stanford tour guides are required to walk (backward!) during their presentations while commencement speakers are usually expected to stand behind the podium the entire time. Aside from these special circumstances, the best choice will be the one that makes you feel the most comfortable, given the situation.

While you don't need to move during your speech, there can be benefits to doing so. Similar to gestures, movement has been shown to facilitate speech recall: actors who move while reciting their lines actually remember their lines better than those who do not move.‡ In addition, movement, like gestures, can be a

---

† When we traveled to Australia for our honeymoon, Nick preemptively asked Melissa to request all of our tables when dining out because he knows he has a nasty habit of unintentionally flipping restaurant hosts the British bird when he raises two fingers and says "For two, please."

‡ Interestingly, movement facilitates speech encoding as well: actors also remember their lines better when they moved while learning their lines, which suggests you should also move while practicing your speech.[14]

useful tool for illustrating your points as well as capturing and maintaining your audience's attention.

In order to avoid predators and notice prey, the human eye evolved to track movement, and as a speaker, you can take advantage of this instinct. If you notice your audience zoning out, you can often regain their attention simply by moving.[15] You can also use movement to capture your audience's attention before presenting key points.

Of course, this trick only works when used occasionally. If you pace back and forth for your entire speech, hoping to never lose your audience's attention, your audience will be just as likely to zone out as if you had never moved at all. Your movement will be more impactful if you mix moments of movement with moments of stillness. The key is contrast: your audience pays greater attention to things that change.[16]

Attire

While your stance, gestures, and movement are essential aspects of your delivery to consider *while* giving your speech, there is another important aspect of delivery to consider *before* you leave home: your attire.

For better or worse, what you wear while giving a speech can have a profound impact on how your audience perceives you and your message. For example, presenters dressed in business formal attire are rated as more professional, more confident, more competent, and more credible than presenters dressed in casual attire, and their presentations are perceived to be of higher quality.[17] In addition, people who see their presentations actually learn more![18] If persuasion is your goal, formal attire can boost your authority and inspire more people to follow you. In one study, people were more than three times as likely to follow a man who walked across the street against a red light when he was wearing a business suit than when he was wearing casual clothing.[19]

Before you go out and buy a closet full of formalwear, however, note that there are trade-offs to formality. While presenters who wear formal attire are viewed as more credible, more intelligent, more competent, more organized, more knowledgeable, better prepared, and more respectable, presenters who wear less formal attire are viewed as more likable, more approachable, friendlier, more flexible, more sympathetic, more fair, more enthusiastic, more understanding, and more relatable.[20]

Of course, the best choice of attire is highly dependent on your audience. Whoever they are (and whatever their expectations), you should carefully adapt your attire to them. In fact, research has shown that people are more likely to help those who are wearing attire similar to their own and less likely to help people wearing dissimilar attire.[21] While many public speaking guides advise that you should always be the best dressed person in the room, this research suggests that a better rule of thumb is to be *among* the best dressed people in the room.

Studies have also shown that you can make your presentation more persuasive by wearing attire that is consistent with your message. For example, one study found that people were significantly more likely to recall a health message when it was presented by someone wearing a stethoscope.[22] In another study, people were twice as likely to pick up a piece of litter when the person asking them to do so was dressed as a security guard.[23]

While it's important to consider the effect your attire will have on your listeners, it's also important to consider the effect it has on you.[†] In one study, participants wore a doctor's lab coat, a piece of clothing associated with attentiveness. Not only did this increase third-party perceptions of attentiveness, but it also led the wearer to act more attentively.[25] Similarly, formal attire can make the wearer feel more powerful and can even affect their thought process, causing them to think more abstractly.[26]

In the end, what should you wear? As always, it depends on your audience, and on you. But as a general rule, wear something your audience can both respect and relate to while making you feel like you're at the top of your game.

[†] For a first-person account of these principles, see Tom Chiarella's piece in *Esquire* entitled "What Happened When I Dressed Like A Priest."[24]

Before your next speech, try on several different outfits, and see which one makes you feel the best. If nothing inspires you, maybe it's time to do a little shopping to find the perfect outfit for this particular occasion. As Paolo Nutini suggests, sometimes all it takes is putting some new shoes on to make everything feel right.[27] And there's even research to suggest he's right![28]

Chapter 4

The Voice

So, today, I'm like gonna like tell a story about like what it was like like growing up in like London. Like…

Believe it or not, this is how one of our students began their narrative speech in our class. Needless to say, it wasn't a very effective speech. Whereas our previous student's nervous energy manifested in his body, this student's nerves came through in their voice. Fortunately, by learning a few tips about voice, our student's future speeches were much improved. It's as easy as remembering the three Vs of voice: volume, velocity, and variation.

Volume

One day, after teaching three classes in a row, Nick came home to have dinner with Melissa. When she asked him how his day was, he proceeded to tell her in the same voice he had been using to project to the back of the classroom all day. Needless to say, she kindly informed him that she was right across the table and he didn't need to use his public speaking voice anymore.

As this story illustrates, there's a difference between the voice we use at the dinner table and the voice we use while speaking to a large room. In both cases, it's important to adapt our voice so that everyone can hear us at a comfortable volume, rather than straining to hear, or covering their ears. Generally speaking, the voice you use when giving a presentation will be louder than usual, which has the benefit of making you sound more confident.[1]

Velocity

In addition to adjusting the volume of your voice, you should also pay close attention to its velocity. Speaking too quickly canmakeithardforpeopletounderstandwhatyou'resaying while speaking too slowly can . . . make . . . it . . . seem . . . like . . . you . . . don't . . . know . . . what . . . to . . . say . . . next.

Speaking Rate

What exactly is a natural velocity for speaking? A wide variety of studies have been conducted to determine listeners' preferences for speaking rate, finding optimal rates ranging from 163 to 225 words per minute (wpm).[†] Slower rates (around 100 wpm), and faster rates (around 300 wpm), are much less preferred.[2]

While many speakers (including Nick) have been perpetually told they need to slow down, these studies suggest that the optimal speech rate is actually somewhat brisk. In addition, many other studies have found benefits to speaking quickly. In one study, listener ratings of a speaker's competence increased linearly with speech rate: the faster a speaker talked, the more competent they were perceived to be.[3] In another study, faster speakers were perceived to be more knowledgeable, intelligent, and objective than slower speakers. The faster speakers were also more persuasive, convincing more listeners to agree with their message.[4]

But what about comprehension, which speaking fast is generally believed to make more difficult? In studies of speaking rate and comprehension, there is little evidence to support this belief.

[†] Curious what your natural speech rate is? It's surprisingly easy to figure it out. Grab something to read out loud, set a timer for 1 minute, and record yourself speaking. Now go back and count the words you hear!

Within a reasonable range (approximately 125 wpm to 275 wpm), most studies find little to no difference in comprehensibility, all else being equal.[5]

Even for non-native speakers with accented speech, who are almost always told they need to slow down, slower speaking rates are not necessarily any more comprehensible. In fact, in several studies, non-native speakers who were asked to speak more slowly actually ended up sounding *more* accented and *less* comprehensible than when they spoke at their natural rate.[6]

Pronunciation

So if speaking rate isn't the problem, what is? Many people mumble while they speak, chewing their words like a cow chews its cud. Unfortunately, their audiences (and their messages) suffer. In one study, listeners who heard a presentation indistinctly enunciated scored 50% worse on a test of comprehension compared to listeners who heard the same speech distinctly enunciated![7] Thus, proper diction is of the utmost importance.

If you know that you're a perpetual mumbler, what can you do?[†] Before you go on stage, say some tongue twisters:

- Six thick thistle sticks.

- He threw three free throws.

- I wish to wash my Irish wristwatch.

- A box of biscuits, a box of mixed biscuits, and a biscuit mixer.

[†] A related question we often get concerns what to do if you have an accent. Although we usually have little trouble understanding them, many of our students are self-conscious about it. And while studies have shown that having an accent isn't as bad as mumbling, it still can have an effect.[8] For speakers who are concerned about their accents, we recommend immersing yourself in English as much as you can. (If you're learning another language, adapt this advice accordingly.) Watch American TV shows and movies, watch TED talks, and listen carefully to the conversations around you. Then repeat what you hear as accurately as you can. Over time, your accent will become less discernible.

There are many more examples you can find on the web.[†] Choose a few that really trip you up—this will be different for every person—then practice saying them before your speech, perfectly enunciating every syllable. After warming up your articulators ("the lips, the teeth, the tip of the tongue," as they say), you'll find it easier to speak clearly, and your audience will find it easier to understand you.

Pauses

As Mark Twain put it, while the right word may be effective, "no word was ever as effective as a rightly timed pause."[9] As it turns out, science has proven him right. For example, making deliberate use of pauses before or after major points can help the audience understand and remember those points.[10]

In the context of public speaking, silent pauses are preferred to pauses filled with filler words such as "umm," "uh," "so," "like," "I mean," "you know," "annnnnd," "anyways," etc.[‡] In a study of silent versus filled pauses, speakers using silent pauses were perceived as more knowledgeable than speakers using "umm" and "uh." In fact, even pausing silently for a full five seconds was still better than saying "umm" (although a shorter silent pause was best).[12] So while it's totally fine—beneficial even—to pause during your speech and collect your thoughts, try to eliminate filler words.

When trying to break a bad habit, psychologists have found that it's more effective to replace a bad habit with a good habit rather than just trying to will away the bad one.[13] In the case of filler words, a good habit you can employ is simply to take a breath whenever you feel the need to pause, instead of filling the silence

---

[†] Including at scienceofspeaking.com/twisters.

[‡] It's important to note that public speaking is different from everyday conversation. In everyday contexts, filler words can serve an important role in regulating conversation, indicating that the speaker is searching for a word, or deciding what to say next, without ceding the floor.[11] For conversational introverts (like both of us), this is an essential tool for getting our fair share of speaking time without having our more extroverted conversation partners take back the floor before we're ready. So filler words aren't always bad—they're just not ideal in a public speaking context.

with "umm" or "uh." And as we've seen before, taking a breath can also help you relax.

This is also a good strategy to use if you "blank out" and forget what you were going to say. When this happens, there's no need to panic, or start apologizing for forgetting, as many novice speakers do. You actually have a much longer time than you think before the audience realizes something went wrong. Remember, they only know what you said, not what you were planning to say. Simply pause confidently, as if your pause were deliberate, collect your thoughts, then continue on with your speech.

If you find that you struggle with filler words, here's an effective technique you can use to make yourself more aware of them and set you on the path to getting rid of them. You'll need a friend and a pen that clicks. Your job is to give a speech. Your friend's job is to click the pen every time you say a filler word, defined as anything that doesn't add value to what you're saying. Faced with the feedback of the clicking pen, it will be much easier for you to recognize these bad habits and find ways of breaking them.

Variation

We've all heard presentations by monotonous speakers, like Ben Stein in *Ferris Bueller's Day Off*, who put everyone in the audience to sleep. You don't want to be one of them! Instead, make your speech interesting by incorporating vocal variation.

Just how important is vocal variation? In a Harvard study conducted nearly 100 years ago, researchers found that five days after hearing a story, listeners remembered twice as many details about it when the reader actively varied his voice![14] More recently, vocal variation has been linked to increased views on TED.com, as well as higher ratings of credibility and charisma.[15]

All aspects of your voice can be varied, including volume, velocity, and your tone of voice. For example, you might raise your volume and velocity to convey excitement or lower them to "share a secret" with the audience. The key is to adjust your quality of voice to match whatever you're saying at the moment.

This is the proper takeaway from the frequently misinterpreted studies by Albert Mehrabian that supposedly demonstrated that 7% of a message is communicated through the words that are said, while 38% is communicated through vocal tone, and 55% is communicated through facial expressions. What the Mehrabian studies actually demonstrated is that when vocal tone or facial expressions are mismatched to emotional words, the audience is more likely to be affected by the vocal tone and facial expressions than the words. Which means it's particularly important to match your tone to your content.[16] As a dramatic example of a failure of tone, surgeons who speak with a less empathetic tone are significantly more likely to be sued for malpractice![17]

While surgeons (and speakers) often believe that showing emotion is inappropriate in a professional environment, the research shows that it's actually essential—as long as the emotion matches the message.

Chapter 5

The Face

Imagine this: the speaker stands up, smiles at the audience, and launches into their presentation. It's about human trafficking in Thailand. Still with a smile, the speaker describes the sad, harrowing conditions victims face. Eventually, they reveal that several of their friends had been involved in trafficking, but the ever-present smile on their face makes the audience shift nervously in their seats, wondering whether these friends were involved as victims or as traffickers…

This is another real-life story about one of our Stanford students, who was simply doing his best to implement the advice he had received in a coaching session—that he needed to smile more during his speeches. Though well-intentioned, this general piece of advice really didn't work with his topic! This is the major takeaway of this final section on delivery: it's important to form a genuine connection with the audience through eye contact and appropriate facial expressions.

Eye Contact

Eye contact is one of the easiest and most effective tools you can use to quickly improve the impact of your speaking. Extensive research[†] has shown that when you make frequent eye contact with your listeners, they will immediately perceive you as more competent, more credible, more intelligent, more attractive, more likable, and more trustworthy.[1] You will also be perceived as less nervous and more confident, and the power and potency of your message will be amplified by your gaze.[2] In other words, eye contact enhances nearly every quality you could possibly want to have as a speaker!

Engaging your listeners with frequent eye contact also makes them more likely to remember what you said, long after your speech is over.[3] If your presentation involves a persuasive component, eye contact can help you win over the hearts and minds of your audience. It will make them significantly more likely to comply with your requests, and important decision-makers will be more likely to make a deal with you.[4] If you're a teacher, making eye contact with your students will lead to increased class participation and higher test scores, while simultaneously improving your end-of-quarter teaching evaluations.[5]

Given the immense power of eye contact, it's clear that your eyes should be trained on the eyes of your audience for as much of your speech as possible. Even when you are using visual aids or notes, you should still spend the vast majority of your talk connecting with the audience. Think of it this way: every moment you spend looking away from your listeners is a lost opportunity to build rapport and sell your message.

An exception to this rule is when you want you want your audience to look at something specific—perhaps at a particularly important piece of data. In that case, you can use a unique power of your humanity to secretly direct their attention. Out of the more than 200 primate species on Earth, only one—*Homo sapiens*—has white sclera, the part of the eye surrounding the colorful iris. According to evolutionary biologists, this unique feature likely evolved to facilitate cooperation by making it easier to tell what our companions are looking at.[6] As humans, we are deeply interested in knowing what our fellow humans are looking at, and we reliably

---

[†] There are more than 40 different studies referenced in this short section, and that's just scratching the surface!

look to see what they're seeing.[7] Therefore, if you look where you want your audience to look, there's a good chance they will look there too. Just be sure to go back to making eye contact soon after!

In any case, like every other aspect of delivery, your eye contact should be dynamic. Rather than mechanically sweeping around the room, hitting each person in the same order every time like a sprinkler, your eyes should scan the room in a random fashion. If you're speaking to a full auditorium, don't worry if your eyes don't make it to absolutely everyone: research has shown that third-party listeners evaluate a speaker more positively when the speaker is looking at *someone*, even if that someone isn't them.[8]

How long should you look at each person? As a general rule, long enough for both of you to feel the connection, but not so long that it starts getting awkward. As a specific rule, no more than three seconds. According to a recent study, this was when things started to get awkward, on average.[9] As an easy, actionable piece of advice, some speakers find that it helps to think of delivering one (brief) thought while giving continuous eye contact to one person, then delivering their next thought to someone else.

Facial Expressions

In addition to speaking with a monotone voice, many speakers present with a monotone face, looking bored to death with what they're saying. This in turn only bores their audience.[†] While some people don't know they're doing it, others actually do it on purpose: it's amazing how many people believe they must be "serious" the whole time they're speaking, limiting themselves to a neutral expression! This certainly isn't the case.

Just as your voice can (and should) be used to express different emotions and add interest and integrity to your speech, so too can your facial expressions. The same basic principles apply: first,

---

[†] More on this in Chapter 15, where we'll see that speaker enthusiasm is the single most important factor in determining an audience's motivation to learn!

make your facial expressions dynamic, and second, make sure they always support your content.†

As our student in the introduction had been told, smiling during your presentation is generally a good thing: smiling speakers are perceived as more likable, more sincere, more competent, more attractive, more intelligent, and more trustworthy than speakers with a neutral expression.[10] But it's even more important to match your expressions to your content. Smile when it's consistent with what you're saying, but don't be afraid to express other emotions as well, like surprise and sadness, or even anger and disgust. Research has shown that emotions are highly contagious, meaning that expressing emotions through your facial expressions can influence your audience to feel these same emotions.[11] So don't be afraid to let them show!

Like every other aspect of delivery, facial expressions are most effective when they're genuine.[12] So rather than predetermining every facial movement ("at the end of this sentence, I'm going to raise my eyebrows to illustrate surprise"), simply free yourself to be naturally expressive, feeling and displaying the emotions that your speech engenders.‡

---

† This is the other proper takeaway from the Mehrabian studies which we introduced on p. 48.

‡ Interestingly, research has shown that this is actually the optimal strategy for all aspects of speaking. For example, in a recent analysis of corporate communications, unscripted remarks were found to be significantly clearer, more engaging, and more trustworthy than scripted remarks.[13] While it's often more nerve-wracking, extemporaneous speaking—in which you know *what* you're going to say, but not exactly *how* you're going to say it—is often the most effective.[14] Of course, this doesn't mean that word-for-word scripts are always bad—for the State of the Union address, they're essential—but if you can speak naturally from an outline, that's usually better.

Conclusion

In speaking, it's not only *what* you say that matters: *how* you say it can be just as important. Luckily, you now have quite a long list of tips and tricks to enhance your physical, vocal, and emotional delivery! Here are a few highlights to keep in mind:

- **The Body**
    - **Stance**: Maintain a solid and self-confident stance in either the Hands at Sides or Peace Offering position. Wherever you put your hands, avoid fidgeting!
    - **Gestures & Movement**: Incorporate visible, purposeful gestures and movement to help your audience understand and remember your speech. Gestures can be used to direct, demonstrate, and draw.
    - **Attire**: What you wear matters too. Wear something your audience can both respect and relate to, while making you feel like you're at the top of your game.
- **The Voice**
    - **Volume**: Speak at a volume appropriate for the venue and audience size—louder than usual but not too loud.
    - **Velocity**: Speak at a comfortable rate while focusing on clear pronunciation and well-timed, silent pauses.
    - **Variation**: Avoid speaking with a monotone voice by varying all aspects of your vocal delivery, which will make your talk more interesting and memorable.

- **The Face**
  - **Eye Contact**: Use frequent, random eye contact to connect with your audience. If there's one aspect of delivery that is most important, it's this!
  - **Facial Expressions**: Don't be afraid to show emotion through dynamic facial expressions, while making sure they always match your content!

Part IV

Organization

Introduction

1, 7, 4, 6, 9, 3, 2, 8, 5, 10.

What are we doing? Why, we're counting to ten of course! Obviously, there's a much better way to do this:

1, 2, 3, 4, 5, 6, 7, 8, 9, 10.

And yet, it's amazing to see how many speakers organize their speeches the first way, without giving any thought to the most logical way to present their content.[1] You wouldn't watch *Game of Thrones* out of order or blend the ingredients of a gourmet three-course meal into a smoothie, so why do we so often fail to appreciate the importance of organization while speaking?

In the next three chapters, we'll give organization the thought it truly deserves. In particular, we'll propose that you think about organizing a presentation in the same way you'd think about giving a thoughtful present—as a gift in a box wrapped up with a bow.

In Chapter 6, The Gift, we'll explore how you can distill your ideas to give each audience something of value. Then, in Chapter 7, The Box, we'll show you how to package these ideas in order to make them understandable and memorable. Finally, in Chapter 8, The Bow, we'll give you some other effective techniques to help your ideas stand out from the rest.

Chapter 6

The Gift

When the holidays roll around, what do you do? Give gifts, of course! Suppose you got every person on your list the same gift—how do you think that would go over? Probably not so well, especially if any of them were in the same room when they opened said gifts! But this situation would never happen because we've all learned since we were little that the best gifts are personalized. You get your foodie friend a nice bottle of wine and your little nephew some fun colors of Play-Doh. Mixing up these gifts would not only be awkward but extremely inappropriate!

And yet, speakers so often fail to consider this basic principle when designing a presentation. They recycle the exact same words, visuals, and tone regardless of whether they're speaking to their boss, a group of friends, or a visiting class of grade schoolers. But in reality, this is just as big a faux pas as the gifting scenario described above. Think of your presentation as a gift of knowledge—just like a physical gift, it should be personalized to each specific audience. This process of personalization is called audience analysis.

How do you effectively analyze an audience? Simply ask yourself two questions: 1) What does this audience already know? And 2) What does this audience want to know? When you figure out what your audience already knows, you'll have a springboard from which to launch your presentation. And when you identify what they want to know, you can focus on the aspects of your topic that your audience will find most interesting.

Consider the extreme example of an audience of children versus an audience of adult peers. In terms of what they know, these groups have vastly different amounts of experience with your topic. As such, your presentation to the children will need to be more big picture than your presentation to your peers, which can dive deeper into topical nuances. In terms of what they want to know, these audiences also differ greatly. While your peers will be interested in the professional ramifications of your latest endeavor, the children just want to learn something fun. Although it may seem difficult, if you challenge yourself to never give exactly the same presentation twice, you'll be well on your way to always successfully delivering a gift of knowledge.[†]

The Iceberg Model

When considering what gift of knowledge to give, it helps to think of your knowledge as an iceberg. We realize this may seem like a bit of a stretch, but hang in there!

Imagine that the cloud of Xs on the next page represents all the ideas you find interesting about your topic. (There are also many other ideas you find interesting about other topics, but those ideas are outside this particular cloud.)

Now, imagine that your cloud of ideas freezes and plunges into the ocean, becoming a giant iceberg of ideas. Because ice is 90% as dense as water, 90% of your iceberg will remain underwater. Only 10% will float above the waterline. Now, you may be wondering: "what do icebergs have to do with my speech?" The answer is: absolutely everything!

While there will always be many ideas that interest you, you will never be able to share them all with your audience. In most cases, you will only have time to share a tiny fraction of your knowledge—the tip of the iceberg, so to speak. The key is to identify which ideas are above the waterline—important enough to share with your audience given the time you have—and which ideas aren't.

[†] Or rather, different gifts of knowledge to different audiences!

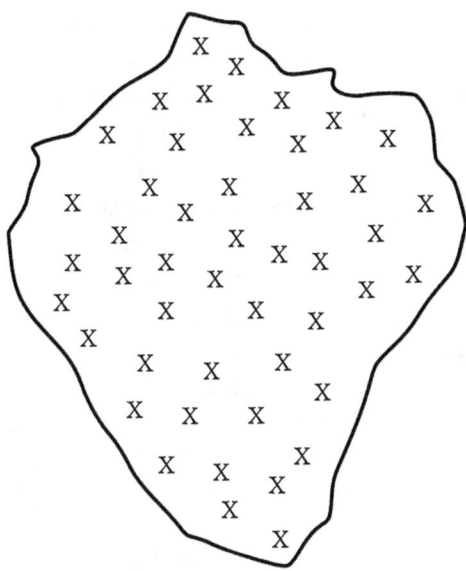

X = ideas that interest you

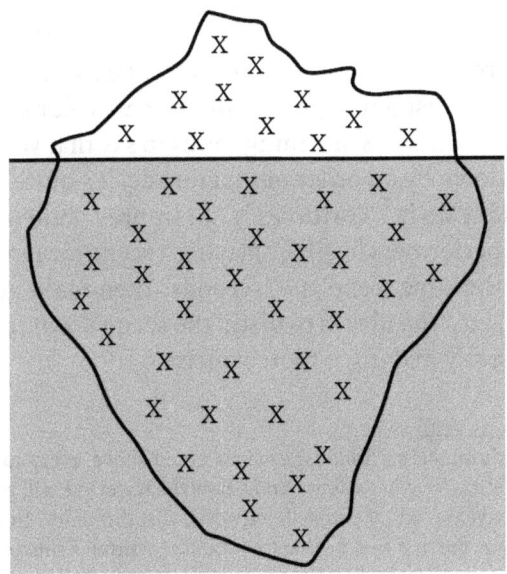

X = ideas that interest you

As Mimi Goss, the iceberg's inventor, explains,

> When you prepare a speech or report, you know all the information—the whole iceberg—or at least as much as you will know before you start speaking or writing. You know the major points above and below the waterline. And, because you have researched your topic, you may now be more interested in points below the waterline. They may seem, by the time you start organizing, more nuanced, quirky, or fascinating.
>
> [...But in] any communication, you are not the most important person. Your audience is. What they need to know is the tip of the iceberg: your main point—in one sentence—and your main supporting points.[1]

As you start to design your speech, keep this iceberg model in mind. Begin to sort your ideas into two categories: ideas above the waterline (essential to communicate to this particular audience at this particular moment) and ideas below the waterline. Of course, ideas below the waterline may still be good ideas. At the very least, they're interesting to you, and may even be interesting to your audience. They just don't quite fit in this particular speech.[†]

Of course, while it's one thing for us to say that you should cut your ideas down by an order of magnitude, it's quite another for you to actually do it.[‡] Fortunately, an improv game can help. In "Half-Life," performers begin by playing a scene for 1 minute. Then they replay the same scene in 30 seconds. Then again in 15 seconds, 7.5 seconds, etc. The idea is to distill the scene down to its essence by progressively making it more concise.

[†] Emphasis on *this particular* speech: as noted above, every speech you give should be different, so what's above and below the waterline will vary each time.

[‡] Over the years, many people have noted this difficulty. In an 1657 letter, Blaise Pascal was the first to note that he "would've written a shorter letter, if only [he] had more time."[2] And when Woodrow Wilson was asked by a member of his Cabinet how long it took him to prepare his speeches, he reportedly replied: "It depends. If I am to speak for ten minutes, I need a week for preparation; if fifteen minutes, three days; if half an hour, two days; if an hour, I am ready now."[3]

The Science of Speaking

While it may seem a bit silly at first, this game can actually be a great exercise for distilling your real world messages too. For example, imagine your talk was scheduled for an hour but is unexpectedly cut down to 30 minutes at the last moment. What information would you keep? What would you cut? What if it's 15 minutes? 7.5 minutes? Once you know which points are important enough to make the cut in 7.5 minutes, you can then go back and develop each of these points to bring your time back up to an hour.

"That's great," you might say, "but wouldn't it be more efficient to just pick a small number of points and spend my time developing those from the get-go? Do I really need to go through all this trouble of considering a large number of ideas and then distilling them?" Well, no, you don't *have* to go through that trouble, but there's compelling research to suggest you *should*.

How do people become creative geniuses? In *Originals: How Non-Conformists Move the World*, Adam Grant provides a surprising answer: they simply come up with a lot of ideas. Grant cites psychologist Dean Simonton, who found that "on average, creative geniuses weren't qualitatively better in their field than their peers. They simply produced a greater volume of work, which gave them more variation and a higher chance of originality."

As Grant explains,

> When the London Philharmonic Orchestra chose the 50 greatest pieces of classical music, the list included six pieces by Mozart, five by Beethoven, and three by Bach. To generate a handful of masterworks, Mozart composed more than 600 pieces before his death at thirty-five, Beethoven produced 650 in his lifetime, and Bach wrote over a thousand. In a study of over 15,000 classical music compositions, the more pieces a composer produced in a five-year window, the greater the spike in the odds of a hit.[4]

Therefore, the first step to giving a remarkable speech is generating a lot of ideas. Before deciding on a few main points, it pays to take a moment to consider all of the points you could cover, rather than just settling for the obvious answer. If Mozart had settled for his first six ideas, there's little chance we'd even know his name.

Of course, as we saw before, once you've generated all of those ideas, you won't have time to present them all. And even if you could, this wouldn't be a good thing: what matters most is quality of ideas, not quantity. This was clearly demonstrated in a recent study of stock traders, which found that the best-performing traders were not the ones that had the *most* information, but rather, the ones who had the *best* information.[5] Your job as a presenter is to take what you know and distill it for the audience, considering the most information and then presenting just the best.

What's the Point?

After your speech is over, what is the *one* thing you want your audience to remember? We'll call the answer to this question your thesis. Ideally, your audience will remember more of your speech than just your thesis (and if you make it interesting, they probably will). But at the very least, you want to make sure they remember the one thing that is most essential.

It's important to note how a thesis is different from a topic. Many speakers simply introduce their presentations by stating their topic, i.e., "Today I'm going to talk to you about *public speaking*." While this is certainly better than nothing, compare it with this: "Today I will show you how *anyone can improve their public speaking by designing their speech like a thoughtful present—a gift in a box wrapped up with a bow*." The first example presents a topic—a general category of ideas—while the second presents a clear thesis—a single idea that takes a stand.

Once you've decided on your thesis, you should divide the rest of your content into a few well-defined supporting points. Of course, the exact number of points will depend on how you want to break down your topic. If you're giving a speech about the brain, you might split your topic down the middle and have one point on the left brain and one point on the right brain. If you're talking about the balance of power in the U.S. government, you might choose to split your speech into three points: the executive branch, the legislative branch, and the judicial branch. If you're giving a speech on how to pick a diamond, you might organize it around the four C's: cut, carat, color, and clarity. All of these are logical ways of organizing a speech. They also each have a reasonably small number of points, which is important: if you present twelve points, no one will remember them all.

If your topic has flexibility in how you divide it, choosing three points can be particularly powerful. Consider the following:

- "Of the people, by the people, for the people."

- "Life, liberty, and the pursuit of happiness."

- "Blood, sweat, and tears."

These are three classic examples of the "rule of three," which states that things are more memorable when they come in sets of three. (Interestingly, the third example began its life as a quartet—blood, sweat, *toil*, and tears—but history has reduced it to a more memorable three![6]) In addition to being more memorable, research has shown that a thesis supported by three claims is actually more persuasive than one supported by four.[7] As such, the rule of three is a useful guideline to keep in mind as you organize your speech. At the same time, it isn't an absolute rule: as illustrated above, it's okay if your topic requires four points, or even just two. The key is that the number is small enough to be memorable.

If you follow the guidelines we've laid out in this chapter, you'll end up with the iceberg on the next page, in which the best information you have—the gift you want to give this particular audience—has been distilled into a thesis and several supporting points. But while a speech based on this iceberg will be far better than most, there's still quite a bit we can do to improve it. For starters, let's give it a story.

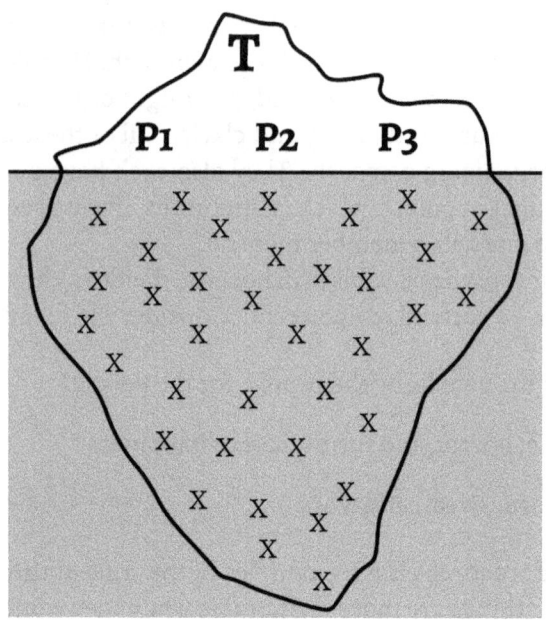

T = your thesis
P1, P2, P3 = your supporting points
X = other points you might discuss — *later*

Chapter 7

The Box

Once you've crafted the gift you want to give your audience—deciding on your thesis and a few main points to support it—it's time to put it all in a nice orderly box, deciding on the way in which you're going to organize everything. While the best way to do this will depend on your topic, this chapter will present some useful guidelines for effectively organizing any presentation.

The Story

In a classic study at Stanford University, participants were presented with a variety of passages to read, each with a different organizational structure.[1] In the first passage, the information was presented in story form, with the theme of the story clearly defined at the beginning.[†] In the second passage, the theme of the story was presented at the end. In the third passage, the theme of the story was absent. In the fourth passage, the information was simply described without setting it in a narrative context. A fifth passage had the sentences mixed up at random. The graphs on the next page reveal the results.

[†] In the military, this practice is called BLUF ("bottom line up front"). It's also similar to the internet practice of tl;dr ("too long; didn't read"), which is a short summary of something for people who don't want to read the whole thing, written either by the author, or by someone else who has read the whole thing.

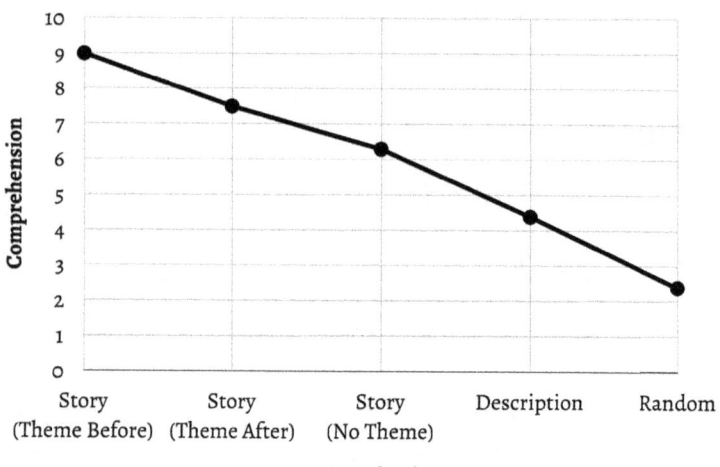

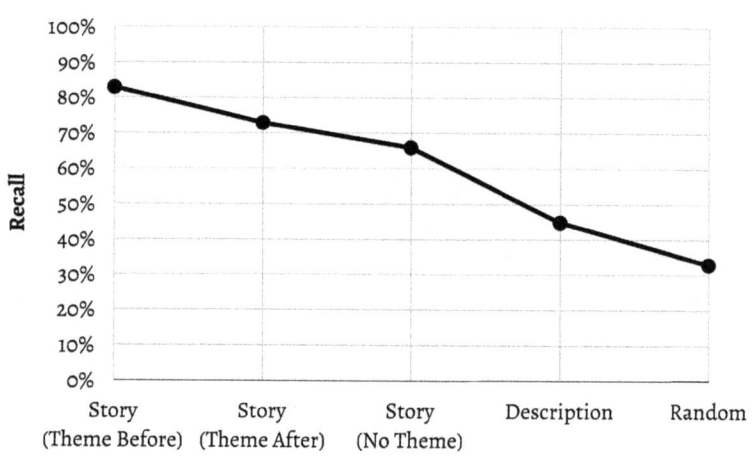

As these graphs clearly show, in terms of both comprehension and recall, a story with its theme presented up front was best, followed by a story with its theme presented at the end, followed by a story with no theme, followed by a description, followed by randomized sentences.

There are several things we can take away from these graphs. First, organization is essential! When the information was presented chronologically, it was significantly more understandable and memorable than when it was presented as a non-narrative description—or in random order. And while this study looked at a chronological organization in particular, we suspect these findings will generalize to a variety of other logical organizational structures.[†] After all, every logically organized speech tells a compelling story, even if it's not strictly chronological.

Second, it's important to have a main theme—and to present that main theme at the beginning of your speech. As we saw before, a story with its theme presented up front was better than a story with its theme presented at the end, which was better than a story with no theme. In the context of speaking, this theme is your thesis and main points. And while some people think that identifying their main points up front will "spoil the surprise" and therefore choose to reveal them only at the end of their speech, the research suggests that your audience will be more likely to understand and remember what you have to say if you let them in on your main points right from the beginning.[‡] (More on how to do this in just a few pages.)

There's one final piece of advice we can draw from this study. In addition to testing participants' comprehension and recall of the

---

[†] For example, progressing through space or zooming in/out.

[‡] If you're someone who still balks at this idea, consider the following example, adapted from a classic study: "First, you sort things into several piles. Then you load the piles sequentially into a machine. As soon as you take them out of the machine, you put them into another machine. Finally, you sort them into a different set of piles. Tedious though this process may sound, it's an essential part of modern life." Do you have any idea what we're talking about? Most people in the study who read a description like this had no clue what it was about. (Neither did we when we first read it!) But when you see the answer on the next page, everything will become totally obvious.

story as a whole, the researchers also tested their recall of particular aspects of the story, depending on how central they were—was it an essential part of the big picture, or was it simply a nitty-gritty detail? The results are presented in the graph below.

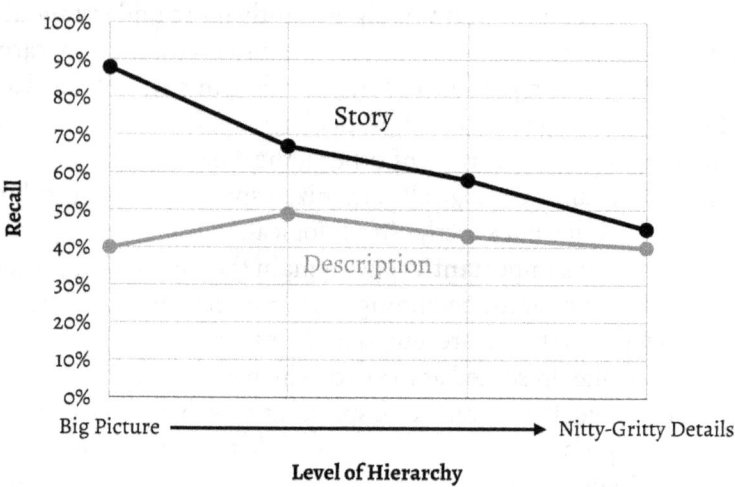

There are several things we can take away from this graph. First, it reconfirms that for all levels of detail, from the big picture down to the nitty-gritty, having a logical organization makes everything more memorable.[†]

Furthermore, it goes on to show exactly the pattern of remembering we want to see: when the information was presented in a logical order, participants remembered nearly 90% of the big picture elements, almost 70% of the second-order points, around

---

[†] What if we told you that on the previous page we were "doing the laundry"? Now, doesn't everything make a lot more sense? In the study, when people were told beforehand that they were going to read a paragraph about doing the laundry, they understood things perfectly from the beginning and were able to remember many of the details. But when the theme of the paragraph was saved until the end, people were totally confused the whole time they were reading—so much so that even after they were told they'd just read a paragraph about doing the laundry, they still had trouble remembering what they'd just read![2]

60% of the third-order points, and about 45% of the nitty-gritty details. While it would be nice to have 90% recall of everything, that's simply not possible, so the best case scenario is greater recall for the most important points—exactly what we see here.

When the information lacks a logical organization, however, this desirable pattern disappears completely. Instead, we see around 40 to 50% recall of all points, regardless of their importance. Since your ultimate goal is to get your audience to remember your thesis and three or so supporting points, this means that unless you have a logical organization, they'll be just as likely to remember four totally random points as they will be to remember the four points you want them to!

As this research shows, organization not only improves your audience's comprehension and recall of all your points, it especially increases recall of your main points without reducing recall of the details. Therefore, regardless of what kind of organization you choose, it's essential to make sure you always have one and to design it so that it leads the audience to remember the important points you want them to.

Transitions

It's clear from the data above that we need to go beyond simply describing our ideas to turning them into a memorable story. But what is it that differentiates a story from a description? A story has a natural flow, a continuous arc from beginning to end. This is what you want in your presentations as well. The key to creating this arc is crafting effective transitions between your points.

On one hand, you don't just want to say, "My first point is…" then talk about your first point, only to stop abruptly and say, "My second point is…" That's jarring and misses a key opportunity to highlight the logical connection between your points. On the other hand, you don't want all of your points to run together without any clear delineation between them. That defeats the whole purpose of organizing your speech and makes it less likely that the audience will remember each of your points.

The key is to strike a delicate balance between making your audience's journey through your speech as smooth as possible and simultaneously "signposting" along the way to clearly indicate where you are in this journey. You can do this by finding (or better yet, designing in) a logical relationship between your points and highlighting this relationship as you transition.

Take, for example, the organization of this section of the book: the gift, the box, and the bow. There's a clear logical progression here: first, decide on your content, then, organize your content, and finally, make your content memorable.† The key is to highlight this progression as you go. For example, we began this chapter by writing, "Once you've crafted the gift you want to give your audience—deciding on your thesis and a few main points to support it—it's time to put it all in a nice orderly box, deciding on the way in which you're going to organize everything." This sentence serves as a bridge between our two points—it starts by wrapping up our first point, then seamlessly spans across to our second point.

In addition to smoothly connecting your points, this bridge approach has an additional benefit: it simultaneously serves as a brief review of where we've been and a brief preview of what's to come. And as we'll see in the next section, this is a time-honored strategy for making your points more understandable and memorable.

The Roadmap

As we saw before, presenting the theme of a story upfront significantly increased what the audience understood and remembered. While not quite as powerful as presenting the theme beforehand, presenting the theme after the story also helped. You might wonder, then, what would happen if you applied both strategies, previewing the theme at the beginning *and* reviewing it at the end. Although this particular strategy wasn't tested in the study, it's an approach that presentation coaches have recommended for ages:

---

† Note the use of transitional words here: first, then, finally. While these are often effective in short-form, when it comes to the longer form of a speech, you'll generally want to include more descriptive transitions.

"Tell 'em what you're gonna tell 'em. Tell 'em. Then tell 'em what you told 'em."[3]

While, at first, this may seem like a lot of repetition, research has confirmed that this timeless three-peat structure is ideal. In a classic study, participants heard the same message repeated one, three, or five times. Unsurprisingly, recall of the message increased linearly with repetition: the more we hear something, the more likely we are to remember it. Agreement with the message, however, peaked at three repetitions. Whether through boredom or annoyance, five repetitions proved to be too much. Therefore, the timeless recommendation of three repetitions provides an ideal balance between memorability and persuasion.[4]

The first of these repetitions is your roadmap, which is essentially a table of contents for your talk. There are several benefits to including a roadmap. First, it acts as a brief overview for your audience, which allows them to begin familiarizing themselves with your content, direction, and perspective. Second, it gives them signposts to clue into during your presentation, helping them stay with you throughout the talk. And third, it provides anchor points for them to recall your main points after your speech has ended.

Just like a good table of contents, we want our roadmap to be concise. If a table of contents read: "Chapter 12: In which the villagers band together, united, to brave the elements and battle the dragon," you'd be exhausted before you even saw the title of Chapter 13! Instead, a simple word or phrase would be better, such as "Chapter 12: The Hunting Party." The same principle applies to presenting. Remember, the roadmap isn't the body of your speech—it's only a preview of what's to come. You want to clue your audience into your points, not give away everything right up front. Giving each point a concise label also makes it easier for you to refer back to it throughout your speech as you transition between points, as well as making it easier for your audience to remember in the future.[†]

[†] It also has the added benefit of making it easier for you to remember your own points while you're speaking!

The Scrapbook

Once they've finished presenting their last point, many speakers are tempted to "get out of Dodge" and rush full steam ahead toward the end of their speech. But there's one more element you'd do well to include, which can be best described as a scrapbook.

Consider a family vacation. While everyone shared the same experiences, some events inevitably stick with some people while others find different events particularly memorable. But if you create a scrapbook of pictures and memories of your vacation, everyone can look back on it together and have a shared experience once again. This shared experience is a powerful memory tool!

In the context of presentations, you want your scrapbook to be brief—like the roadmap, it isn't the body of your talk. You simply want to highlight your main points one last time to give your audience the best chance of remembering what you want them to take away. (Although it may sound a bit overbearing, it's true: you want to take this last opportunity to define what they take away, rather than leaving what they remember to chance!)

Some people like to repeat the exact same structure from their roadmap while others prefer a subtle rephrasing—perhaps referring back to something particularly memorable from each main point. Both techniques can work well as long as you make it clear you're referring back to your main points (as opposed to adding completely new information).

Here's a scrapbook for this chapter. If you remember only one thing, remember that organization is essential for helping your audience understand and remember your points. Research has confirmed what speaking coaches have been saying for centuries: it's important to have a logical organization which helps guide your audience through your speech and to preview and review this journey for them by providing a concise roadmap and scrapbook.

Chapter 8

The Bow

"Hi, my name is..., and today I'm going to tell you about..."

How many times have we all heard this boring intro? We don't know about you, but an intro like this immediately makes us want to pull out our phones, or worse yet, take a nap.

While we've already given you a solid organizational foundation that will make your speeches more understandable and memorable than most, this chapter will reveal several other effective techniques you can use to take your talks to the next level—beginning right at the beginning.

The Hook

In a recent analysis of Twitter users, researchers found that "users are most receptive to content as they first start scrolling through their news-feed." In particular, "memory response is highest in the first 30 seconds of a Twitter session." Even more specifically, they found that the very first thing users see is perceived as 14% more relevant, 28% more emotional, and as a result, 32% more memorable than the rest of the content seen in a viewing session.[1]

While this data was primarily intended to sell so-called "First View" ads on Twitter, it's also quite relevant to speaking, suggesting that the first 30 seconds of your presentation are essential. As it turns out, this insight isn't unique to Twitter: it's been proven many times over that first impressions matter—a lot.

In one study, researchers found that listeners already had opinions about a speaker in less than half a second after hearing them say a single word: "hello."[†] Not only were these snap judgments made about a wide variety of personality traits (attractiveness, confidence, competence, likability, and trustworthiness), they were also highly consistent across listeners.[3] In another study, viewers made similar judgments about a person before they even uttered a single word. After seeing someone's face for just one tenth of a second, viewers already had opinions about them. Furthermore, these opinions changed very little over time. Lasting impressions were made in the first tenth of a second![4]

Many other studies have attested to the longevity of first impressions. For example, in one recent experiment, viewers' first impressions based on a single photograph of a person significantly predicted their impressions after a live interaction with that person a month later.[5] In another study, students' initial impressions of their classmates after a brief interaction significantly predicted their impressions at the end of the quarter, even after nine additional weeks of interaction.[6] And even after viewing only 6 seconds of a lecture, students' first impressions significantly predicted the professor's end-of-quarter teaching evaluations.[7]

Given what we know about first impressions, it's important to make sure that the start of your speech makes a good one. While there's no one right way to begin, here are several suggestions for what you might do and what you definitely shouldn't:

DO:

- Tell an engaging **story**.

- State an interesting **fact** or **statistic**.

- Cite a relevant **quotation**.

[†] In a study by dating site OkCupid, they found that messages that began with the usual greeting, "Hi," had an average response rate of 25%, whereas messages with an unusual greeting like "Howdy" had an average response rate of 45%![2]

- Ask the audience a **question**.†
- Say something **unexpected**.‡
- Use multimedia: show an **image** or play **audio** or **video**.
- Ask the audience to **imagine** something.

DON'T:

- Start with a filler word (most commonly, "So...").
- Introduce yourself ("Hi, my name is...").
- State your topic ("Today, I'll be talking about...").

To be clear, you should most definitely introduce yourself and your topic (or better yet, your thesis that takes a stand), but it shouldn't be the very first thing you do.§ Start your speech with an engaging hook, then circle back to these essential introductions.

The Finale

Recently, while watching *Sing It On*, a TV show which follows groups competing in the International Championship of Collegiate

---

† Several recent studies have found that when people are curious about the answer to a question, they remember more about everything they hear, not just the answer to the question.[8]

‡ A wonderful, if probably apocryphal, example: "God damn, it's hot out here today!" exclaimed the preacher, beginning his sermon. "That's what I heard a man in this very crowd say this beautiful Sunday morning, and that's why today, I will preach on the sin of blasphemy!"[9]

§ But what if you're expected—or even required—to do this? In this case, you have one of two options: you can start with what's expected and then launch into your engaging hook, or if you want to be adventurous, you can push back against the status quo and start with an engaging hook instead. In a recent study, researchers found that subtly subverting established presentation guidelines can (in some cases) actually make you appear more competent.[10] Of course, this isn't to say you should disregard all guidelines, but it does mean that it's not always a bad idea to play with them, particularly if you're playing with ways to improve them. But if you're going to do this, just remember: while it can sometimes be good to push the envelope, it's usually not good to rip it to shreds.

A Cappella, we were exposed to the idea that show order matters. According to the seasoned performers on the show, in a competition where the judges deliberate afterward, it's best if your group performs at the end because that way, the judges are more likely to remember you. Getting an early slot, on the other hand, is the kiss of death—you have absolutely no chance of winning.

Seeing how convinced the performers were of this theory, we wondered whether there was any evidence to back it up. In fact (and unfortunately for early performers), there is. For example, in a study of figure-skating results from 1994 to 2004, the last to perform had a 14 percent chance of winning, compared to a 3 percent chance of winning for the first performers. This suggests that simply going last can increase your chance of winning by almost a factor of five![11] It also means that what you say at the end of your speech will have an inordinate impact on the audience.

In psychology, there is a principle known as the "peak-end rule," which states that our overall evaluation of an experience (like a speech) is largely determined by our evaluations of its peak—the most intense moment—and its end.[12]

In a classic demonstration of this rule, psychologists randomly divided colonoscopy patients into two groups. The first group underwent a typical colonoscopy procedure, while the second group underwent a modified procedure in which the tip of scope was left inside the patient for an additional three minutes, but not moved. While these additional three minutes were still uncomfortable, they were less painful than what came before. So while the total amount of time in discomfort was greater, the end of the procedure was significantly more bearable. Interestingly, patients who experienced this modified procedure rated the whole experience as less unpleasant than patients who had experienced the traditional procedure—even though they had spent longer in pain! As a result, they were more likely to return for subsequent procedures.[13]

While we're sure your speech won't resemble a colonoscopy, the same basic principles apply. When thinking back on your presentation, your audience's evaluation of it will largely be based on the peak moment of your speech and the end. So it's absolutely critical that you stick the landing!†

While there's no one right way to end your speech, here are several general suggestions for what you might do and what you definitely shouldn't:

DO:

- Provide a clear **call to action**.
- Tell the audience where to find **more information**.
- Bring it **full circle** back to your hook.
- End with a **bang**!

DON'T:

- Add a whole new point after the scrapbook.
- Trail off uncertainly...‡
- Make the event organizers drag you off the stage.

Memory Tricks

An engaging hook will create a good first impression, and an effective finale will leave the audience wanting more, but how do you get the audience to remember your content? In this final section on organization, we'll explore a few effective memory tricks that you can use to make your main points more memorable—not only for your audience, but also for yourself!

---

† Interestingly, studies have shown that when it comes to pleasurable experiences, the end needs to be even better than the rest of the experience to have a positive effect. If your ending is good, but the rest of your speech was better, your ending will actually drag down the audience's perception of your speech as a whole. This means it often pays to save the best for last![14]

‡ The worst speech ending we ever saw? "Umm, I guess that's the end of my speech, but there are more slides..."

Simplicity

Compare these two different ways of introducing the three essential aspects of vocal delivery:

1. There are three things to keep in mind about vocal delivery: making sure you don't talk too loudly or too softly but at a volume appropriate for the room and audience size; finding a Goldilocks tempo at which to talk, not too fast, not too slow, but just right; and keeping the audience interested by varying all aspects of your voice.

2. There are three things to keep in mind about vocal delivery: volume, velocity, and variation.

Which of these do you think is more likely to stick with the audience? One of the easiest and most effective ways to make your ideas more memorable is to find short, simple labels for them. Using a concise word or phrase to represent each of your main points will immediately make your ideas catchier than presenting those same points in complex sentences. And in addition to helping your audience remember your main points, simple labels can help you remember them as well.

Alliteration

In addition to being short and simple, "volume," "velocity," and "variation" have another benefit: they all start with the same letter. This list[†] illustrates another easy and effective technique for making your main points more memorable: alliteration, or repetition of the same first letter.

We could've labeled these points: loudness, speed, and dynamism. But while the meaning of these three words is the same, your likelihood of remembering them is definitely not.

In a recent study of language learning, researchers found that alliterative phrases were almost 20% more likely to be remembered

---

[†] Not to mention the title of this book.

than non-alliterative phrases. That's impressive! But that's not all: drawing students' attention to the fact that the phrases were alliterative increased this effect even further. In a follow-up study, phrases that had been explicitly identified as alliterative were almost 60% more likely to be remembered![15] Therefore, it not only pays to alliterate, but to draw attention to the fact that you have done so, just as we did with the three Vs of voice.

Another recent study demonstrated that alliteration can do more than just make your ideas more memorable: it can also make your ideas more attractive, simply because alliterative ideas "have a ring to them" and "just sound right." Participants were asked to evaluate product deals that featured alliteration in comparison to deals that did not alliterate. Despite the fact that the alliterative deals were more expensive, participants believed they represented a better value.[16] Sometimes, it literally pays to alliterate!

Acronyms

Using an acronym that spells out your main points can be another effective way to make them memorable. Studies of acronym use in the classroom have shown that when teachers use acronyms to present key concepts, students are more likely to remember those concepts weeks later on their final exams. And not only are they more likely to remember the words in the acronym: they are also more likely to define them correctly.[17]

Research into acronyms has uncovered a few key principles for using them effectively. First, pick a memorable sequence of letters—a word or a classic acronym like SOS—rather than a random sequence, which will be no more memorable than the content itself. Second, choose a sequence of letters you can logically connect to your topic, and explicitly present this connection to your audience. For example, to help people remember the key principles of dog training, try DOG or BARK, not XBH or CAT.

Finally, take time to make sure that both your acronym, and the content it supports, are cemented in your audience's mind. It's not enough to throw out an acronym one time in the middle of your speech and hope it sticks. Instead, be sure to repeat your acronym—and what it stands for—throughout your speech to give your audience the best chance of remembering it.[18]

Rhyming

Which of the following statements is more likely to be true?

1. Woes unite foes.

2. Woes unite enemies.

Obviously, these statements are equally true. Or are they? In one recent study, participants rated rhyming statements as 20% more accurate than non-rhyming statements of identical meaning![19] Taking this even further, a follow-up study found that rhyming statements were rated as more likable, more original, more memorable, more persuasive, and more trustworthy than their non-rhyming counterparts.[20]

While it's certainly not necessary (or advisable) to turn your entire speech into a sonnet, phrasing key points so they rhyme can be another way to make your ideas more memorable.

Parallelism

"Of the people, by the people, for the people." This description of democracy from Abraham Lincoln's Gettysburg Address is one of the most well-known phrases in American memory, in large part due to its use of repeated words and grammatical structure.[†]

Seven score and fifteen years later, you too can employ parallelism to make your key points more memorable. Wherever possible, rephrase your main points to include repeated words and grammatical structure, and your audience will be more likely to remember them down the road.[21]

[†] As a contemporary example, consider *Survivor*'s tagline, "Outwit, Outplay, Outlast." With more than 500 episodes since its premiere, it's still going strong!

Extended Metaphor

Throughout the past three chapters, we have used an extended metaphor to explain how you can effectively organize any presentation by thinking of it as a gift in a box with a bow.† Our hope is that by using this extended metaphor, you'll be more likely to remember our points down the road.

It also demonstrates how you too can use extended metaphor to neatly package your points, help your audience remember them, and make it more likely that they'll regift them in the future, increasing your impact even further.‡

---

† Okay, technically it's an extended simile, but given that "extended metaphor" is the more popular phrase, we're erring on the side of memorability.

‡ These are just a few of the many sentence-level strategies you can use to make your points more likely to stick with your audience. If you want to learn more, we highly recommend Mark Forsyth's *The Elements of Eloquence: Secrets of the Perfect Turn of Phrase*, which explains many of the classic rhetorical devices that have made things stick throughout the ages.[22] For memorable phrase-making, there is no better guide!

Conclusion

Without organization, your presentations have little chance of being understood or remembered. To effectively organize any presentation, just think of it as a gift in a box with a bow.

- **The Gift**: This is the one, overarching idea you want the audience to take away from your talk. As with any gift, it should be personalized to the audience. Begin by considering everything you could talk about, then use the iceberg model to cut it down to a clear thesis and several supporting points.

- **The Box**: This is the organizational structure of your presentation. Since stories with explicitly presented themes are most memorable, find your story and then tell it with smooth transitions. To help the audience understand and remember, incorporate both a roadmap and scrapbook.

- **The Bow**: These are the embellishments that make your speech memorable and help it stand out from the rest. Begin with a unique, engaging hook that grabs the audience's attention and end with an impactful, memorable finale. Along the way, consider using one or more memory tricks to help both you and your audience remember your points.

Part V

Visual Aids

Introduction

Take a moment to review this slide:

Review of Test Data Indicates Conservatism for Tile Penetration

- The existing SOFI on tile test data used to create Crater was reviewed along with STS-87 Southwest Research data
  - Crater overpredicted penetration of tile coating significantly
    - Initial penetration to described by normal velocity
      - Varies with volume/mass of projectile (e.g., 200ft/sec for 3cu. In)
    - Significant energy is required for the softer SOFI particle to penetrate the relatively hard tile coating
      - Test results do show that it is possible at sufficient mass and velocity
    - Conversely, once tile is penetrated SOFI can cause significant damage
      - Minor variations in total energy (above penetration level) can cause significant tile damage
  - Flight condition is significantly outside of test database
    - Volume of ramp is 1920cu in vs 3 cu in for test

BOEING 6

What do you think it's trying to say?

On January 23, 2003, a team of engineers from Boeing presented this slide to NASA.[1] A week earlier, during the launch of the Space Shuttle *Columbia*, a piece of spray-on foam insulation (SOFI) had broken off from the liquid fuel tank and struck the left wing of *Columbia*. In the intervening week, the engineers reviewed a variety of data in order to determine whether it was safe for *Columbia* to re-enter Earth's atmosphere. This is the key slide that presented their findings.

A week later, *Columbia* disintegrated as it re-entered Earth's atmosphere, killing all seven of its crew members. Knowing this, let's take a closer look at the slide:

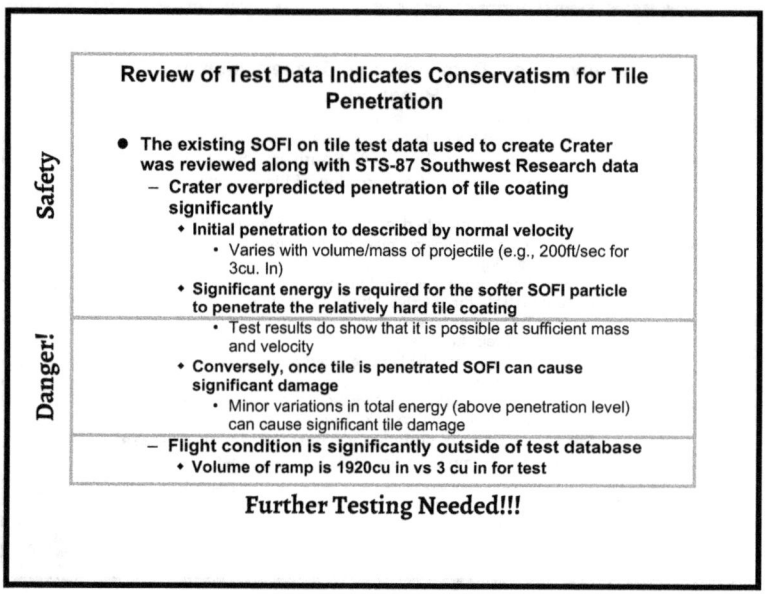

In the top half of the slide, which we've labeled Safety, the engineers "indicate conservatism." After reviewing data from a variety of sources, they have determined that the Crater research model used to predict damage consistently "over-predicted." This means it often reported there would be damage when there actually wasn't any. This fact, along with the engineers' somewhat obvious assertion that "it's difficult for soft things to penetrate hard things" leaves the audience with the sense that *Columbia* will be safe.

Halfway down the slide, however, buried deep in the fourth level of bullet point hierarchy, the engineers reveal that test results do show "it" is possible at sufficient mass and velocity. What is "it"? A potentially catastrophic penetration of the tiles protecting the wing! The news only gets worse from there: once the protective tiles are penetrated, "minor variations in total energy" can cause "significant damage."

At the bottom of the slide, the engineers note that the "flight condition is significantly outside of [the] test database." While tests were conducted with a 3 in^3 piece of insulation, the piece that hit the wing was 1,920 in^3 (640 times larger)! In order to draw a reasonable conclusion, further testing will obviously be required.

On a later slide, the engineers present their ultimate conclusion: *contingent on further analysis*, a safe return to Earth is indicated. Unfortunately, the only piece of this complex message that made it up the hierarchy to the decision-makers at NASA was that a safe return was indicated. They made the call to bring *Columbia* home, with tragic consequences.[2]

While not all presentations have the lives of seven astronauts at stake, world-changing decisions are made on the basis of similar slide decks every day. And while we've all seen slides that are reasonably good, we've also all seen slides that are very bad. As a society, we have come to accept that sitting through an endless stream of mind-numbing bullet points is an inevitable part of the human experience. It doesn't need to be this way!

In the next three chapters, you will learn some essential principles for making your message POP by Picking, Optimizing, and Presenting effective visual aids.

Chapter 9

Pick

Let's pretend you have a speech to give, and you've been designing it as you read this book. So far, you've calmed your nerves, considered your physical, vocal, and emotional delivery, picked a topic, personalized your content for your audience, and given your talk interest and flow. Do you feel ready to present yet?

If the answer is no, it's probably because we haven't covered another crucial aspect of presenting: visuals. While you now know how to *tell* the audience something of value, it's equally important to find ways to *show* them. Fortunately, although many people overlook them, there are actually a wide variety of visuals you can pick from ranging from the obvious (slides) to the obscure (dance).

In order to select the best visuals for a particular presentation, consider both yourself as a speaker and your topic. If you feel comfortable with your ability to stand and deliver and your topic is powerful and easy to understand, perhaps you don't need visuals. As a great example of this, consider Lincoln's Gettysburg Address. Would Lincoln have benefitted from adding slides? Probably not—even if he could've used PowerPoint, his use of a simpler style of presentation allowed the audience to focus entirely on his message. Adding slides would have only detracted.[†]

On the other hand, if you feel most at home when you're explaining charts and graphs and your topic involves presenting lots

---

[†] If you want to see what this might've looked like, Peter Norvig has a marvelously terrible example at norvig.com/Gettysburg.

of data, it's probably best if you do use slides. Imagine Al Gore's *An Inconvenient Truth* without a single graphic to support him. Quite a bit would be lost in translation!

To help you pick the best visual strategy for any given presentation, consider the following types of visuals.

Types of Visual Aids

While PowerPoint is one of the most commonly used presentation tools in the world, it certainly isn't the only one. In the next few pages, we'll look at a few different kinds of visual aids you can consider for your next presentation.

Slides

Slides are one of the most common types of visual aids in use today. When used well, they can be versatile and effective.

- **PowerPoint** is the classic example of slideware, used for 30 million presentations every day.[1] In addition to all of the basic features of slideware, it includes a unique feature called SmartArt, which can be a great tool for quickly making your ideas more visual.[†]

- **Keynote** is Apple's slideware program, originally designed for Steve Jobs' keynote addresses. Available on MacOS and iOS, it's similar to PowerPoint but has slightly different features. Some things are easier to do in PowerPoint, while others are easier to do in Keynote. If you're a Mac person, it's worth trying both and seeing which works best for you. The answer might be different for different presentations—we regularly go back and forth between the two.

- **Google Slides** is Google's slideware solution, which lives in the cloud in your Google Drive. It's similar to PowerPoint

---

[†] For more on this, see p. 109.

and Keynote, but again, they're all slightly different. Google Slides is becoming increasingly popular because it allows multiple people to collaborate on a presentation at the same time. Living in the cloud, it's also easy to access from any computer. And unlike PowerPoint and Keynote, it's free! Be careful though, because like anything that's free, Google Slides lacks some of the features that paid solutions like PowerPoint and Keynote give you.

- **Prezi** is another cloud-based presentation solution, built around a "zooming user interface." Instead of designing individual slides, you design one big mind map and a series of transitions that pan and zoom around it. This allows you to create not only static screens similar to slides but also dynamic transitions between them that clearly show how each of your ideas is related to the others. (You can see examples of this in action at prezi.com/personal/gallery.)

While PowerPoint, Keynote, Google Slides, and Prezi are the current market leaders, there are many other competitors out there. A search for "PowerPoint alternatives" returns many options you can experiment with if you're looking for something a bit different.

Drawings

Another effective way to present your ideas visually is simply to draw them. There are a few different ways you can do this.

- The **whiteboard** (or **blackboard**) is a classic presentation tool that has remained popular throughout the ages because of its infinite adaptability. In addition to being flexible, the act of drawing in real-time guarantees your content is appropriately paced, as opposed to slides, which make it easy to present way too much at once. Keep in mind, however, that it requires you to draw all of your visuals each time you present and can complicate delivery because you must ensure that you aren't facing the board the entire time.

- **Transparencies** are totally old school. In fact, they've been out of style for so long that we should probably take a moment to explain what they are: a transparency is a sheet of clear plastic you can print your content on and then project using an overhead projector, which shines light through the plastic and displays the printed figures on the screen. While they've generally fallen out of use, they did have some unique benefits—most notably that you could write on them in real time during the presentation in addition to printing on them ahead of time. In some cases, transparencies have been replaced by **document cameras**, which project real-time video of a piece of paper that you can both print and write on. **Interactive whiteboards** can also have this dual capability.

Props and Demos

Props and demos can be a great way to bring your presentation to life, pulling it off the screen and into the real world.

- Hearkening back to show and tell in kindergarten, **props** can be a great alternative (or addition) to two-dimensional visual aids. If there's a portable object related to your presentation, feel free to bring it and show it off.[†] Props can also be passed around the audience or even given out for them to keep, where appropriate.[3]

- **Demos** can be another great way to get your audience engaged in your content. Whether it's a live action chemistry or physics experiment or a walkthrough of your company's product, leading the audience through a demonstration can be a great way to illustrate complex ideas.

[†] A recent study found that people place significantly higher value on an object when it's physically present as opposed to simply pictured or named![2]

Audio and Video

Audio and video can also be effective ways to draw the audience into your presentation.

- Although not strictly a *visual* aid, **audio** can be a great way to engage your audience's senses. We've seen speeches that begin with whale song, presenters who play live music during their presentation (Benjamin Zander's TED talk is a stunning example of this), and when Nick was taking public speaking, he began one of his speeches by singing!

- **Video** can also be a powerful visual aid. If there's a video that illustrates the concepts you're presenting, by all means, show it to the audience. Just make sure that it doesn't steal focus: keep it short compared to the length of your speech, using only what's necessary to make your point. In addition, consider muting the video and narrating it yourself so you can more carefully control the message.

If you want to include audio or video in your presentation, make sure it will play successfully. The best option is to download the audio or video to your computer, edit it so it contains only what you need, and embed it directly into your presentation. Then, when you get to the venue, test it before your presentation to make sure it plays and that the volume (if applicable) is comfortable.

Audience Involvement

Inviting the audience to be a part of your presentation can also be a great way to make everyone feel engaged.

- For example, you might use an audience **volunteer** to help you with a demonstration. This not only makes the presentation more engaging for the volunteer but also for the entire audience who gets to live vicariously through them.

- The entire **audience** can also be used as a visual aid. For example, you might ask them to raise a hand to indicate their answer to a question, then have them look around to get a sense of the responses of their peers. This places everyone right in the middle of your presentation.

Dance

At first glance, this may seem like an outrageous idea, but when done right, the effect can be powerful.

- Science writer John Bohannon has a "modest proposal": that we use **dance** instead of PowerPoint to explain our complex ideas.[4] In 2007, Bohannon created the Dance Your Ph.D. competition, in which students around the globe explain their scientific research using dance.[5] Some of the submissions are pretty amazing! While it may not always be the easiest way to present, dance can be a powerful tool in your visual toolbox. And as strange as this suggestion may sound, realize that every speaker is already using this method to some degree in every presentation, simply by using gestures and movement. Bohannon is just suggesting that we take these concepts further!

Imagination

Dating back to the very origins of language, one of the oldest forms of "visual aids" is generating images in your listeners' minds using nothing more than your words.[†]

- The human **imagination** is a powerful tool you can use to create visuals simply by speaking. By painting a vivid picture

---

[†] The ancient Greeks called this technique *ekphrasis*, defining it as "a speech that brings the subject matter vividly before the eyes."[6]

of how the things you are talking about look, smell, sound, taste, and feel, you can actually engage many of the same brain processes that are engaged when the audience actually sees, smells, hears, tastes, and feels these things.[7] As a result, when you ask the audience to imagine something, you make them significantly more likely to believe it.[†]

[†] As an added benefit, a recent study found that the more image-based language you use, the more charismatic you will seem.[8]

Chapter 10

Optimize

Once you've decided what kind of visual aids you want (if any), it's time to start creating them. As you begin to craft your visual aids, it's important to keep in mind their purpose. But what exactly is their purpose?

Unfortunately, many speakers act as if the primary purpose of visual aids to aid *them*. They use their visual aids as a script, projecting their talking points for all to see. But while this may help the speaker remember what they want to say, it actually makes it harder for the audience to understand them! Research has shown that adding written words on top of spoken words actually interferes with learning.[1] It's like having two different people talking to you at the same time, telling you the same thing but in slightly different ways: your brain has to work even harder than usual to sort it all out! So while lists of bullet points may help the speaker, they certainly don't help the audience. Which is a problem, because aiding the audience is the real purpose of visuals!

Visual aids are simply that—*visuals* that *aid* the audience. Unlike adding written text to speech, which can confuse the audience and interfere with learning, studies have shown that adding visuals to speech can greatly improve it.[2] While the brain has a single channel for processing both written and spoken words, it has a separate channel for processing visuals. Engaging the visual and verbal channels at the same time increases the amount of information the audience can process.[3]

Putting these ideas into practice, here's a visual representation of these principles:

Adding visuals to speech improves learning, while adding text interferes with it.

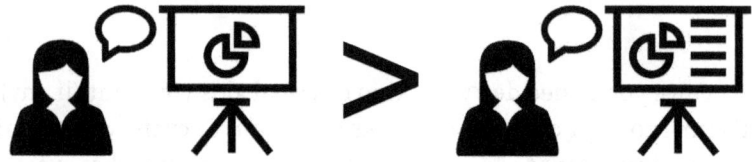

A Visual Aid Designer's Toolbox

Based on this research, it's clear that your visuals should primarily be visual. But what kind of visual should you use? According to Dan Roam, author of *The Back of the Napkin*, it all depends on the type of question you're trying to answer.

When the question is...

- "who?" or "what?" we can use a **picture**
- "how much?" we can use a **chart**
- "where?" we can use a **map**
- "when?" we can use a **timeline**
- "how?" we can use a **flowchart**
- "why?" we can use a **scatter plot**
- "what's the point?" we can use an **equation**

Who or What?

The most basic questions your visuals can help you answer are questions of "who?" or "what?" To illustrate the answers to these questions, you can simply show the audience a **picture** of who or what you're talking about.† This can be a photograph or a drawing—anything that shows the qualities you want to illustrate.

To show qualities,
use a picture

Even the simplest drawings can be enough to illustrate the relevant qualities of what you're talking about. For example, the pictures above clearly illustrate that we're talking about a happy construction worker as opposed to a dour businessman and a single-family home instead of a skyscraper.

This brings up an important point. With any visual, you want to make sure it's clarifying what you're saying, rather than introducing ambiguity. If in actuality, we *are* talking about a dour businessman, the drawing of the happy construction worker doesn't help our audience understand—it actually gets in the way. Unsurprisingly, studies on the benefits of visual aids find that they only improve learning when the speech and visuals are related.[5] In fact, adding irrelevant images actually reduces learning![6]

---

† A recent study suggests that simply adding a picture of what you're talking about immediately makes what you say about it more believable.[4]

As cute as they are,
these cats are distracting you

Too often, we see speakers fill their presentations with generic stock images that have only the slightest relevance to what they're saying—if any. If an image isn't directly relevant to what you're saying at the moment, it has no place in your presentation!

In addition, your pictures should be designed to show just the right level of detail. You want to be sure to emphasize what is relevant to your message while deemphasizing what is not. If your presentation hinges on explaining the nitty-gritty details of something, it's important to illustrate those details. But if they're irrelevant to the audience's understanding, it's actually better to leave them out.[7] A great way to emphasize key details is to add labels to your pictures, as illustrated below.

Similarities and Differences Between Airplanes and Spaceships

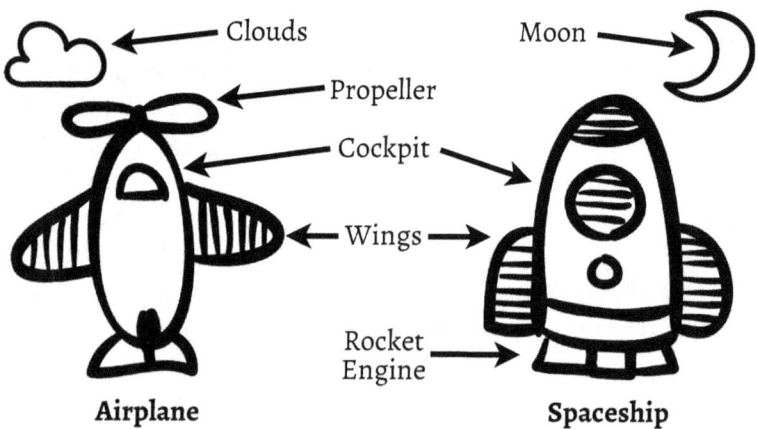

How Much?

Another important question your visuals can help you answer is: "how much?" Here, the answers come in the form of numbers.

Sometimes, all you need is one number. In this case, you can simply present the number, but there are a few pieces of advice for how to do this effectively. In studies that track where viewers look while interacting with a graphic, researchers have found that when you cite individual numbers, it's better to present them as numerals (1, 2, 3) than as words (one, two, three) because numerals stand out and draw greater attention.[8] This is contrary to traditional rules about writing numbers, which dictate that many kinds of numbers should be written out as words. But if you glance over this paragraph, you'll notice that the numerals 1, 2, and 3 immediately jump out at you!

The only exceptions to this rule are when the number is hard to understand (very large or very small), or when you actually want the number to fade into the background. For example, in the sentence "after hundreds of tests, we found a 40% improvement," the number "40%" stands out, while the word "hundreds" fades into the background.

What if the number is very big or very small? A good technique for presenting numbers larger or smaller than those we encounter every day is to use an analogy to bring them into the human scale. For example, which measure of accuracy sounds more impressive: "throwing a rock from the sun to the earth and hitting the target within one third of a mile of dead center," or "throwing a rock from New York to Los Angeles and hitting the target within two thirds of an inch of dead center"? In a recent study, while 58% of people thought the first version sounded "very impressive," 83% of people who heard the second version thought so![9]

Of course, numbers become more meaningful when they are compared to other numbers. For example, the statement "Meryl Streep has 20 Academy Award nominations" is a meaningful one that clearly demonstrates she is a talented actress. However, this number becomes even more meaningful when we compare it to other numbers: "Meryl Streep has 20 Academy Award nominations, which is 8 more than the runners-up, Katharine Hepburn and Jack Nicholson, who are tied with 12."

The best way to visually present such a comparison is to use a **chart**. Here are a few things to keep in mind as you design one.

To show quantities,
use a chart

First, above all else, show the data. Let the numbers speak for themselves by presenting them in the clearest way you can. While it's tempting to add extra bells and whistles (like 3D elements), these detract from your message instead of adding to it.[10] In fact, a recent survey of PowerPoint audiences found that 2D charts were preferred to 3D charts because the former are much easier to read.[11] All you need for an effective chart is an elegant presentation of the data and clear labels to help people digest it.

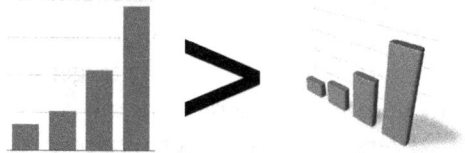

is easier to interpret than

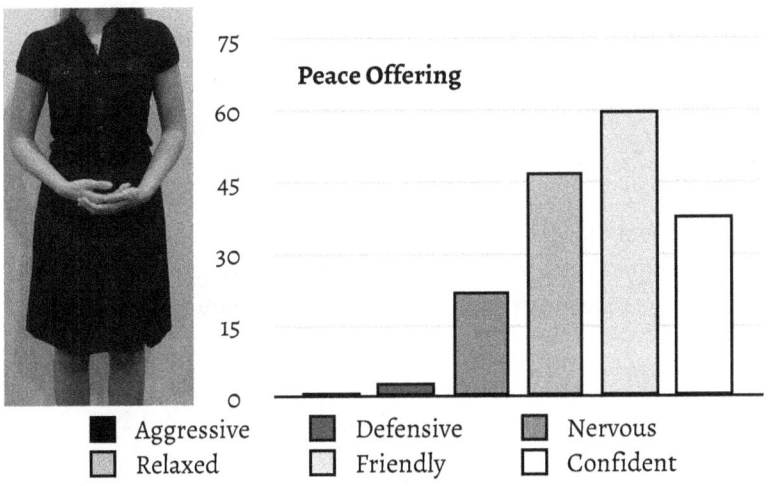

On that note, research has found that people learn better when corresponding words and graphics are presented near each other on the screen. For example, when labeling a graph, it's better to put the data labels directly on the graph than to rely on a legend, which is farther away.[12] A legend requires the viewer look back and forth between the legend and the chart, increasing the effort required to understand it. It's easier to see what's going on when the relevant label is near the corresponding data. For this reason, when presenting the data from our stance survey in Chapter 3, we put the labels right on top of the bars.

In addition, make sure you pick the right kind of chart. Although there are nearly 100 different kinds of charts you can generate in PowerPoint, you really only need two basic families to make most numerical comparisons: the bar chart and the pie chart. If you want to make comparisons between different things, use a bar chart. If you want to make comparisons between parts of a whole, use a pie chart.

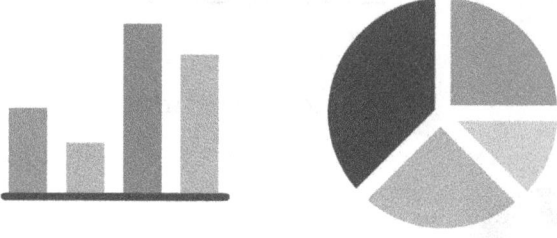

Where?

The next question your visuals can help you answer is "where?" Everything in your presentation is related, and it's helpful to illustrate these relationships visually. To do this, you can use a **map**.

To show positions in space,
use a map

In PowerPoint, there is a feature called SmartArt that allows you to generate diagrams to illustrate a wide variety of relationships. Simply pick the option that best represents the relationship you want to illustrate, fill in the blanks, and you're all set! If nothing fits how you envision things, you can always use simple lines and shapes to design your own.

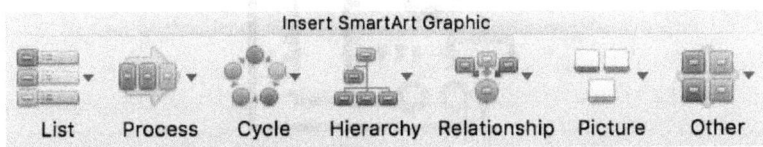

Here are some different examples of the types of maps you can use in your presentations:

- **Geographic Map**: Sometimes it's useful to show a literal map of how things are related to each other in space.

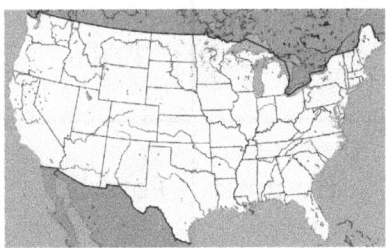

- **Social Network**: Or perhaps you want to illustrate how people are related to each other by using a social network, family tree, or org chart.

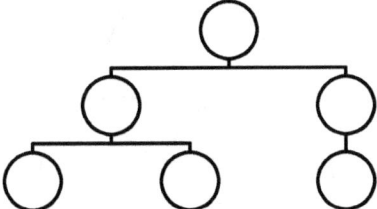

- **Schematic**: A schematic is like a social network of objects that shows how individual parts work together as a whole.

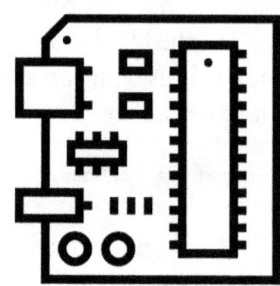

- **Concept Map**: Concepts can also be mapped to show how various ideas are related to each other. Sometimes concept maps look like social networks, with ideas instead people. Others can be placed on their own coordinate system.

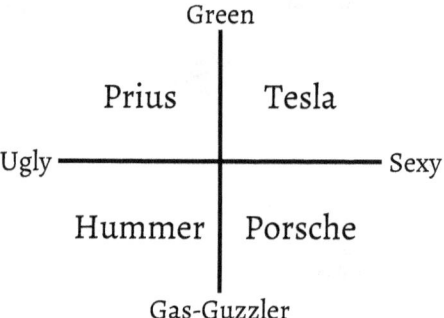

- **Venn Diagram**: A Venn diagram is another kind of concept map that shows similarities and differences.

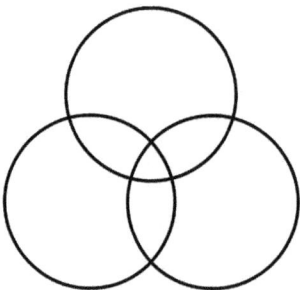

When?

In addition to talking about positions in space, you may also want to talk about positions in time. To represent this visually, you can use a **timeline**. PowerPoint's SmartArt allows you to quickly generate these as well.

To show position in time,
use a timeline

Of course, *every* presentation necessarily answers the question of when, even if only about itself. At the very least, every presentation has a beginning, middle, and end—an introduction, body, and conclusion—with many sub-points along the way.

Unsurprisingly, studies have shown that people learn better when they are given visual cues that illustrate this structure.[13] At the very least, include a title slide, a roadmap slide, slides for each of your main points and the transitions between them, and a scrapbook slide. Mirroring your structure visually will help the audience follow the arc of your presentation.

One effective technique for visually organizing your points is to introduce a timeline of your speech with your roadmap, then return to this timeline between points and highlight the point to which you are transitioning (see left below). Another effective method is to have a kind of "progress bar" at the bottom of every slide that has an icon for each main point, with the current point highlighted (see right below).

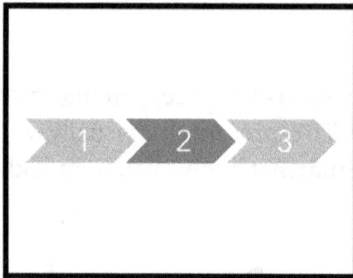 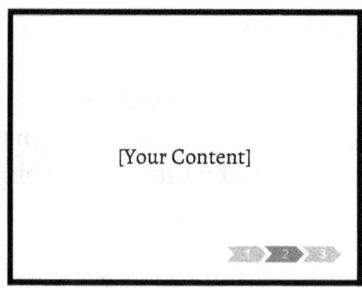

As you design timelines for your presentations, keep in mind your audience's expectations about the directionality of time. Generally speaking, most audiences you encounter will expect time to progress from left to right horizontally, top to bottom vertically, clockwise in a circle, or from behind them to in front of them.

But while these views are common, they are not universal. Linguists have discovered that different languages have different ways of representing time, which affect how their native speakers view it. For example, people who primarily read in a right-to-left language like Arabic are more likely to represent time as moving from right-to-left than left-to-right. The indigenous Aymara people in South America view the past as being in front of them and the future being behind them.† And the Kuuk Thaayorre people in Australia view time as moving from east to west (with the sun), regardless of the direction they are facing.‡ While it's unlikely you'll give a presentation in Kuuk Thaayorre anytime soon, it's always important to consider your audience and represent things in the way that will be most understandable to them.

---

† As strange as this may seem to us, there's logic here. Because we can see the past, and can't see the future, it's as if we're walking backward into the future.

‡ As Lera Boroditsky reports, the Kuuk Thaayorre also use cardinal directions (north, south, east, and west) to describe space at all scales, saying things like, "There's an ant on your southeast leg" or "Move the cup to the north-northwest a little bit." When greeting each other, the Kuuk Thaayorre ask "Where are you going?" and the answer should be something like "South-southeast, in the middle distance." This means they need to stay oriented at all times. Even in unfamiliar landscapes and inside unfamiliar buildings, the Kuuk Thaayorre always know which direction they're facing. [14]

How?

One of the most important questions you can answer in your presentations—and with your visuals—is "how?" Here, the answers come in the form of cause and effect—how things influence each other. This can be visually represented with a **flowchart**.

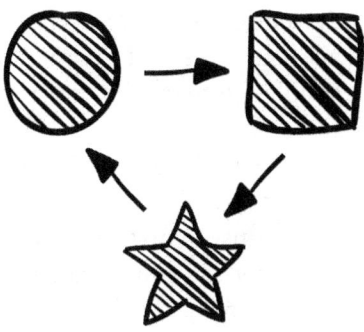

To show cause and effect,
use a flowchart

To really get a sense of the purpose and power of flowcharts, consider the bullet point-filled slide below.

How to Overcome Your Nerves

- Even if you don't feel confident, fake it (stand up straight, speak loudly, look at the audience, etc.)
- The audience will see you as confident and respond by paying more attention to your talk
- You'll gain real confidence from the audience's positive reaction

This slide isn't very effective—there are simply too many words on it. The message is buried in a block of text. It also lacks any visual component, which we know greatly enhances learning.

If you read closely, you'll see there's a logical relationship between these three points, but the current slide design makes this difficult to catch. There's a starting point (faking confidence) which leads into a cyclical relationship between the following two points (increased audience attention leads to real confidence which leads to increased audience attention, and so on). And while an astute audience would probably figure this out eventually, visuals could greatly accelerate this.

Enter the flowchart. Recall that PowerPoint has SmartArt, a highly effective, easy-to-use tool for designing visuals to show a wide variety of relationships. In no time, you can easily whip up a graphic like the one below and simultaneously make your point clearer and more compelling.

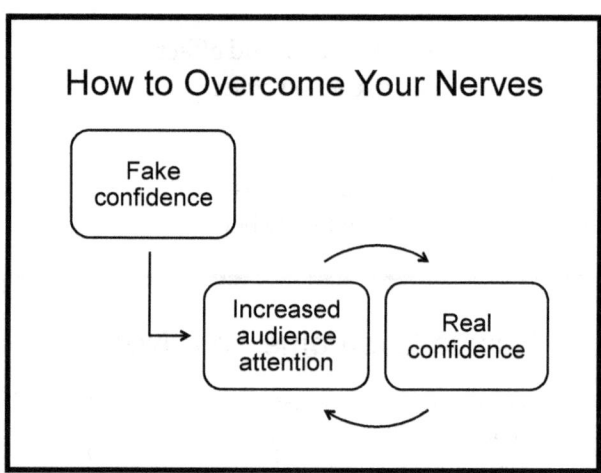

By cutting down the text on this slide, you increase the value of each word because only the most important ones make the cut. And by keeping text to a minimum, you also free up more slide real estate to devote to helpful visuals that make your message even more impactful.

Of course, as always, cutting down on words is a guideline to be checked against your intuition, rather than a rule to be slavishly followed. If the text is essential, and you are sure it will improve the audience's understanding, by all means, include it: even the visually redesigned slide still includes some words. But if the text—or any other element of your presentation, for that matter—doesn't add anything to your audience's understanding, it's better to get rid of it than have it distracting them.

Why?

Another important question your visuals can help you answer is one of the thorniest questions we all face: the ever-important question of "why?" Here, the answers come in the form of correlation and causation, prediction and deduction. The classic way of presenting this visually is to use a **scatter plot**. For example, the simple graph below might be used to support a discussion of the positive correlation between the x and y variables, as well as what's going on with the outlier in the lower right.

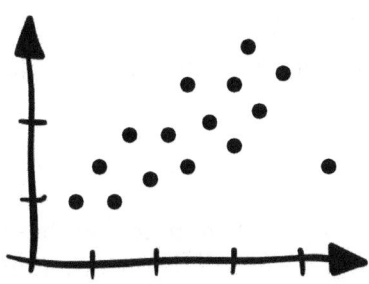

To show correlation and causation,
use a scatter plot

In the case of the scatter plot, it's more important than ever to label everything clearly, including the axes (with units) as well as any important conclusions you want to call out. Don't assume the audience will automatically see what you see. Remember, while you've been working with these ideas for a long time, it's probably the audience's first time seeing them. Make your ideas as easy to digest as you can.

What's the Point?

There's one more kind of graphic, one which we've used several times already in this chapter—the **equation**. The equation answers the question: what's the point? What's the moral of the story, the one thing you want the audience to take away?

To show the moral of the story,
use an equation

An equation is simply two other graphics connected by mathematical symbols like +, -, =, >, and <. By connecting visuals mathematically, you can easily illustrate overall conclusions.

What Else?

As always, it's important to note that these are not the only kinds of graphics, just some of the most common.[†] These basic forms are meant to open your mind to what's possible ("I never thought to illustrate it that way!") rather than limit you ("I'm answering 'why,' so I have to use a scatter plot!"). In line with the overall philosophy of this book, this chapter is simply a collection of tools you can use when they're helpful. It's ultimately up to you to decide which tool will be most effective for any given task.

[†] After all, each of the nearly 100 different kinds of charts in PowerPoint was created for a reason!

Formatting

Although often overlooked, the importance of good design cannot be overstated. In a recent study, researchers found that while your content determines whether your audience trusts you, what determines whether they *dis*trust you is your visual design.

On one hand, if your content is good—if you present relevant, unbiased information in clear, simple language—your audience will trust you. At the same time, if your design is lacking—if your visuals lack structure and have a busy layout with too much text—your audience will distrust you, regardless of your content. Therefore, even if you have the best content in the world, if your visuals aren't up to snuff, they can cause the audience to immediately distrust you and disregard your message before they've even heard it. As always, it's not enough to have good ideas—you also need to know how to present them effectively.[15]

In this section, we'll look at some principles for good design, including font, color, titles, consistency, and simplicity.

Font

With regard to font, a recent literature review found no clear winner in the battle between serif and **sans serif** fonts in terms of readability—although both sides have strong proponents who argue otherwise.[16] As long as you don't go too crazy, your font choice will probably be reasonable. More important to consider is the size of the font. Venture capitalist Guy Kawasaki proposes this tongue-in-cheek algorithm for calculating minimum font size: "find out the age of the oldest person in your audience and divide it by two."[17] A more practical approach is simply to replace as many words as you can with images, then make the remaining words as large as you can (within reason).

Color

In terms of color, a study comparing the perceived attractiveness of different colors in PowerPoint slides found that graphs drawn in cool colors (e.g., blue and green) were preferred to graphs drawn in warm colors (e.g., yellow and orange). And while there was little difference in attractiveness between slides with white and black backgrounds, low-contrast slides (e.g., grey on grey) were rated as the least attractive.[†]

On that note, while color can be a powerful way to differentiate various elements of your visuals aids, it should never be used by itself. First, approximately 5% of your audience will be color blind. If you're interested in learning more about how this affects their ability to see your presentation, Vischeck (vischeck.com) is a free online tool that lets you simulate what your slides will look like to someone who is color blind. In addition, even if you and the rest of your audience aren't color blind, you may have to contend with faulty technology: even a healthy projector can distort colors quite badly, and a sick one can drop one or more color channels entirely. While this doesn't mean you can never use color as a way to differentiate things, it does mean you should always pair it with something else (i.e., size or shape).[‡]

Titles

Titles are another tool you can use to dramatically improve the comprehensibility of your graphics—and your ideas. In this vein, Michael Alley has proposed a new model for titling visuals called the "assertion-evidence approach."

[†] Interestingly, research has found that making your content easier to read by increasing the color contrast will not only make your audience happier—it will actually make your content seem more believable![18]

[‡] In addition, as always, be aware that different colors mean different things in different cultures. For example, while in most countries, green represents growth and life, in other countries it represents just the opposite: death. And while in many countries, black is the color of death, in other countries, it's just the opposite: white.[19]

Too often, he says (and we certainly agree), speakers give their visuals generic titles like: "X vs. Y," or worse yet: "Results."[†] In fact, a recent study found that more than 80% of slides in science and engineering presentations feature this kind of generic title.[20] While these titles are accurate—you're showing your results using an XY scatter plot—they fail to tell the audience what they really want to know: why they should care. Your audience wants to know what your main message is!

To fix this problem, Alley proposes we explicitly address the audience's question by putting the answer right in the title. In the assertion-evidence approach, the title of the graphic makes an assertion (e.g., "Bigger audiences in rehearsal lead to better speech performance"), and the graphic provides visual evidence to support the assertion (e.g., a scatter plot of rehearsal audience size versus speech grade). The visual evidence can be any kind of graphic—the only requirement is that it supports the assertion.

As it turns out, there's good evidence to support Alley's assertion. Studies have shown that when an audience watches a presentation designed this way, they actually understand and remember significantly more than an audience that sees a presentation with conventional titles. This is true even when the words the presenter says are exactly the same![21] It also works in the real world: when the lecture slides in a geology class were redesigned using this approach, final exam scores improved significantly![22]

Interestingly, studies have shown that you as the *presenter* will also come away with a better understanding of your topic if you design your slides using the assertion-evidence approach. This is because it forces you to think more deeply about your topic in order to formulate your assertions and present your evidence.[23]

So whenever you're tempted to use a generic title, think about what your main message is, and consider using that as the title instead. Not only will your audience understand and remember more—you may even learn something as well!

[†] Or worst of all, "   ".

Consistency

An easy way to ensure consistency across your presentation is to use your slideware's "Master Slide" feature. This allows you to pre-define the format of different slide types upfront, ensuring that all of your slides will have the same style from the beginning.

An important exception to this rule of consistency is when you deliberately choose to deviate from your usual formatting in order to emphasize a particular idea. Done well, this can be a powerful technique for highlighting your insights and gaining a bit more control over what your audience remembers.

For example, in a recent study, Carmen Simon invited people to view a presentation with twenty slides, each illustrating one point. Two days later, she asked them what they remembered. Of the 20 points she presented, viewers remembered an average of 4, at random. Then Simon redesigned the slides to highlight the key points she wanted the viewers to remember by making them look different from the rest of the presentation (for example, by changing the background color). This time, while viewers still only remembered 4 points, the points they remembered were no longer random. Viewers were much more likely to remember the points Simon had differentiated.[24]

When you set up a pattern, then break that pattern, the thing that breaks the pattern receives more attention. This is why it's important to have consistent formatting throughout your presentation, except at points where you want to draw attention to something. If your basic formatting is inconsistent, you'll be drawing attention to irrelevant details.

When you think you're completely done designing your slides, run through them one more time with the eagle eyes of an editor, looking for differences in formatting, typos, or anything that might otherwise receive unwanted attention. (Or better yet, get someone else to look over your slides. A second pair of eyes will often catch things you've missed![†])

[†] Nick recently caught this typo on the title slide of a student presentation (before it was presented, fortunately): "Data Scientist: The Sexist Job of the Year." The student meant to write "Sexiest"!

Simplicity

While it's tempting to add additional flourishes to your presentation, such as fancy backdrops or dramatic animations and transitions, studies have shown that people learn better when this kind of extraneous material is excluded.[25]

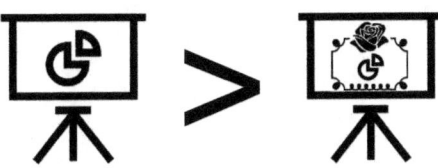

As a general rule, you should include only as much information in your visual aids as is required to clearly make your point. Paraphrasing Einstein, "everything should be made as simple as possible, but no simpler."[26] Visual information that is irrelevant to the point being made, but still important, can be presented on a separate slide.

In fact, research has confirmed that this strategy is ideal because people learn better when information is broken up into manageable segments.[27] This means you should spread your message across multiple slides, rather than cramming too many things onto one. As we saw earlier, this was one of the critical flaws in the Boeing engineers' *Columbia* presentation: three totally different ideas were presented on the same slide—safety, danger, and further testing needed. The audience fixated on the first point, safety, which ultimately led to tragic consequences.

To solve this problem, Nancy Duarte, who designed the visuals for Al Gore's Academy Award-winning presentation, *An Inconvenient Truth*, makes the radical proposal that you should present only one idea per slide!† Though radical, it's a proposal we wholeheartedly endorse.‡

---

† Often, you'll hear the rule of thumb that you should have about one slide for every minute of content. But Duarte's proposal is more effective—and more practical. Design one slide for every idea, then keep that slide up for as long as it takes to explain it, whether that's 1 minute, 5 minutes, or 5 seconds.[28]

‡ At a recent engineering seminar, we saw a particularly egregious violation of this advice. The format of the seminar dictated that the presenter have no more than two slides, while the student's academic adviser had demanded that all of his lab's data be presented. As a result, the student included six different graphs on one slide. Each graph was animated so that it flew in at full size, then a second later, collapsed to a tiny thumbnail at the bottom of the slide, before bullet points appeared to tell the speaker what to say.

Chapter 11

Present

Once you've picked and optimized your visuals, there's only one thing left to do: present them! Fortunately, the vast majority of what you need to know about presenting with visual aids, you already know from reading Part III. There are, however, a few more things to consider when visuals are added.

Don't Present to Your Slides

When presenting with visuals, making eye contact with the audience becomes even more important. Far too many speakers spend the majority of their speech staring at their slides instead of connecting with their audience.

If there's something critical for the audience to see on your slides, you can use your eyes to direct their eyes there. And it's also a good idea to glance at your slides when advancing them to make sure you're on the correct slide. Just be sure that when you're done, you go back to making eye contact! Remember, each moment you look away from the audience is a lost opportunity to build rapport and sell your message.

Don't Block Your Slides

While you don't want your slides to upstage you, it's also important to not upstage your slides. We've all seen presentations where the speaker stands directly in front of their slides, blocking important information while the projector gives their face a ghostly glow. Don't be that speaker!

Instead, place yourself so that everyone in the audience can see both you and your slides at the same time. Keep this in mind at all times, regardless of whether you choose to move or stand still.

Take Control

Too often, speakers take a backseat to their slides. They have no idea what slide is next, so they bring their presentation to a screeching halt as they wait to see what slide appears. Then, they read their next point directly from it. Instead, you should know your presentation well enough that you can speak continuously without seeing your next slide. This way, you can bring in each slide just when you need it.

Another good technique for maintaining control is to take advantage of your slideware's "Presenter View." This will project your slides for the audience to see while simultaneously showing you a variety of helpful information on your computer screen, including the current slide, the next slide, and the amount of time you've been speaking. While you then need to be careful not to pay too much attention to your computer, Presenter View can make working with visuals a lot less stressful.

Use a Remote

Using a remote control to advance your slides can also help you remain in control of your presentation. A remote gives you the freedom to deliver your speech exactly how you want to instead of being chained to your computer. For less than $10, you can get a remote that allows you to go forward, backward, and even black out the screen, all from the palm of your hand.

There are a few things to keep in mind when using a remote. First, don't fiddle with it! Your audience will notice and be distracted. Second, recognize that a remote is meant to free your delivery, not to restrict it. With the exception of counting to ten on your fingers—which you probably shouldn't be doing anyway—you can still do all of your great gestures while holding the remote.

Keep It Relevant

As we saw before, visuals only improve learning when they are directly relevant to what is being said. While this issue generally arises when designing slides, it can also become a problem when presenting them. Too often, we'll see presenters leave an image on the screen long after they're done saying anything related to it, which only distracts the audience from the new and interesting information being presented verbally.[1] In this case, it's better to find another image that relates to the new information or, if there isn't one, to simply black out the screen.[†]

The same thing can happen when the presenter jumps the gun and advances to a new slide before they're done making their previous point. In fact, sometimes they do this because they're aware that the old slide isn't relevant, without realizing that the new slide is just as irrelevant and even more distracting. This is because the audience immediately begins reading the new slide, missing out on what the speaker is saying. The same advice applies here as well: either find a relevant image or black out the screen until you're ready to talk about the new slide.

[†] You can do this with a remote, or by pressing "B" on your keyboard. You can also white out the screen by pressing "W," or include a blank slide of either color in your slide deck. (Note that the B and W keyboard shortcuts are one of the aforementioned features that are lacking in Google Slides.)

Prepare for Technical Difficulties

For any presentation you give with slides, you should also be fully prepared to give it without them. It sounds terrifying, we know, but sometimes, it's your only choice. On several occasions, we've found ourselves in a situation in which we were told there was going to be a projector only to find that there wasn't one when we got there. Fortunately, we knew our stuff well enough to adapt.

During a presentation at State Science Fair in high school, Melissa experienced an even more harrowing glitch. Despite checking her slides shortly beforehand, she realized in the middle of her presentation that the file had been corrupted, and the data on her graphs was completely wrong. Fortunately, she had prepared well enough that she knew her numbers by heart. Citing her numbers from memory, she used gestures to indicate what each graph was supposed to look like. Despite this terrible glitch in her slides, her overall presentation impressed the judges enough for them to crown her state champion![†]

As scary as it sounds, sometimes you just need to roll with the punches and give your speech without slides. If there's a whiteboard, or something else you can write on, you can hand-draw your essential graphics as you need them, or you can simply rely on your expert delivery techniques to make your speech memorable without visuals.

If you want to minimize the chance of technical difficulties, it's always a good idea to bring your own equipment, with backups. At the very least, bring your slides on a flash drive, ideally in multiple formats (the original, as well as a more foolproof format like pdf, which will work on pretty much any device). But a safer plan is to bring your own computer, ideally with your own cables (everything you need to output to standard VGA and/or HDMI, including any

---

[†] On the other end of the spectrum, we once saw a presentation where the speaker spent twice his allotted time just trying to make his slides work, meaning that by the end of his speech, he had used up three times his fair share of time! (At no point did the speaker propose he might be able to present without slides.) At some point, you have to know when to cut your losses and give the best presentation you can with what you have.

special adapters you may need). If you don't know what cables you'll need to connect to the venue's audiovisual system, ask. (Even if they assure you they have the cables, it's never a bad idea to bring your own as a backup.) If your presentation relies on sound, make sure to bring an audio cable as well.[†]

Practice

To make all of these aspects of delivery run smoothly, it's absolutely essential that you practice. Not just by flipping through your slides and saying to yourself, "here's where I'll talk about my results," but actually giving the entire presentation exactly as you will during the real event. If you have access to the room, practice in the room; if you have someone you can practice in front of, practice in front of them; if you'll be using a remote, use the remote. The closer your rehearsal is to the real thing, the less likely it is that something will go wrong.

[†] And remember to plug it in and test it. Although it sounds obvious, this is one of the most common things people forget!

Conclusion

In order to make your visuals stand out, simply remember to make them POP by picking, optimizing, and presenting them.

- **Pick**: In order to pick the best visual strategy, begin by asking yourself whether visuals will actually help this particular presentation. If so, what type will be most effective? While slides are one of the most common choices, there are many other options to enhance your presentation including drawings, props and demos, audio and video, audience involvement, and even dance and imagination.

- **Optimize**: While crafting your visuals, remember that there are many different kinds: pictures, charts, maps, timelines, flowcharts, scatter plots, equations, and more! In addition, be sure to keep your formatting consistent throughout, except when you want to differentiate an important point, and make sure your visuals can be seen from afar.

- **Present**: Continue to practice your excellent delivery techniques. In addition, keep these visual-specific tips in mind: don't present to your visuals, don't block your visuals, take control, use a remote, keep it relevant, prepare for technical difficulties, and practice!

Part VI

Pitching

Introduction

As Daniel Pink writes in *To Sell Is Human*, "We're all in sales now." In a survey of 7,000 full-time workers in the U.S., Pink found that "people are now spending about 40 percent of their time at work engaged in non-sales selling—persuading, influencing, and convincing others in ways that don't involve anyone making a purchase." Furthermore, "people consider this aspect of their work crucial to their success."[1]

Even if you don't think of yourself as someone who sells, you're actually doing it all the time. And it's not just in the workplace. It happens whenever you try to convince your friends to see a movie with you or to eat at your favorite restaurant. Whether you realize it or not, you're actually pitching every day.

In the next three chapters, you'll learn how to pitch your ideas even more effectively than you already do. You'll learn the importance of presenting a clear ask to a particular audience while approaching them with a personalized angle. You'll also learn how to push your audience away from the status quo while pulling them toward inspiring solutions. Finally, you'll learn the importance of revealing your expertise and presenting your pitch with efficiency.

Chapter 12

Ask, Audience, and Angle

As author and speaker Scott Berkun writes, "Ideas demand change. By definition, the application of an idea means that something different will take place in the universe. Even if your idea is undeniably and wonderfully brilliant, it will force someone, somewhere to change how they do something."[1]

This insight is key to successful persuasion. Too many speakers go into a pitch thinking that as soon as they present their amazing idea, the audience will be magically swept up by its brilliance and change what they're doing in exactly the way the speaker wants them to. Unfortunately, this is rarely the case.[2]

In a classic study, participants were exposed to a three-hour energy conservation workshop that showed them how easy it was to conserve energy at home. Afterwards, participants showed "greater awareness of energy issues, more appreciation for what could be done in their homes to reduce energy use, and a willingness to implement the changes that were advocated." But when researchers visited the participants' homes to follow up, they found that in all but a few cases, "behavior did not change."[3] Unfortunately, many other studies have found similar results.[4]

"But, wait!" you might say, "These people didn't hear *my* pitch! I can turn them into true believers!" Maybe so, but even this is unlikely to help. Unfortunately, many studies have found that actions are often only very loosely correlated with beliefs.[5] For example, when 500 people were interviewed about their personal responsibility for picking up litter, 94% said they felt they had one. But when this sense of responsibility was actually put to the test with a piece of litter planted by a researcher just outside the interview location, only 2% actually stopped to pick it up.[6]

If information alone doesn't lead to action, what are we to do? In the next few chapters you'll learn many techniques for effective persuasion, beginning with carefully crafting your ask.

The Ask

The first step to crafting a winning pitch is to determine exactly what you want your audience to do. This is your "ask." And while your ask is closely related to your idea, it's important to realize that they are not the same thing.[†]

If it isn't already blatantly obvious, here's our idea: "science can help you speak better." While this is a good idea (at least we think so!), if we simply present it to you and leave it at that, it's not entirely clear what we want you to *do* with this idea. To clarify what we mean, consider the following ways we might convert this idea into a specific ask:

- Buy this book.
- Read this book.
- Apply its lessons the next time you give a presentation.
- Give this book to someone who is afraid of speaking.
- Invite us to give a workshop at your company.
- Invite us to give a TED talk about the science of speaking.
- Offer a class on the science of speaking at your school.
- Use this book as the textbook in your class.

[†] This distinction between your idea and your ask is closely related to our earlier distinction between your topic and your thesis.

- Develop a science-based rubric for grading speeches.
- Conduct further speaking research.
- Fund further speaking research.

The first thing you'll notice about each of these asks is that they all ask people to *do* something instead of just asking them to rearrange bits in their brain. While it's certainly possible those rearranged bits might eventually lead to one of these outcomes—that believing "science can help you speak better" might lead a university administrator to explore offering a class on the science of speaking—it's even more effective to design your pitch around the specific outcome you want in the first place.

Make It Specific

Research has shown that the more specific you make your ask, the better. In a classic study, students were asked who in their dorm would be most and least likely to donate to a food drive (i.e., who were the "saints" and who were the "jerks"). Then two different requests were randomly sent out to the students. One was a general letter that simply asked them to bring a can of food to a well-known plaza on campus. The other was a more detailed letter which included a specific request for a can of beans, a map to the precise spot on the plaza, and a suggestion that they think about a time when they'd be near that spot so they wouldn't have to go out of their way.

Of the students who were given the general letter, 8% of the "saints" donated—and 0% of the "jerks." Of those who were given the specific letter, 42% of the "saints" donated, as well as 25% of the "jerks." There are two things to note here: 1) "saints" who received a specific letter were more than five times as likely to donate as "saints" who received a general letter, and 2) "jerks" who received a specific letter were more than three times as likely to donate as "saints" who received a general letter![7]

Of course, while you want your ask to be specific, it's also good to give your audience some flexibility within that level of specificity:

even those who received the specific letter were given a week-long window in which to donate, rather than a specific time. This is important because other studies have found that a goal that is specific yet flexible is more likely to be met than one that is specific and rigid.[8]

Start Small

As the ancient Chinese philosopher Lao-Tzu wrote, "A journey of a thousand miles begins with a single step."[9] The research on persuasion confirms this: another way you can make your pitch more successful is to make your initial ask small.

For example, in a study of door-to-door solicitation of donations for the American Cancer Society, 29% of people donated when asked if they would be willing to help. But when five words were added to the request, almost twice as many people were willing to donate! Those five words? "Even a penny will help." By starting with a small ask, you make it much more likely that your audience will be willing to accept it. And contrary to what you might expect, presenting this small ask didn't reduce the average size of donations, it simply increased the number of them and resulted in a greater sum of contributions![10]

Another benefit of starting with a small ask is that it can also make your audience more likely to accept a larger one down the road. In a classic study, participants were asked to put a small sign in their window that said "Be A Safe Driver." Because it was such a small request, almost everyone agreed to do so. Two weeks later, when they were asked to put an ugly 3 ft by 6 ft billboard on their lawn that said "Drive Carefully," 76% agreed to do so. When others were asked to put the billboard up without having previously been asked to put up the small sign, only 17% agreed.[11] Simply starting with a small ask made people four times more likely to accept a large one later!

Just Ask

We know what you're thinking: "This sounds complicated. What if I pick the wrong ask, and it gets rejected?" If so, you're in good company, because most people (including us) have similar concerns about rejection.[†]

Fortunately, rejection is less likely than we think. A variety of studies have found that people are generally twice as willing to help as we think they are![13] Unfortunately, this means that we often don't ask for help when we need it, even when people are ready and willing to provide it. And to make matters worse, while people who need help *underestimate* the likelihood that a request for help will be accepted, people in a position to provide help *overestimate* the likelihood that someone who needs help will ask for it![14] So just ask, and you shall (be more likely to) receive.[‡]

The Audience

Another thing you'll notice about the list of asks above is that many of them are directed at a particular audience. While the first four can apply to anyone, the remaining seven have a specific audience in mind. "Fund further speaking research" is only a reasonable ask if your audience actually has the power to do that. To achieve your goals, you need to pitch to the right audience.

If you want a raise, you need to pitch to your boss. If you want money for your startup, you need to pitch to investors. If you want Whole Foods to bring back salted frozen peas,[§] you need to pitch to their buyer. Once you've determined your ask, think about who

---

[†] Given that our brains process rejection in much the same way as they process physical pain, this seems quite reasonable.[12]

[‡] In *Rejection Proof: How I Beat Fear and Became Invincible Through 100 Days of Rejection*, Jia Jiang chronicles his quest to overcome rejection by consciously seeking it out for 100 days by making seemingly ridiculous requests of strangers. One of his most interesting findings, however, was that people were far more willing to say yes than he expected—including a woman who made him a Krispy Kreme donut in the shape of the Olympic rings![15]

[§] It's a long story...

can effectively act on it to help you get what you want. Then, design your pitch specifically for that audience.

Make It Relevant

For example, if you're pitching your new dating app to a group of students, a reasonable ask might be for them to try your app and provide feedback. On the other hand, if you're pitching your app to a group of venture capitalists, a reasonable ask might be for them to provide millions of dollars in funding. If you mix up these two asks and audiences, asking students to provide millions of dollars in funding, your pitch is going to fall flat.

A great example of effective audience analysis comes from our new home state of Texas. In 1985, Texas was one of the most littered states—each year, it was spending $20 million dollars to clean up trash on its highways! Something had to change. So the Texas Department of Transportation asked advertising executive Tim McClure to create an ad campaign to address the problem.

McClure began by asking himself two questions. The first was, "Who is doing the littering?" He found that the litterbugs were mostly 18- to 35-year old males, whom he characterized as "bubbas in pickup trucks" who believed it was their God-given right to throw beer cans from their pickup trucks.

The second question he asked himself was, "What does this group care about?" Well, they're anti-establishment rebels, so they certainly aren't going to care to do anything the Texas Department of Transportation asks of them. But they're also tough guys, fiercely proud of their home state.

To effectively appeal to these tough but littering Texans, McClure recruited other Texan tough guys—sports stars, musicians, and other Texas icons—to star in a variety of ads featuring the slogan: "Don't Mess with Texas." One popular ad even featured a B-17 bomber from the Confederate Air Force hunting down an unfortunate litterer!

The campaign was so successful that in the 30 years since it debuted, "Don't Mess with Texas" has become ingrained in Texas culture. It's a phrase universally known and recited, synonymous with Texas toughness—even though it started as an environmental campaign! And as for the littering? In the first four years of the campaign, littering in Texas dropped by a whopping 72%! All because of McClure's astute audience analysis.[16]

As McClure expertly demonstrated, once you've decided on your ask and your audience, the next step is to figure out why your audience will care.[†] In the case of the students in our example above, it might be that your app can get them more dates. For venture capitalists, on the other hand, it might be that they can get a good return on investment. Once again, if you mix up these motivations and tell venture capitalists that your app will get them more dates, your pitch is going to be far less successful.

While mixing up these two motivations may seem silly, a similar kind of mix-up happens all too often. According to advertising pioneer John Caples, "The most frequent reason for unsuccessful advertising is advertisers who are so full of their own accomplishments (the world's best seed!) that they forget to tell us why we should buy (the world's best lawn!)."[18] Of course, this focus on your accomplishments is understandable—you've spent a long time perfecting "the world's best seed." But honestly, that's really not what matters. What matters is what the audience gets out of it—what Chip and Dan Heath call the "benefit of the benefit." As the saying goes, "people don't buy quarter inch drill bits. They buy quarter-inch holes so they can hang their children's pictures."[19]

A great real-world example of this principle can be seen in Sam Mendes' ad for FaceTime on the iPhone 4.[‡] Rather than explaining the technical specifications of the hardware and software, it simply

---

[†] It's important to note that this is often quite different from why *you* care. And though it can often be hard to believe, that's okay. What matters is not so much *why* they care, as *that* they care. Interestingly, a recent study found that when it comes to politics, "(a) political advocates spontaneously make arguments grounded in their own moral values, not the values of those targeted for persuasion, and (b) political arguments reframed to appeal to the moral values of those holding the opposing political position are typically more effective." By reframing your arguments to appeal to the values of your audience, rather than your own, you can make them much more persuasive.[17]

[‡] You can see it at scienceofspeaking.com/facetime.

shows a series of emotional examples of the technology in use: a father on a business trip seeing his children, grandparents seeing their granddaughter prepare for graduation, a woman helping her friend pick clothes for a date, a soldier seeing his wife's ultrasound, and a deaf man signing to his fiancée over the phone. Despite the fact that it uses no words whatsoever, it's one of the most effective pitches we've ever seen.

Personalize It

As you let your audience know how they'll benefit, it's best if you can make it personal. For example, in 1982, psychologists tested two different sales pitches for cable television. One group of homeowners was told:

> Cable television will provide a broader entertainment and informational service to its subscribers. Used properly, a person can plan in advance to enjoy events offered. Instead of spending money on the babysitter and gas, and putting up with the hassles of going out, more time can be spent at home with family, alone, or with friends.

A second group of homeowners was told:

> Take a moment and imagine how cable television will provide you with a broader entertainment and informational service. When you use it properly, you will be able to plan in advance which of the events offered you wish to enjoy. Take a moment and think of how, instead of spending money on the babysitter and gas, and then having to put up with the hassles of going out, you will be able to spend your time at home, with your family, alone, or with your friends.

Even though these two messages are very similar, the results were not: while only 20% of homeowners in the first group subscribed to cable, a whopping 47% of homeowners in the second group subscribed. Simply personalizing the pitch by asking the audience to imagine the benefits for *them* more than doubled the number of subscribers![20]

Studies have also shown that using people's names—in particular, their first names—makes them significantly more likely to comply with your requests.[21] So while you can't always refer to everyone in the audience by their first name, it may be beneficial to use the first names of key decision-makers.

Interestingly, you don't even need to use their name to have an effect: sometimes, all it takes is the first letter. For example, one study found that people whose names begin with the letter R were 260% more likely to donate to support relief efforts for Hurricane Rita than people whose names began with other letters.[22] Similarly, research has shown that our names can influence our profession (Dennis is more likely to become a dentist), where we choose to live (Florence is more likely to move to Florida), who we marry (Charles is more likely to marry Charlotte), and what products we buy (Herman is more likely to like Hershey's).[†] Thus, if you know you're pitching to Steve, it may be a good idea for you to surreptitiously slip some additional Ss into your speech.

Regardless of how you personalize your pitch, your audience will appreciate that you have done so. This is why crowds go wild when rock stars say the name of their town during a concert (and why rock stars never fail to do it). Even if the rest of the show is the same in every town, the fact that they took the time to recognize your town is meaningful.

Simply showing the audience that you've taken the time to personalize your pitch has also been found to increase an audience's willingness to accept your ask. For example, in one study, adding a handwritten sticky note requesting completion of a survey more than doubled the response rate. (It also decreased the response time and improved the quality of the answers.) Adding a "Thank You!" to the note along with the researcher's initials increased the response rate even further.[‡]

[†] Aren't human beings wonderful?![23]

[‡] In support of persuasive *speaking*, a recent study found that a request made in person was 34 times more effective than a request made by email![24]

Find Common Ground

Another thing that will make your audience more likely to accept your ask is seeing you as similar to them. For example, one study found that people are almost twice as likely to return a survey that was sent to them from someone with a similar name, i.e., Cynthia Johnston is more likely to return a survey from Cindy Johanson than one from Robert Greer.[25]

This similarity effect extends beyond names to all kinds of social groupings. In another study, fans of the English football[†] team Manchester United were asked to write down what they liked about their team and then walk to another building. Along the way, they saw a jogger trip and fall, presumably injuring himself. The jogger was wearing one of three different shirts: a plain white shirt, a Manchester United shirt, or a shirt of their rival, Liverpool. When the jogger was wearing a white shirt, a third of the participants stopped to help him. When the jogger was wearing a Manchester United shirt, the overwhelming majority stopped. And when the jogger was wearing the shirt of their rival, almost everyone left the jogger to fend for himself![26] Therefore, if you can find common ground with your audience and make that explicit in your pitch, they will be more likely to accept your ask.

But what if we, as Stanford fans, want to pitch something to Cal fans? Does that mean we're simply out of luck? Fortunately, no. In the jogger study, if Manchester United fans were asked what they liked about being football fans instead of what they liked about their team, they became twice as likely to help someone wearing a Liverpool shirt. This is because they had been primed to think of themselves as football fans, and even a Liverpool fan is part of that group. So while singing "All Right Now" won't help our pitch to the Bears, we may be able to increase our success by mentioning that the West Coast is the best coast.

[†] Also known as soccer in the United States.

The Angle

Once you've determined your ask and your audience, the next step is to develop your angle—the approach you will take to convince your audience to accept your ask. In the next two chapters, we'll explore a variety of effective angles you can use to push and pull your audience closer to accepting your ask while presenting your expertise and pitching with efficiency.

Chapter 13

Push and Pull

The Push

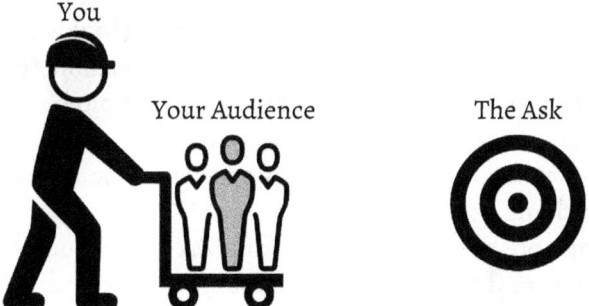

Countless studies have demonstrated that when given a choice between sticking with the status quo and changing, people have an overwhelming bias for the status quo. In Austria, where there is an opt-out system for organ donation, there is a 99.98% participation rate. In neighboring Germany, where there is an opt-in system, the rate is only 12%.[1] Regardless of which option is the default, the vast majority of people stick with it.

As we've seen before, it's not enough to simply present your audience with a new option and hope they choose it. To effectively convince them it's worth changing from the status quo, you must first convince them there are issues with it.

Reveal the Issues

In a classic study, students were shown one of several different pamphlets about tetanus. The first, which simply proposed it was a good idea to get a tetanus shot and gave a specific plan for how to get one, wasn't particularly effective. A second pamphlet, which added a description of the frightening consequences of getting tetanus, was much more effective. This shows that it's not enough just to give people the option to change: it's also important to explain the consequences of not changing. By revealing issues with the status quo, you push your audience away from it.

Extensive research has revealed that this focus on the consequences, on what the audience stands to lose if they don't change, can be significantly more effective than simply presenting the benefits of changing. This is because people are highly loss averse. What this means in plain English is that it hurts more to lose $100 than it feels good to gain $100. Therefore, your pitch will often be more persuasive if you frame it in terms of what your audience will lose by sticking with the status quo rather than what they will gain by changing.[2]

While pushing people away from the status quo, it's critical to make sure that you're pushing them in a particular direction, specifically, toward your ask. In the tetanus shot study, a third pamphlet, which included the frightening consequences but no specific plan, was also ineffective. Faced with a problem but no clear solution, the audience is more likely to block out or deny the problem instead of acting to solve it.[3] If we simply said, "giving a speech can be an embarrassing experience," all we would do is increase our audience's aversion to speaking. A better pitch would be: "giving a speech can be an embarrassing experience if you don't know how, but if you read our book, you'll have all the tools you need to succeed!"

Avoid Criticism

As you push your audience toward your ask, it's important to avoid criticizing them. This means that you don't want to characterize what they've done in the past (or what they're doing now) as a mistake. You don't want to say, "you suck, and here's the only way you can stop sucking!" (While nobody says it in quite those words, some people get surprisingly close.) That's no way to win over your audience. As in the tetanus example above, this is likely to cause people to tune out, or worse yet, to argue against you. Whenever you can, you want to present your new idea as being consistent with your audience's current beliefs and practices, as opposed to being a radical departure from them.[4]

As social psychologist Eric Horowitz explains:
> Imagine you're a dedicated social liberal who is attempting to show a conservative friend the joys of gun control. You put your trump card on the table right away: Gun control saves lives. All evidence from around the world and within the U.S. points to that conclusion. You smirk, knowing that there's no way somebody can deny that argument. But things appear different to your friend. The upshot of your argument is that he has spent years supporting a set of policies that kill people. And yet he knows there's no way that could be true because he's a good person who wants what's best for the world. So what you're saying has to be false. It's not even worth considering.[5]

Rather than succeeding in convincing your friend, the paradoxical result of such an argument is that your friend will feel even more strongly that they are right in opposing gun control.[6]

Furthermore, a recent study found that, regardless of political affiliation, "politics makes us stupid."[7] First, participants were asked to solve a tricky math problem about the effectiveness of a skin cream in treating rashes. Next, they were asked to solve an analogous math problem that either confirmed or challenged their beliefs about gun control. Regardless of political affiliation, people were significantly more likely to get the answer wrong when it challenged their existing beliefs. Interestingly, being good at math didn't help. In fact, it actually made things worse: the people who were the best at math were the ones most influenced by their partisan bias! As one author summarized, "the smarter the person is, the dumber politics can make them."[8]

In another study, people were classified as either liberal or conservative and ranked on the basis of "science intelligence," defined as the ability to comprehend science. Across the political spectrum, people with low science intelligence were generally in agreement about the causes and risks of global warming: everyone was equally unsure about the causes and moderately concerned about the risks. However, as science intelligence increased, opinions diverged. While highly intelligent liberals believed there was solid evidence of human influence and an extremely high risk of serious consequences, highly intelligent conservatives believed there was little evidence of human influence and a low risk of serious consequences. The more intelligent the participants were, the more likely they were to toe the party line.

This means that as much as we'd all like it to be true, education alone won't help us bridge the partisan divide. If anything, these studies suggest it only makes the problem worse. So what can we do to make it better? Fortunately, there is a glimmer of hope. In addition to classifying people based on "science intelligence," researchers also classified people based on "science curiosity." While science intelligence is the "ability to comprehend science," science curiosity is the "desire for the pleasure of finding out what science knows for its own sake." Although these variables are obviously somewhat related, there's not a perfect correlation between them: you can be high on both, low on both, high one but low on the other, or somewhere in the middle for both.

While science intelligence increased partisan bias, science curiosity decreased it. Where the answers of highly intelligent participants diverged, the answers of highly curious participants converged. While highly curious liberals and conservatives still weren't in complete agreement, they were much closer to seeing eye-to-eye.

This is good news for the future of our country, and it suggests that we should devote even more effort to cultivating curiosity.†
But what does this all mean for effective pitching?

It means that rather than fighting against the existing beliefs of our audience, we'll have much greater success if we arouse their curiosity. We can do this by approaching the issue in new and interesting ways and presenting our audience with arguments they may never have considered. Indeed, in the global warming study, people across the political spectrum were much more likely to read an article that challenged their beliefs when the title of the article inspired curiosity by presenting itself as surprising. For example, if you swear by the old advice to imagine your audience in their underwear while speaking, you'll be more likely to read an article titled: "Scientists Report *Surprising* Evidence: Imagining Your Audience in Their Underwear Will Make You More Nervous" than one titled "Scientists Find *Still More* Evidence That Visualizing Your Audience in Their Underwear Is a Bad Idea."[9]

Get Emotional

In Chapter 5, we saw that emotion is a key part of an effective presentation. This is especially true in the case of persuasion. While it can be tempting to believe that we can just "stick to the facts" and leave emotion out of it entirely, research has shown that, in fact, we can't. And by that, we don't just mean that we shouldn't—we actually literally mean that we can't.

In *Descartes' Error: Emotion, Reason, and the Human Brain*, neurologist Antonio Damasio debunks the pervasive myth that decisions can be based on facts alone. Damasio tells the story of a patient who had part of his prefrontal cortex removed as a result of a brain tumor. In the process, the patient lost all ability to process emotion. As a result, he also found himself unable to make even the simplest of decisions. Asked to choose between two dates for an appointment, he spent almost 30 minutes going through a tedious

---

† For more on cultivating curiosity, see Chapter 16.

logical cost-benefit analysis about which date was better. Even after all of this effort, he was still unable to choose one.

As Damasio explains, emotion is essential to decision-making because it's what actually gives value—either positive or negative—to the alternatives. As we consider various options, our emotions mark the expected consequences of each one as either positive or negative, and this emotional calculus is what ultimately leads us to choose one option over another. Without emotions to mark one date as preferable to the other, Damasio's patient was totally unable to make a decision.[10]

While the decision-makers you are pitching to will likely have their prefrontal cortices intact and will naturally use their emotions to guide their decisions, you can enhance this process by using emotional appeals. By appealing to decision-makers in this way, you can influence their emotional calculus and make them more likely to accept your ask.†

For example, in a recent study, people were presented with one of two donation requests. One group was given statistics about hunger in Africa (e.g., "More than 11 million people in Ethiopia need immediate food assistance"). A second group was told:

> Any money that you donate will go to Rokia, a 7-year-old girl from Mali, Africa. Rokia is desperately poor, and faces a threat of severe hunger or even starvation. Her life will be changed for the better as a result of your financial gift.

Despite the fact that eleven million people logically need far more money than one girl, people presented with the emotional appeal gave twice as much money as people presented with the numerical one![12]

In addition to being more persuasive, emotional stories are also more memorable, which increases their chance of having a

---

† While the idea of encouraging your audience to feel might make you uncomfortable, research suggests that it's actually what they want. In a recent study involving Twitter, researchers found that the more emotional words (like "fight," "hate," "love," and "peace") there were in a tweet, the more likely it was to be retweeted. In fact, with each additional emotional word, the spread of the tweet increased by 20%![11]

lasting impact. For example, in a recent classroom experiment, each student was asked to give a one-minute persuasive speech, then everyone was distracted by a short video clip. When the clip was over, the students were asked to write down everything they remembered about each of the speeches. Here are the results:

> In the average one-minute speech, the typical student uses 2.5 statistics. Only one student in ten tells a story. [...But] when students are asked to recall the speeches, 63% remember the stories. Only 5% remember any individual statistic.[13]

While every speech you give will necessarily include facts, it's important not to overlook the power of feelings too.

The Pull

While negative emotions can be a powerful force for pushing your audience away from the status quo and toward your ask, it's important to ensure that your pitch isn't framed entirely in the negative. In fact, one study found that a pitch presented positively, in which the speaker "spoke with a friendly tone of voice, smiled often, nodded her head in agreement, and appeared cordial and inviting" was *twice* as effective as a pitch presented negatively, in which the speaker "spoke antagonistically, appeared intimidating, and was insistent."[14] So while the push is necessary, it is by no means sufficient.

Provide Solutions

When Nick was an undergraduate, he wrote a column for *The Stanford Daily* entitled "Positive Sustainability." In his opening piece, he lamented the fact that almost every article written about the environment is entirely negative, essentially saying, "We're All Going to Die!" If you're lucky, you might find an article that tells you how to be a little less bad—how to waste a little less water or use a little less gasoline. But the only thing you can possibly do is be less bad: the articles give you no way to be good.

In response, Nick presented an analogy. Imagine what would happen if your local gym took the same "less bad" approach, running a campaign with the slogan: "In thirty days, we can make you less weak! You'll still be weak, but at least you'll be less weak!" No one would sign up, because no one wants to be less weak—they want to be strong. As he wrote at the time, "Humans, Americans, and especially Stanford students aren't inspired by negatives—we're inspired by positives."

This led straight into the core philosophy of his column:
> We are in desperate need of a vision, and not one of environmental doom and gloom, as is reported daily in the media. Rather, what we need is a vision of environmental hope. A vision of an ecologically sound world that actually works. . . . A world in which all environmental, economic, and social indicators are getting steadily better, not worse, and where people are getting happier, not more depressed. What we need is a blueprint for a world of good.[15]

In the columns that followed, Nick presented his blueprint for a world of good. In addition to clearly explaining the issues with the status quo, he also clearly presented solutions to them. And not only that: the solutions he presented were designed so that they were clearly superior to the status quo. His argument wasn't just that we should consider electric cars because we need to use less oil, it was also that we should consider electric cars because they have the potential to be better cars, period, even in the absence of any concerns about oil!

While we've seen that pushing your audience away from the status quo is important, it's equally important to pull them toward something inspiring. As you're crafting your angle, look for ways to present your ask so that it represents a clear win over the status quo. You should not only show how your idea will solve the issues, but also how it will take the audience to a better place.

Appeal to the Best in Them

When crafting appeals to pull their audience toward their ask, speakers often underestimate their audience and severely limit the kinds of appeals they consider. They act as if they are speaking to an audience of Kevin O'Leary[†] clones, treating them as if they are motivated by nothing but cold hard cash.[16]

In reality, there are many things that motivate your audience. While no one has yet discovered a perfect theory of human motivation, Abraham Maslow provided a reasonable starting point. In his famous 1943 "Theory of Human Motivation," Maslow proposed that humans are motivated by a variety of basic needs. These range from physiological needs (for food, water, sleep) to needs for safety, love, esteem, understanding, and self-actualization (fulfilling our potential).[17] In later writings, he added the need for self-transcendence (contributing to something greater than ourselves), and metamotivation based on values such as truth, beauty, and justice (among others).[18] Instead of ignoring this diversity of motivations, we need to understand and embrace them, appealing to all of them in our pitches.

Even venture capitalists, who need to make a profit, aren't solely motivated by money. Like everyone else, they want to feel good about themselves (esteem), to become the best person they can be (self-actualization), to contribute to something greater than themselves (self-transcendence), and to see more truth, beauty, and justice in the world (metamotivation). Therefore, as you're

---

[†] Better known as "Mr. Wonderful" on ABC's *Shark Tank*.

thinking about how to motivate your audience, be sure to consider all of the things that might motivate them, not just the most obvious ones like money.[19]

Invite Them to Join the Bandwagon

One of the most effective persuasive pulls you can use in your pitch is what psychologists call "social proof." In a classic study, when one man stopped on the New York sidewalk and gazed skyward, few people stopped to see what he was looking at. When five people stopped and gazed skyward, the number of people stopping to join them quadrupled.[20]

In another study, psychologists tested two different methods of persuading hotel guests to reuse their towels. The first was a sign with a traditional environmental message about saving water and energy. The second was a sign informing guests that the majority of guests at the hotel had reused their towels. Guests who saw the social proof sign were 26% more likely to reuse their towels than those who saw the environmental message. Guests who saw a third sign informing them that people who had previously stayed in *their room* had reused their towels were even more likely to reuse them.[21] Thus, the best appeal is not just that "many people are doing this," but that "many people *like you* are doing this."

There's one important caveat, however. If we told you "everyone uses filler words," that sets the use of filler words as an acceptable norm, even if we simultaneously lament how terrible this is. In a study about the most effective way to deter theft of petrified wood from Arizona's Petrified Wood National Park, visitors who read a sign saying "Many past visitors have removed the petrified wood from the park, changing the natural state of the Petrified Forest" were actually three times more likely to steal a piece of wood from the forest than visitors who didn't see any sign![22] Therefore, instead of focusing on the number of people contributing to the issues, it's better to focus on the large (or growing) number of people who are adopting your solution (e.g., "Many people have succeeded in replacing their filler words with pauses!").

In the end, as you craft your pitch to move your audience toward to accepting your ask, it's important to consider both push and pull—to push your audience away from the status quo while simultaneously pulling them toward inspiring solutions.

Chapter 14

Expertise and Efficiency

While push and pull are excellent tools to help motivate your audience, alone, they are not enough to truly persuade them. It's equally important to share your expertise and pitch with efficiency.

Expertise

A good way to learn about pitches (both good and bad) is to watch ABC's *Shark Tank*, which features entrepreneurs pitching to a group of wealthy investors in order to get money to "start, grow, or save their business." One of the primary lessons we can learn from *Shark Tank* is the importance of presenting your expertise and explaining the value you bring to the table. This is where *Shark Tank* entrepreneurs often fail spectacularly: they present their idea without clearly explaining why they are the best person to implement it. As a result, the sharks say, "there's no patentable intellectual property here, so what's stopping me from taking the $500,000 you're asking for and hiring the best people in the world to do this better than you, crushing you like the cockroach you are while owning 100% of the company myself?" (Nobody said sharks play nice!) Far too many entrepreneurs are unprepared to answer this question. And as a result, they walk away with nothing.

You should always be ready to answer this question—to pitch not only your idea but also yourself. Why should the audience believe in you? What unique qualities do you bring to the table? If the next person through the door is pitching the same idea, why should an investor choose you and not them?

Establishing your expertise is important, but what's the most effective way to do it? According to "The Pitch Coach," David Rose, one good way to establish credibility as an expert in the field is to begin by stating a few things your audience already knows about the field and then going a step further to tell them something they don't know.[1] This shows the audience that you bring real value to the table. In a similar vein, you should be absolutely sure that you don't say anything your audience knows is not true because that will immediately destroy your credibility.[†] Many entrepreneurs have bombed on *Shark Tank* for exactly this reason.

Pass the Sinatra Test

Another way to establish your expertise is simply to cite your past successes. But while you probably have many great examples you could give, you won't time to talk about them all. Enter what Chip and Dan Heath call the "Sinatra Test," based on Frank Sinatra's song "New York, New York," in which he sings, "If I can make it there, I'll make it anywhere." An example of expertise passes the Sinatra Test when it alone is sufficient to establish credibility in a given domain. For example, if you've catered an event for the White House, you're in the running for any catering contract in the world, even if it's the only event you've ever done. If you can make it at the White House, you'll make it anywhere.[3]

By identifying and sharing the single most compelling example of your past experience, you can simultaneously establish your expertise while leaving yourself ample time to talk about what you actually want to pitch in the present.

[†] In his book *Steal the Show*, Michael Port elaborates on this idea, advising speakers to "give a presentation that doesn't have any holes to poke." In particular, he writes, "if I say 'No one likes earwax-flavored ice cream,' you could refute my theory because it's possible that someone does, as crazy as it sounds, like earwax-flavored ice cream." Therefore, you generally want to avoid absolutes like "everyone," "no one," "always," and "never."[2]

Show Your Potential

But what if you don't have such an example? What if you know you have the potential but don't (yet) have the credentials to back it up? You're in luck, because psychologists have found that a decision-maker's perception of a presenter's *potential* matters even more than their perception of a presenter's past *experience*.

For example, in one study, researchers found that a decision-maker was more likely to hire an applicant who had no relevant experience and a score of 92/100 on a test called the Assessment of Leadership *Potential*, than an applicant who had two years of relevant experience and a score of 92/100 on a test called the Assessment of Leadership *Achievement*.[4]

While this doesn't mean that past experience is irrelevant, it does mean that potential is also important. Therefore, finding ways to highlight your potential can be an effective way to bolster your audience's perception of your expertise, particularly where it may otherwise be lacking.

Avoid Hedging

Another way to establish your credibility is to avoid hedging when presenting your pitch. Using qualifying language like "kind of," "probably," "maybe," and "I think" will only weaken your point. In fact, in a recent analysis of corporate earnings calls by data scientists at Quantified Communications, they found that up to 2.5% of stock price movement can be attributed to the language a CEO uses, including whether they speak directly or hedge.[5] In another study, hedging led not only to negative perceptions of the pitch but also of the speaker delivering it![6]

At the same time, while using weak language diminishes your effectiveness, it turns out that admitting your weaknesses does not. In the courtroom, when jurors hear a lawyer mention a weakness in his own case before the opposing lawyer does, they perceive him to be more trustworthy, and view his case more favorably than when he didn't mention the weakness. The same is true of expert witnesses: when the prosecution's expert witness volunteers a weakness in her testimony before it is brought up by the defense, the jury is significantly more likely to side with the prosecution.[7]

When presenting your weaknesses, studies have found that it's best if you present them alongside corresponding strengths. For example, "I may be new to this industry, but that means I have fresh ideas to contribute."[8]

Use Testimonials

The most common complaint we hear from our students regarding expertise is that it feels awkward to be so self-promoting. And there's something to this concern: studies have shown that self-promotion is often viewed negatively and that people who are modest are better liked than those who are boastful.[9] On the other hand, there is also evidence that presenters who do not make positive assertions about themselves and their work are also perceived negatively.[10] So what are we to do?

In many cases, our best option is simply to strike a balance between the two extremes and walk a fine line of sharing our expertise without coming across as boastful.[11] But in other cases, there may be an even more elegant way out of this dilemma: if a third party presents your credentials, your audience will see you as both more competent and more likable than if you present the same credentials yourself.[12] Therefore, when possible, it pays to present your expertise through testimonials, reviews, or better yet, in-person introductions by people who know your work.

Cite Experts

One final way you can bolster your own expertise is to cite the expertise of others. In a recent study, participants were asked to make a series of difficult financial decisions. Alongside some of these decisions, the researchers presented advice from a prominent economist. Not only did this advice strongly influence the participants' decisions, it actually significantly reduced activity in the parts of their brains devoted to critical thinking. When given advice from an expert, the participants essentially out-sourced their decision-making to the expert's brain.[13] Therefore, by citing experts who support your cause, you can make your audience more likely to accept your ask.

Efficiency

Just as you don't want to oversell yourself, you also don't want to oversell your idea. When crafting your pitch, aim for efficiency: find the most effective angle for your audience and present it as concisely as you can.

As we saw in Part IV, the ideal structure of an effective argument is 3 x 3: three claims, repeated three times. While three claims are more persuasive than two, adding a fourth claim actually makes your argument less convincing. And while memory of a message increases with repetition, agreement with a message peaks at three repetitions.

These findings are particularly important to remember in the context of persuasion, where there is a natural tendency toward overselling. Some people believe that if they cram in as many claims as possible and repeat them as many times as they can, their argument will be even more persuasive. But as the research shows, this is not the case. Therefore, it's important to carefully craft your message in order to avoid overselling it.

In addition to having too many claims and repeating them too many times, there are several other pitfalls that result in less persuasive messages, including too many choices, too many arguments, and mixed motivations.

Too Many Choices

One common mistake is to offer your audience too many choices. Presenters often think that the more options the audience is given, the more likely they will be to choose one of them. In reality, it's precisely the opposite. For every retirement fund added to an employee's investment options, they become *less* likely to select *any* of them.[14] When shoppers are presented with a display of either six or twenty-four flavors of jam to sample, 30% buy jam from the smaller display, while only 3% buy jam from the larger display.[15] While it's tempting to give your audience more choices, cutting down the number of choices is actually better for everyone. In fact, when Proctor & Gamble decreased the number of different kinds of Head & Shoulders shampoo it offered from twenty-six to fifteen, sales increased by 10%.[16]

If you do want to offer your audience a choice, there are several things you can do to make your preferred choice more likely. First, if at all possible, make it the default. As we saw before, people are much more likely to stick with the default than to make a choice that deviates from it. If it's possible to arrange your ask so that your audience must opt out of it, they'll be more likely to accept it than if they have to opt in.[17]

If it's not possible to make your preferred choice the default, there are still other ways you can improve your chances. One is to make the choice an active choice, rather than just an option to opt-in. In one study, when people were given the option to save money on their health insurance by getting a flu shot, 42% chose to do so. When they were asked to make an active choice between getting a flu shot and not getting a flu shot, 62% chose to do so. Finally, when the consequences of each option (i.e., decreasing flu risk and saving money vs. increasing flu risk and not saving money) were explicitly presented alongside the choices, 75% chose to get a flu shot.[18]

Averaging Arguments

In addition to adding more choices, speakers are often tempted to present additional benefits, for example, "buy now, and we'll throw in a free gift." While this seems like a logical way to increase persuasion, it often backfires. Consider the following irrational findings. Customers are willing to pay more for an iPod than they are for an iPod that also comes with a free music download. And a $750 fine for littering is perceived as more severe than a $750 fine plus 2 hours of community service.[19]

The psychological explanation for these findings is that rather than having an *additive* effect, piling on additional benefits (or punishments) can actually have an *averaging* effect. Although the addition of a free music download obviously adds value to the iPod, the fact that the value of the music is much lower than the value of the iPod drags down the customer's perception of the combined deal. Therefore, rather than piling on additional (and weaker) arguments, it's better just to stick with your best arguments and make sure they all have equal force.

Mixed Motivations

Worse yet, when certain kinds of appeals are combined, they can negate each other entirely. This often happens when intrinsic and extrinsic motivations are combined. For example, when a group of homeowners was informed that they were using more energy than their neighbors, they decreased their energy use by 6%. Perhaps they felt bad about using more energy, or they wanted to be better than their neighbors: whatever their motivation was, it was entirely intrinsic. When a second group of homeowners was given extrinsic motivation for using less energy in the form of a monetary incentive, their energy use decreased by a similar amount. However, when a third group of homeowners was given both the intrinsic and extrinsic motivations at the same time, they didn't reduce their energy use at all![20]

Similar effects have been found in studies of charitable giving: when egoistic ("it will make you feel good") and altruistic ("it will help others") reasons for giving are provided at the same time, people give less than when only one of these reasons is provided.[21] When motivations are mixed like this, listeners see the message for what it is—an attempt to persuade—and become less likely to accept your ask.

In a particularly dramatic demonstration of the dangers of mixing intrinsic and extrinsic motivation, psychologists introduced a monetary fine for parents who were late to pick up their children from daycare in an attempt to decrease the number of late pickups. As a result of the fine, the number of late pickups actually *doubled*! What happened is that the introduction of extrinsic motivation (a monetary fine) broke the parent's intrinsic motivation for picking up their children on time (a sense of social obligation). To make matters worse, when the fine was removed, the number of late pickups did not return to normal. Even a temporary mixing of motivations can have permanent consequences![22]

Therefore, while both intrinsic and extrinsic motivations can be effective, it's important to stick to one or the other. More generally, you always want to ensure that all aspects of your pitch are consistent with each other.

Argumentative Archery

In the end, persuasion can be compared to archery. In an Olympic archery competition, the archer fires three arrows, each stabilized by three feathers. The feathers represent your claims, which all work together to support your thesis, the arrow. In your roadmap, body, and scrapbook, you fire this arrow three times.

The goal is not to fire as many arrows as you can, covered in as many feathers as possible, in order to blanket the target and hope that you hit the bullseye. The goal is to carefully craft each arrow and feather so they will work together to fly true and hit the bullseye every time.

Conclusion

In order to successfully persuade your audience, you should consider the ask, the audience, and the angle, including push and pull and expertise and efficiency.

- **The Ask**: First, turn your idea into an ask. The most effective asks are small and specific yet flexible.

- **The Audience**: Next, tailor your pitch to the audience. Make your ask relevant, personalize it, and find common ground with the audience.

- **The Angle**: Use both push and pull and expertise and efficiency to persuade your audience to accept your ask

    - **Push and Pull**: Reveal the issues with the status quo to push the audience toward your ask while avoiding criticism of their current views and actions. Don't be afraid to use emotion. At the same time, provide inspiring solutions that pull your audience toward your ask. Appeal to the best in them, and invite them to join the growing bandwagon.

    - **Expertise and Efficiency**: Show the audience that you have the experience and potential to make it happen. Be careful not to oversell your message, and make your pitch as efficient as you can.

Part VII

Technical Communication

Introduction

Glissé, coupé, passé, glissé, coupé, jeté.

For people like us, who specialize in reconstructing and teaching social ballroom dances from the 19th through the 21st centuries, this sentence is packed with meaning, efficiently describing the mid-19th century Polka Mazurka.

To most of you, however, it probably means nothing. The sentence is written entirely in jargon—technical language specific to a field of study that is difficult for anyone outside that field to understand. The words above make sense to social dance historians, but not to anyone else! Alright, let's try again:

1: Slide left foot to side (2nd). 2: Draw right to left, at the same time passing left to side (2nd raised). 3: Hop on right, at the same time bringing left toward right ankle (3rd raised). 4 & 5: Repeat 1 & 2. 6: Leap from left to right, turning half round.[†]

This version, adapted from M. B. Gilbert's description of the Polka Mazurka in *Round Dancing* (1890), is slightly better, written mostly in words you understand, but at the same time, it still includes some jargon. What the heck is "2nd raised"?

Let's try one more time:

Count 1: Move your left foot to the left, keeping it on the floor.

[†] You might wonder why we included this second example, instead of simply giving you the final version. While few presenters are as bad as the first example, this is second example is eerily similar to the technical presentations we see every day. The presenter is attempting to translate their topic, but hasn't quite gotten there. Don't worry: in the next two chapters, we'll get you there!

Count 2: Move your right foot toward your left foot so it takes the place of your left foot while moving your left foot to the left again, slightly raised off the floor, foot pointed.

Count 3: Lift your left foot toward your right leg, just above your right foot, as you jump in place on your right foot.

Counts 4 and 5: Repeat counts 1 and 2.

Count 6: Jump from your right foot to your left foot, turning half way around to the right.

This version, while still far from perfect, is approaching something you might actually be able to visualize. If you're ambitious, you might even try to dance it. (If you want to see what it looks like in practice, there's a video of us dancing it in 19th century attire at scienceofspeaking.com/mazurka.)

While this version still describes something very complicated, it does so in words we all understand. In fact, it does so using only the thousand most commonly used words in English.[†] Of course, effectively communicating technical knowledge to a general audience doesn't require limiting yourself to the thousand most common words in English.[‡] It does, however, require translating technical language into words your audience can understand, and making the topic interesting to them. That's what the next two chapters are all about.

[†] In his popular webcomic *xkcd* (xkcd.com/1133), Randall Munroe used these same thousand words to describe the "US Space Team's Up Goer Five" (also known as NASA's Saturn V rocket). Later, Munroe used the same approach to describe a wide variety of technical topics in his book *Thing Explainer: Complicated Stuff in Simple Words*.[1] While we certainly don't recommend that you actually talk like this, Munroe's approach can be a useful exercise for getting you to think about your technical topic in much simpler ways. If you want to try it out yourself, Munroe has created a web tool (xkcd.com/simplewriter) that checks your writing against a dictionary of those words.

[‡] In a TED talk about the power of words, wordsmith John Koenig proposes that we evaluate the usefulness of words based on the question "how many brains will this give me access to?" As he notes, "a word is essentially a key that gets us into certain people's heads. And if it gets us into one brain, it's not really worth it. ...Two brains, eh, it depends on who it is. A million brains—okay, now we're talking. A real word is one that gets you access to as many brains as you can. That's what makes it worth knowing."[2]

What is Technical Knowledge?

At Stanford, after students give their pitch, it's time for their next assignment: a technical speech. Whereas the scientists and engineers often protest the pitch, now it's everyone else's turn to gripe. "I'm not a scientist or engineer, so I don't have any technical knowledge! How can I possibly give a technical speech?"

The truth is that *everyone* has technical knowledge. While it's obvious that a theoretical physicist has technical knowledge about quantum gravity and a civil engineer has technical knowledge about earthquake-safe buildings, these aren't the only kinds of technical knowledge. A gamer has the unique ability to explain the ins and outs of LoL and WoW. A ballerina knows the difference between a chaînés and a soutenu. And a football player knows the difference between a bubble screen and a buttonhook.

What all of these people have in common is a specialized vocabulary unique to their fields. If they talk to a general audience like they talk to their colleagues, the general audience will have trouble understanding them. This leads us to the definition of technical knowledge—any information that requires translation for a general audience to understand it. Technical communication is the process of sharing this technical knowledge in a way that is understandable to a general audience.

As we'll see in the following two chapters, the key to effective technical communication is simultaneously exciting your audience and enlightening them.

Chapter 15

Excite

While our simplified description of the Polka Mazurka is much more understandable than the first, there's still a critical piece of information missing: why you should care about it. As it turns out, there are many answers to this question, which are covered extensively in Nick's first book, *Waltzing: A Manual for Dancing and Living*. Dances like the Polka Mazurka are far more than historical curiosities: they are actually some of the most powerful tools that human beings have ever discovered for improving our lives and relationships.[†] In addition to being good fun and great exercise, social dancing provides countless benefits, including relieving stress, building trust, and even making you smarter![2] Now, doesn't the Polka Mazurka seem much more exciting?

Unsurprisingly, a large body of research has shown that we are more likely to understand and remember things that we find interesting.[3] If your audience isn't interested in what you have to say, you have little chance of communicating successfully.

But this way of stating things puts the blame on the wrong person, suggesting that the audience's disinterest is *their* fault.

[†] In a book on the importance of language to human evolution, anthropologist Robin Dunbar writes, "Language allowed us to find out about each other, to ask and answer questions about who was doing what with whom. But of itself, it does not bond groups together. Something deeper and more emotional was needed to overpower the cold logic of verbal arguments. It seems that we needed music and physical touch to do that."[1]

In fact, it's precisely the opposite: it's *your* job as the speaker to get your audience interested. In this chapter, you'll learn some effective ways to do this.

Make It Relevant

One day, when Nick was in a class on differential equations at Stanford, the instructor turned around during a lesson on Laplace transforms and said: "By the way, Laplace transforms are totally useless. You will never use them in the real world." As stressed out students, we silently screamed in unison, "Then why the #@%! are we learning about them?!" Later that night, when Nick relayed this story to his father, a professor of Aeronautics and Astronautics at Stanford, he was absolutely appalled. "I use Laplace transforms every day!" he exclaimed. What does he use them for, you ask? To make air travel safer using GPS.

What a tragically wasted opportunity for learning! According to the instructor, Laplace transforms were completely irrelevant. All that was in it for us was lots of hard work with zero reward. According to Nick's father, what was in it for us was safer airplanes (and countless other engineering innovations). How much better that lesson on Laplace transforms could've been if it had been introduced in such a relevant way!

The first step toward exciting your audience is to show them how your topic is relevant to them—how listening to your speech will enrich their lives. Relevance can be established in a variety of ways. If listening to your speech will directly benefit your audience—for example, by showing them how energy efficiency can save them money—then that's your relevance right there.

But this isn't the only way to establish relevance. This is because, as we've seen before, our immediate self-interest isn't all that interests us. If you announce that you've found a cure for cancer, you'll immediately have the interest of everyone in the room, even those of us who don't have cancer. Your speech can also be relevant simply because it's entertaining or inspiring. (There are multi-billion dollar industries that exist solely for these purposes!)

When coaching our students on technical speeches, we always ask them how their topic is relevant to their audience. It's tragic how often these students reply "I don't know," or worse yet, "it's not." Our response to these students, and to you, is two-fold.

First, if you think your topic is irrelevant, that's BS. With a little bit of creative thinking, you can find a way to make any topic relevant to any audience. Second, and more importantly, if you truly believe your topic is irrelevant to your audience, why are you even giving the speech? Remember, speaking is all about communicating something of value to your listeners. If you truly believe your topic is irrelevant to them, you're better off picking a different topic or audience.

Arouse Their Curiosity

The rings of Saturn are one of the most spectacular features of our Solar System, unlike any other planetary structure we've studied. So what are the rings of Saturn made of, anyway?

Before a definitive answer was discovered, three internationally acclaimed groups of scientists came to three wholly different conclusions. One group, at Cambridge University, proclaimed the rings were made of gas. Another group, at MIT, was convinced they were made of dust. A third group of scientists, at Cal Tech, insisted they were made of ice.

So what was the final answer to this mystery? We'll get there, but first, let's see what's going on here. This example, from Robert Cialdini, demonstrates the power of mystery in generating interest in a topic. While you probably weren't particularly interested in the rings of Saturn a minute ago, now, you want to know the answer. As Cialdini explains, "Mystery stories do not need personal relevance—they bring their own."[4]

So how can we use the power of mystery to make our presentations more engaging? One easy and effective method is proposed by George Loewenstein, a behavioral economist at Carnegie Mellon. Summarizing decades of research, Loewenstein explains that curiosity arises when we perceive a gap in our knowledge. For example, as people who are knowledgeable about technical communication, you could immediately arouse our interest by telling us that you discovered a new way of getting an audience excited about any topic. By pointing out a gap in our knowledge, you make us want to fill it.

This technique is most effective when the gap in our knowledge is small. On one hand, if you have memorized all but 3 of the 50 state capitals, you'll likely be eager to learn the 3 that you're missing. On the other hand, if you only know 3 capitals, learning the remaining 47 may seem more daunting than pressing.[5]

So what if your audience is in the latter category, with little knowledge about your topic? What if the gap is more like the Grand Canyon? The key is to start by filling in that canyon until all that remains is a manageable gap. This is exactly what happened when we provided background information on the mystery of Saturn's rings, introducing you to the topic and the three opposing theories but leaving a small but essential gap unfilled: the final answer to the mystery.

Which is dust, by the way. Well, ice-covered dust, which may help explain the initial confusion. Now, there's certainly nothing inherently exciting about dust, even when it's covered in ice. But when a little bit of background information left a small gap in your knowledge, ice-covered dust became much more interesting.

Show Your Enthusiasm

Remember Nick's differential equations instructor, who failed to make Laplace transforms relevant? Unfortunately, that incident was just one of many. On the last day of class, it got even worse. Just before dismissing us, he turned to us and said, "I have *not* enjoyed teaching you this quarter." Emphasis on the "not."

As shocking as this comment may seem, it honestly didn't come as much of a surprise. The instructor had made it perfectly clear since the first day that he had little interest in teaching the class. As a result, we had little interest in being there.

One of the easiest and most effective ways you can generate excitement about your topic is to show your own enthusiasm for it. In fact, in a study of the many different factors that influence a student's motivation to learn, instructor enthusiasm emerged as the single most powerful motivator![6]

Showing your enthusiasm for your topic is essential, but what's the best way to do this? As it turns out, you already know the answer. In another experiment, instructor enthusiasm was experimentally manipulated by presenting two versions of the same lecture, one with "enthusiastic qualities" and the other without. What were these enthusiastic qualities? "Vocal delivery with variation in pace, volume, and intonation; eyes that open wide and 'light up'; demonstrative gesturing; large body movements; facial expression of emotion; and a high level of overall energy and vitality," i.e., everything you learned to do in Part III.[7] Students who saw the lecture with these enthusiastic qualities were much more likely to want to learn more about the subject.[†]

Another study presented students with two versions of an entire quarter-long class. On every measure, students rated the enthusiastic version of the class as significantly better. Not only was the professor rated as more enthusiastic—he was also rated as more knowledgeable, more tolerant, more accessible, and more or-

---

[†] If you want to see a great example of enthusiasm in action, Benjamin Zander's talk at TED 2008 is second to none.[8] Even if you have zero interest in classical music, his infectious enthusiasm will leave you wanting to learn more.

ganized. In addition, students not only reported that they learned more in the enthusiastic class and were more likely to recommend it to their friends—they also believed that the class had clearer goals, fairer grading, and a better quality textbook, even though none of these aspects of the course had changed![9]

Robert Cialdini proposes a neat little trick for infusing your presentations with more enthusiasm. As he writes:

> After a few years in the classroom, I noticed that there were some lectures I dreaded giving because the students were bored by the material. There were other lectures that I loved to deliver because the students enjoyed the material. I am sure that the self-fulfilling prophecy phenomenon played a role. On certain days, I expected to be uninteresting and, dispirited by the prospect, I was. On other days, I expected to be interesting and, enlivened by the prospect, I was.
>
> Anyway, the trick was to reconfigure my lectures so that I inserted into each one something that I genuinely looked forward to presenting because students loved it, such as a humorous anecdote, a riveting example, or an especially clever experiment. The key was to have at least one such high point per session. ... The intention was to motivate students to look forward to class by motivating myself to do the same. I found I was a much better teacher when I had a special reason to want to be in each class session.[10]

Sometimes, the best way to excite your audience is to find a way to get yourself excited again.[†]

[†] It's also tragic how often our students find their own content boring. If you're not excited to give your speech (setting aside the inevitable nerves, of course), it may be worth re-evaluating why you're giving the speech at all.

Shoot for the STARs

In his talk about malaria at TED 2009, Bill Gates began by establishing the gravity of the situation, noting that over 200 million people are suffering from malaria at any given time and countless millions have already died. And yet, he lamented, we spend more money developing baldness cures for rich men than fighting this deadly disease for the poor.

At that moment, he released a jar of mosquitoes into the room, explaining, "malaria is of course transmitted by mosquitos. I brought some here, just so you could experience this. We'll let those roam around the auditorium a little bit. There's no reason only poor people should have the experience."[11]

This is what Nancy Duarte calls a STAR moment, short for "Something They'll Always Remember." In *Resonate: Present Visual Stories That Transform Audiences*, she notes that a STAR moment is "so profound or so dramatic that it becomes what the audience chats about at the watercooler or appears as the headline of a news article." This moment can come in many different forms—a prop, a demo, a shocking statistic, an evocative image, an emotional story, or even a well-crafted sound bite—the key is that it keeps the conversation going long after the speech is over.[12]

The STAR moment is an important idea, with an important caveat. The point of a STAR moment is to create "Something They'll Always Remember." This is great, as long as this moment is what you want them to remember.

For example, while we'll always remember the Bill Gates mosquito moment, to be honest, that's really all we remember. "While talking about malaria, Bill Gates released mosquitoes into the auditorium." That's the one sentence we remember about his speech. Which is certainly better than nothing, because it inspired us to rewatch the talk years later and include the example in this book. But before going back and watching the talk again, we didn't remember any of the specific statistics, only vaguely recalled some of his proposed solutions, and had completely forgotten that the second half of his talk was about charter schools.

In the field of educational psychology, there has been extensive research on precisely this problem. Used the right way, a STAR moment can be a powerful tool for exciting your audience. However, when crafting your STAR moment, you need to be careful to ensure that this moment actually helps your audience remember what you want them to remember, instead of distracting them from your main message.

In one study, students were asked to read several different explanations of lightning formation. In one version, the description was informative but not very interesting, with dry text and boring diagrams. In another version, the basic explanation remained the same, but interesting details were added to "spice it up," such as:

> Approximately 10,000 Americans are injured by lightning every year. Witnesses in Burtonsville, Maryland, watched as a bolt of lightning tore a hole in the helmet of a high school football player during practice. The bolt burned his jersey, and blew his shoes off.

After reading one of these explanations, students were tested on their knowledge of lightning formation. As it turns out, students who read the basic explanation actually remembered twice as much about the mechanics of lightning formation as students who read the version with interesting but irrelevant details![13] As interesting as they were, the irrelevant details actually drew the students' interest away from the main message. For this reason, psychologists call them "seductive details."

The key, then, is not to pepper your speech with seductive details. It's to find creative ways to make your topic exciting by making it relevant, arousing curiosity, showing your enthusiasm, and creating STAR moments that encapsulate your message.[†]

[†] For a great example of an effective STAR moment, see Sir Ken Robinson's story about Gillian Lynne on p. 191.

Chapter 16

Enlighten

In a study by Stanford graduate student Elizabeth Newton, participants were assigned to one of two roles: "tapper" or "listener." The tappers tapped out the rhythm of a well-known song, like "Happy Birthday," and the listeners tried to guess the song.

When the tappers were asked how successful they thought they were, they believed their listeners would be able to guess the song 50% of the time. In reality, over the course of the entire experiment, only 3 songs were correctly identified by the listeners, for a total success rate of 2.5%. The tappers overestimated their success by a factor of twenty![1] As Chip and Dan Heath explain,

> When a tapper taps, it is impossible for her to avoid hearing the tune playing along to her taps. Meanwhile, all the listener can hear is a kind of bizarre Morse code. Yet the tappers were flabbergasted by how hard the listeners had to work to pick up the tune. The problem is that once we know something—say, the melody of a song—we find it hard to imagine not knowing it. Our knowledge has "cursed" us. We have difficulty sharing it with others, because we can't readily re-create their state of mind.[2]

The curse of knowledge is essential to understand (and account for) when it comes to technical communication. As you speak about your topic, it makes perfect sense to you because you can't avoid "hearing the tune." But often, all your audience hears is gibberish. At least until you translate it for them.

Translate the Language

Technical communication is like giving your audience a tour of a foreign land. One of the first things a visitor to this new land will notice is that the inhabitants speak a different language, or at least a different dialect with different slang.

Imagine that your friend from Australia is giving you a tour of her country. While you're there, you hear a variety of new terminology, like "ankle biter," "Hungry Jack's," and "power point" (not the presentation software). As someone who is new to these Aussie turns of phrase, you'll greatly appreciate it if your friend translates them for you.[†] The same is true in a technical presentation: your audience will greatly appreciate it if you translate the language of your field so they can understand what you're talking about.

Unfortunately, many presenters fail to do this, leaving their audience drowning in a sea of jargon. The curse of knowledge leads them to assume that their audience already knows the language, so they don't realize there's anything that needs translating. This results in the speaker saying something like:

> The slow French waltz is a slow pirouette followed by a pas de bourée, all in relevé.[3]

This sentence is clearly too technical, filled with specialized dance terminology that a general audience has no hope of understanding. To be comprehensible, this sentence requires translation. Here's a version of the same sentence in everyday language:

> The slow French waltz is a slow turn in place followed by three steps forward, all on tiptoe.

This version at least has a fighting chance of being understandable to a general audience. (Of course, further description and a

---

[†] Ankle biter = child
Hungry Jack's = Burger King
power point = power outlet

demonstration would likely still be appreciated. You can see us dancing it at scienceofspeaking.com/waltz.)

In some cases, this translated description will be sufficient. If all that matters is that the audience understands the basic idea of the dance, this everyday description gets that done. But sometimes, an important part of your goal in giving your technical presentation is actually to teach your audience some new terminology. In this case, a hybrid approach may be best:

> The slow French waltz begins with a slow turn in place, called the slow pirouette. This is followed by the pas de bourée, which is really just a fancy name for taking three steps forward. All steps are taken on tiptoe, in what dancers call relevé.

While it is still as understandable as Version 2, Version 3 has the added benefit of teaching the audience the meaning of "pirouette," "pas de bourée," and "relevé" along the way.[†]

As you prepare your technical presentation, think about what you really want the audience to take away from it. If the technical language is not important for them to know, simply translate it into plain English. But if it's important that the audience learns the language—perhaps to understand something else down the road—the hybrid approach will be your best choice.[‡]

If you do choose to introduce new terminology, make sure you give the audience enough of a chance to let it sink in. Don't just define a new term once and assume they will remember what it means when you use it again ten minutes later. While you don't need to repeat the same definition over and over again, you should

---

[†] Of course, Version 3 is just an illustration of this concept. If you really want your audience to understand these three terms, you'll need to devote more than one short sentence to each!

[‡] A recent study supports this hybrid approach for a different reason: using technical language can make you seem more competent.[4] This is something we see quite often in our classes. When students translate their technical speeches entirely into conversational language, eliminating all technical terms, we often wonder how much they know, and whether we're really learning anything. On the other hand, when our students fail to translate their speeches at all, speaking almost entirely in jargon, we're absolutely sure we're not learning anything. This is what makes the hybrid approach ideal—it clearly establishes your expertise while still making your speech understandable to the audience.

design all of your explanations so the audience will still understand what you're talking about later on, even if they didn't catch your initial definition.

But how can you know what your audience knows? While the curse of knowledge ensures you'll never know exactly what they know, here's an exercise you can use to get a better idea.

Begin by finding a friend who's willing to help: the ideal candidate is someone who is intelligent but uninformed about your topic. Your job is to explain your ideas to them in a way you think they will understand. Your friend's job is to stop you every time you say something they don't fully understand.

In response, you must find a simpler way to explain things, revising your approach until your friend is satisfied that they completely understand you. If you want, you can also encourage your friend to actively ask you questions along the way. This will give you a better sense of what a general audience finds interesting about your topic and what they want to know more about.

To take this exercise one step further, when you're done explaining your topic to your friend, have your friend explain it back to you. Not only will you get to see what your friend took away from your explanation, but you may even get some new ideas about how to explain things more clearly. In any case, you'll have a much better sense of what people outside your field know about it and how you can adapt your presentation accordingly.

Draw a Map

As we noted before, whenever you give a technical speech, it's like you're transporting your audience to a foreign land. Not only does this land have a different language: it also has a different geography. Therefore, while you give the audience a tour of this new land, it's important to give them a map and directions so they can easily identify where you are and where you're going.

When someone asks you to give them directions, you naturally do several things: you start from where the person is standing, break down the route into manageable pieces, present them in a logical order, and refer to key landmarks to make it memorable.

You say, "keep going straight until you reach city hall, then take a left and a right, and it's right in front of you." Not "find city hall, then take a left..." Or "it's a mile thataway." Or "take a few lefts and rights and you'll be there." But when it comes to technical communication, it's easy to make analogous mistakes.

The first mistake is that the curse of knowledge often leads us to believe that our audience knows more than they do, so we leave out essential steps in our directions. Instead, you want to make sure you give your audience enough background information. The amount of background you give should be inversely proportional to their familiarity with the topic: people within your field will not require much background, while people who are new to the subject may require quite a lot.[5] If your audience already knows how to get to city hall, it's efficient to give them directions from there. But if they don't have any idea where city hall is, it's essential that you first get them there.

If there isn't time to cover all of the details of this background (and there won't be!), it's perfectly fine to put your audience on an express bus to city hall, so to speak, rather than guiding them street by street. This means giving them just enough background to get them to a reasonable starting point, without worrying about all of the nitty-gritty details along the way. Remember, you're not giving them a semester-long course on the subject. You just need to give them the background that is essential for understanding what your presentation is about.

Once you've gotten your audience to city hall, so to speak, you still need to clearly direct them to the destination. This means having a logical organizational structure that guides the audience toward greater understanding. It also means clearly defining the destination, which in this case is a clear thesis. What is the one sentence you want your audience to take away from your presentation, the one key thing you want them to remember? Define this one point clearly up front, then design your other points to support it. By explicitly crafting each part of your message to help your audience understand and remember your thesis, they'll be much more likely to take something of value from your speech.

Show the Highlights

When giving someone a tour of a new place, you don't have time to show them everything. In planning your itinerary, you want to prioritize showing them the sights that are essential for them to see in the time they have. Say your Australian friend is now visiting you, and it's her first time in San Francisco. Your friend will have far more fun seeing the Golden Gate Bridge, eating at Pier 39, and watching Train perform at The Fillmore than seeing your local dog park, eating at your new favorite vegan sushi spot, and going to the latest city council meeting.

While you as the San Francisco native may be bored to death by the Golden Gate Bridge, Pier 39, and The Fillmore, these are exactly what your friend is interested in seeing. And while you may be very interested in your dog park, vegan sushi, and local politics, these will likely bore your friend. With the time you have available for your tour, you want to make it as interesting and informative as you can, which means showing them the highlights.

The same is true in your technical communication. As we saw in Chapter 6, you only have time to show your audience the tip of the iceberg. At Stanford, we saw far too many technical presentations that focused on the mundane day-to-day details of the speaker's research—the protocol, the raw data, the significance tests—when all the audience really wanted to know was why it all mattered. Yes, the protocol, the raw data, and statistics are important—to you, your adviser, and your peer reviewers. But for a general audience, the big picture matters much more.

As always, it all depends on your audience. If you're giving a presentation to your research group, then by all means dive deep into the details because that's what this particular audience will find the most exciting and enlightening. But if you're giving your presentation to a general audience, really think about what's important for them to take away and focus on that, even if it means glossing over the finer details.

Make It an Experience

Giving your friend from Australia a tour of San Francisco, you're not just going to sit her down in your apartment and describe the city using words and gestures. You're actually going to take her out to experience the Golden Gate Bridge, Pier 39, and The Fillmore herself.

Similarly, the more experiential you can make your technical presentation, the better. It's the difference between reading a description of the Polka Mazurka and actually watching us dance it, or better yet, dancing it yourself. Here are a few ways you can make your presentation more experiential.

Visual Aids

As you learned in Part V, visual aids are a powerful way to increase what your audience understands and remembers about your presentation. As you're thinking about how to use visuals to explain your technical topic, remember that there are many different kinds, from PowerPoint (and other slideware solutions) to whiteboard drawings, props and demos, audio and video, audience involvement, and even dance and imagination. Here are a few memorable examples of these visuals in action:

- **PowerPoint**: In his technical speech at Stanford, one of our students used a variety of simple, image-based slides to clearly explain the complex topic of self-driving cars, complete with an animation of the rotating LIDAR.

- **Whiteboard**: While making the case that everyone can draw, another one of our students drew a variety of simple but beautiful sketches on the whiteboard to illustrate the basic principles of drawing.

- **Props**: At TEDGlobal 2009, Michael Pritchard showed off his water-sterilizing LifeSaver bottle by filling it with water from the River Thames seasoned with pond water, sewage runoff, and rabbit droppings, pumping the bottle, pouring a glass of crystal clear water from it, and taking a sip.[6]

- **Demos**: In his 2007 keynote address introducing the original iPhone, Steve Jobs did a masterful job demoing the new and exciting features of the device, including the revolutionary multi-touch interface and the ability to prank-call Starbucks directly from Google Maps.

- **Audio**: In his technical speech at Stanford, one of our students explained audio compression by playing the same piece of music processed with different bit depths and sample rates so we could directly hear the differences between them with our own ears.

- **Video**: Also at Stanford, star running back Christian McCaffrey used video to help explain the complexities of one of Stanford's signature plays on the football field.

- **Audience Involvement**: In a presentation on the pentatonic scale, musician Bobby McFerrin "played the audience" by training by them to sing different tones as he jumped on different parts of the stage, essentially turning them into a giant human piano.

- **Dance**: When Nick was a student in public speaking class, he gave his final presentation about the life lessons social dancing can teach us.[†] Instead of just talking about these lessons, he actually brought in a dance partner and illustrated these life lessons through dance.

- **Imagination**: In a talk about the safety protocols of backcountry skiing, one of our students transported the audience to the scene by asking us to close our eyes and vividly

---

[†] Developing this presentation inspired him to write what eventually became *Waltzing: A Manual for Dancing and Living*.

describing the biting cold, the howling wind, and blinding white snow in every direction.

Examples

In Chapter 13, we saw that concrete, emotional examples ("Rokia faces the threat of starvation") can be much more effective than abstract descriptions of a general trend ("11 million people in Ethiopia need immediate food assistance"). The same principle applies to technical communication: one of the most effective ways you can make your speech more experiential is by including concrete examples that illustrate your main points.[7]

In his popular TED talk on education, Sir Ken Robinson uses a striking example to illustrate how our current educational system fails to appreciate the richness of human potential. He tells the story of a young Gillian Lynne, the choreographer of *Cats*:

> When she was at school, she was really hopeless. And the school, in the '30s, wrote to her parents and said, "We think Gillian has a learning disorder." She couldn't concentrate; she was fidgeting.
>
> [...S]he went to see this specialist. ... [S]he was there with her mother, ... and she sat on her hands for 20 minutes while this man talked to her mother about the problems Gillian was having at school. ... In the end, the doctor went and sat next to Gillian, and said, "I've listened to all these things your mother's told me, I need to speak to her privately. Wait here. We'll be back; we won't be very long," and they went and left her.
>
> But as they went out of the room, he turned on the radio that was sitting on his desk. And when they got out, he said to her mother, "Just stand and watch her." And the minute they left the room, she was on her feet, moving to the music. And they watched for a few minutes and he turned to her mother and said, "Mrs. Lynne, Gillian isn't sick; she's a dancer. Take her to a dance school."[8]

A decade after seeing this talk, we still remember this concrete example, and with it, Robinson's main point that there are many different kinds of abilities, and we should cultivate them all.[†]

Whenever possible, present concrete examples that relate to your topic. Rather than just telling us how your new discovery saves lives, tell us about one person whose life it saved. Or instead of just telling us what your result is, tell us an interesting story about how you got to that result. By making your topic more concrete, you will also make it much more memorable.[9]

[†] In other words, this is a great example of a successful STAR moment!

Conclusion

The key to communicating technical knowledge is to simultaneously excite your audience about your topic and enlighten them by explaining it in an easily understandable way.

- **Excite**: If your audience isn't excited about your topic, you have little chance of communicating successfully. It's your job to get them excited by keeping the following tips in mind.
    - **Make It Relevant**: Clearly show the audience how they stand to benefit from listening to your presentation.
    - **Arouse Their Curiosity**: Reveal a small gap in their knowledge, and they will be eager for you to fill it.
    - **Show Your Enthusiasm**: Deliver your presentation enthusiastically to get your audience excited about it!
    - **Shoot for the STARs**: Include Something They'll Always Remember, while making sure this is actually what you want them to remember.
- **Enlighten**: Think of your technical speech as if you're giving the audience a tour of a foreign land. It's your job to make sure they have a good time.
    - **The Curse of Knowledge**: Remember that when you know something well, it's hard to imagine what it's like not to know it.
    - **Translate the Language**: Translate jargon into plain English. If the vocabulary is important for your audience to remember, use a hybrid approach in which

you use the technical terms but also define them in everyday language.

- **Draw a Map**: Make sure to logically organize your speech to give your audience a clear lay of the land, and direct them to a specific destination, i.e., your thesis.
- **See the Sights**: Think about what is most important for someone new to your topic to take away from your presentation, and focus on that, even if it means leaving out some of the details.
- **Make It an Experience**: Make your presentation as concrete and experiential as you can by using visual aids and specific examples

Part VIII

Conclusion

The Science of Speaking Cheat Sheet

Following our own advice from Chapter 7, here is a brief scrapbook reviewing all of the major points we've covered in this book.

Nervousness: Everyone gets nervous about public speaking, but there are many techniques you can use to calm your nerves. Thoroughly preparing will help, as will leaning on friends and family for support, vividly visualizing yourself giving your speech, finding ways to relax, practicing one-moment meditation, power posing, and developing your speaking skills. In addition, remember that nervousness can be a good thing, your speech doesn't need to be perfect, the audience isn't out to get you, nervousness isn't constant, and if all else fails, you can always fake it. Developing a pre-speech ritual can also help, as well as simply knowing that there are techniques to help you.

Delivery: The key to mastering delivery is to remember how to effectively use your body, voice, and face. Begin with a solid, self-confident stance with your hands at your sides or in the Peace Offering position. Then add visible, purposeful gestures and movements to direct, draw, and demonstrate. Wear something your audience can both respect and relate to while making you feel like you're at the top of your game. Next, hone your verbal delivery by considering volume, velocity, and variation. Finally, use eye contact to connect with your audience, and don't be afraid to add emotion by using facial expressions while making sure your delivery always matches your content.

Organization: Organizing your presentation is as easy as wrapping a gift in a box with a bow. After analyzing what kind of gift of knowledge you want to give this audience, use the iceberg model to distill your content and choose a thesis and several main points to support it. Next, decide what story you want to tell, and craft smooth transitions to help you tell it. In order to make your points more understandable and memorable, don't forget to include a roadmap and scrapbook to preview and review your main points. Finally, to make and leave the best impression, craft an impactful hook and finale, and consider using some timeless memory tricks like alliteration, acronyms, and extended metaphor.

Visual Aids: Remember to make your visuals POP by picking, optimizing, and presenting them. Consider the many different kinds of visual aids you can use, including slides, drawings, props and demos, audio and video, audience involvement, and even dance and imagination. In addition, consider the many different kinds of visual forms, including pictures, charts, maps, timelines, flowcharts, scatter plots, and equations. Keep your formatting consistent throughout, except when you want to differentiate an important point, and make sure your visuals can be seen from afar. Remember not to present to or block your visuals, take control (perhaps by using a remote), keep it relevant, prepare for technical difficulties, and practice!

Pitches: Present a clear ask to a particular audience while approaching them from a personalized angle. Craft a small, specific, flexible ask that is personalized to your audience. Then push them away from the status quo, and pull them toward your proposed solution. Reveal the issues while avoiding criticism, and don't be afraid to use emotion. At the same time, present inspiring solutions that appeal to the best in your audience, and invite them to join the growing bandwagon. Finally, present your expertise, and pitch with efficiency. Show your experience (or better yet, potential), while avoiding hedging and citing experts. And avoid giving your audience too many choices or arguments, particularly those that mix motivations. Engage in argumentative archery!

Technical Communication: Regardless of their field, everyone has technical knowledge—information that must be translated for a general audience. Excite your audience by making it relevant, arousing their curiosity, showing your enthusiasm, involving the audience, and shooting for the STARs (Something They'll Always Remember). Then enlighten them by acting as a tour guide through the foreign land of your topic by translating the language, drawing a map, showing them the highlights, and making it an experience. Always remember the curse of knowledge!

Epilogue

Nearly 200 pages later, we've reached the end of this book. We've combated nervousness, revolutionized visuals, and finessed technical communication. But even though it's the end, we don't see it as the end. Quite the contrary—this is the beginning.

This is the beginning of you going out into the world and sharing your brilliant ideas. The next time a presentation opportunity arises, we hope you'll seize the chance to make it your own and have a lasting impact on your audience. No matter what topic you're presenting on, we truly believe you have a unique skillset and viewpoint that people will benefit from. And now that you have the science of speaking on your side, you have the tools to turn your ideas into a speech that's memorable and impactful.

And while we certainly hope you employ the tips and tricks we've discussed in formal presentation settings, we also encourage you to use them on a smaller scale too. On the first page of this book, we said that "All the world's a stage," and we honestly believe this. You have countless opportunities to use bits and pieces of what you've learned in this book throughout your everyday life. When you're wanting to try out a new restaurant in town. When you're explaining job duties to a new hire you're mentoring. When you're at a party making small talk about your hobbies. Each of these situations—along with countless others—is an opportunity to make a genuine connection, have a meaningful interaction, and make a difference.

Because at the end of the day, regardless of the venue, the audience size, and the stakes, this is really what speaking is all about—it's an opportunity to bring people together. A chance to take a break from our busy lives and connect on an deeper level about something interesting. You truly cannot put a price on that. Now, take what you've learned, and go out and be brilliant!

— Nick & Melissa

References

Chapter 1. All the World's a Stage

[1] *All the world's a stage*: Shakespeare, W. (1599). *As You Like It*.
[2] *We spend up to 80% of our waking hours communicating*: Klemme, E. T.; Snyder, F. W. (1972). "Measurement of Time Spent Communicating." *The Journal of Communication*, 22, 142-158.
[3] *Communication skills are the #2 factor in engineers' success*: Riley, L. A.; Furth, P. M.; Zellmer, J. T. (2000). "Assessing Our Engineering Alumni: Determinants of Success in the Workplace." New Mexico State University.
[4] *Business school recruiter survey*: Alsop, R. (2006, September 20). "MBA Survey: Something Old, Something New." *The Wall Street Journal*. http://www.wsj.com/articles/SB115860376846766495
[5] *Oral communication skills have been identified as being particularly important*: Coffelt, T. A.; Baker, M. J.; Corey, R. C. (2016). "Business Communication Practices From Employers' Perspectives." *Business and Professional Communication Quarterly*, 79(3), 1-17. / / / / / / *In addition, many studies have found that speaking is significantly more effective than other forms of communication. For example: a request made in person is 34 times more effective than a request made by email*: Roghanizad, M. M.; Bohns, V. K. (2017). "Ask in Person: You're Less Persuasive Than You Think Over Email." *Journal of Experimental Social Psychology*, 69, 223-226. / / / / / *Negotiations in person are more effective than negotiations over video, which are more effective than negotiations over email*: Rockmann, K. W.; Northcraft, G. B. (2008). "To Be or Not to Be Trusted: The Influence of Media Richness on Defection and Deception." *Organizational Behavior and Human Decision Processes*, 107(2), 106-122. / / / / / *Conflicts are more likely to escalate when they play out over email than when they play out face-to-face or over the phone*: Friedman, R. A.; Currall, S. C. (2003). "Conflict Escalation: Dispute Exacerbating Elements of E-mail Communication." *Human Relations*, 56(11), 1325-1347. / / / / / / *When a "hire me" pitch is presented in writing, the candidate is viewed as significantly less intelligent, likable, and hirable than when the same pitch is spoken*: Schroeder, J.; Epley, N. (2015). "The Sound of Intellect: Speech Reveals a Thoughtful Mind,

Increasing a Job Candidate's Appeal." *Psychological Science*, 26(6), 877-891. / / / / / *This may be because when we read someone else's writing, we hear it in an unnaturally monotone voice*: Schroeder, J.; Epley, N. (2016). "Mistaking Minds and Machines: How Speech Affects Dehumanization and Anthropomorphism." *Journal of Experimental Psychology: General*, 145(11), 1427-1437. / / / / / *Which makes it harder to discern tone*: Kruger, J.; Epley, N.; Parker, J.; Ng, Z.-W. (2005). "Egocentrism Over E-mail: Can We Communicate As Well As We Think?" *Journal of Personality and Social Psychology*, 89(6), 925-936.

Chapter 2. Nervousness

[1] *Andrea Bocelli*: Hardy, R. (2012, July 12). "My Baby is Like My Voice, a Gift from God: Andrea Bocelli on Singing and His New Daughter." *The Daily Mail*. http://www.dailymail.co.uk/tvshowbiz/article-2172829/Andrea-Bocelli-singing-new-daughter.html

[2] Branson, Richard. (2013, July 15). "Overcoming Shyness." *Richard's Blog*. http://www.virgin.com/richard-branson/overcoming-shyness

[3] *Cicero*: Cicero. (55 BCE). *De Oratore*.

[4] *The Trier Social Stress Test, which includes preparing and giving a speech, is a reliable way to induce stress*: Kirschbaum, C.; Pirke, K.-M.; Hellhammer, D. H. (1993). "The 'Trier Social Stress Test' — A Tool for Investigating Psychobiological Stress Responses in a Laboratory Setting." *Neuropsychobiology*, 28, 76-81.

[5] *Feelings of uncertainty amplify emotions*: Bar-Anan, Y.; Wilson, T. D.; Gilbert, D. (2009). "The Feeling of Uncertainty Intensifies Affective Reactions." *Emotion*, 9(1), 123-127.

[6] *Nervousness and preparation are directly correlated*: Byrne, M.; Flood, B.; Shanahan, D. (2012). "A Qualitative Exploration of Oral Communication Apprehension." *Accounting Education: An International Journal*, 21(6), 565-581.

[7] *Practicing with an audience is better than practicing alone, and the bigger the audience, the better*: Smith, T. E. (2003). "Keeping It 'Real': Does Practicing Speeches Before an Audience Improve Performance?" Miami University Master's Thesis.

[8] *Positive feedback reduces speaking anxiety*: Byrne, M.; Flood, B.; Shanahan, D. (2012). "A Qualitative Exploration of Oral Communication Apprehension." *Accounting Education: An International Journal*, 21(6), 565-581.

[9] *Social support can significantly reduce speaking anxiety*: Heinrichs, M.; Baumgartner, T.; Kirschbaum, C.; Ehlert, U. (2003). "Social Support and Oxytocin Interact to Suppress Cortisol and Subjective Responses to Psychosocial Stress." *Biological Psychiatry*, 54(12), 1389-1398.

[10] *Holding hands reduces speaking anxiety*: Lougheed, J. P.; Koval, P.; Hollenstein, T. (2016). "Sharing the Burden: The Interpersonal Regulation of Emotional Arousal in Mother-Daughter Dyads." *Emotion*, 16(1), 83-93. / / / / / *Getting a shoulder massage reduces speaking anxiety*: Ditzen, B.; Neumann, I. D.; Bodenmann, G.; von Dawans, B.; Turner, R. A.; Ehlert, U.; Heinrichs, M. (2007). "Effects of

Different Kinds of Couple Interaction on Cortisol and Heart Rate Responses to Stress in Women." *Psychoneuroendocrinology,* 32(5), 565-574.

[11] *"You can do it":* Jarrett, C. (2014, July 9). "Self-Motivation: How 'You can do it!' Beats 'I can do it!'" *BPS Research Digest.* https://digest.bps.org.uk/2014/07/09/self-motivation-how-you-can-do-it-beats-i-can-do-it / / / Dolcos, S.; Albarracin, D. (2014). "The Inner Speech of Behavioral Regulation: Intentions and Task Performance Strengthen When You Talk to Yourself as a You." *European Journal of Social Psychology,* 44, 636–642.

[12] *Students with high public speaking anxiety produce more negative, less vivid self-images than students with low public speaking anxiety*: Ayres, J.; Heuett, B. L. (1997). "The Relationship Between Visual Imagery and Public Speaking Apprehension." *Communication Reports,* 10(1), 87-94.

[13] *Speaking anxiety is positively correlated with negative thoughts and negatively correlated with positive thoughts, and visualization can increase the ratio of positive to negative thoughts*: Ayres, J. (1988). "Coping with Speech Anxiety: The Power of Positive Thinking." *Communication Education,* 37(4), 289-296.

[14] *Speaking anxiety and heart rate are lower when a speaker maintains a positive attitude toward speaking*: Hu, S.; Romans-Kroll, J.-M. (1995). "Effects of Positive Attitude Toward Giving a Speech on Cardiovascular and Subjective Fear Response During Speech in Anxious Subjects." *Perceptual and Motor Skills,* 81(2), 609-610.

[15] *Students who visualized giving a successful speech reported reduced anxiety levels*: Ayres, J.; Hopf, T. S. (1985). "Visualization: A Means of Reducing Speech Anxiety." *Communication Education,* 34(4), 318-323. / / / / / *Visualization is an easier intervention for teachers to implement than clinical methods such as systematic desensitization (SD) and rational emotive therapy (RET), but it has similar effects*: Ayres, J.; Hopf, T. S. (1987). "Visualization, Systematic Desensitization, and Rational Emotive Therapy: A Comparative Evaluation." *Communication Education,* 36(3), 236-240.

[16] *Both guided visualization and self-constructed visualization are effective*: Ayres, J. (1995). "Comparing Self-Constructed Visualization Scripts with Guided Visualization." *Communication Reports,* 8(2), 193-199.

[17] *Visualization the day before a speech and a week before a speech are both effective*: Byers, P. Y.; Weber, C. S. (1995). "The Timing of Speech Anxiety Reduction Treatments in the Public Speaking Classroom." *The Southern Communication Journal,* 60(3), 246-256.

[18] *Students who learn to visualize not only report lower anxiety immediately, but also four and eight months later*: Ayres, J.; Hopf, T. S. (1990). "The Long-Term Effect of Visualization in the Classroom: A Brief Research Report." *Communication Education,* 39, 75-78.

[19] *Students who visualized giving a successful speech were perceived by the audience as displaying less rigidity and inhibition*: Ayres, J. (1992). "Visualization: Reducing Speech Anxiety and Enhancing Performance." *Communication Reports,* 5(1), 1-10.

[20] *Listening to relaxing music while preparing for an impromptu speech reduces speaking anxiety*: Knight, W. E. J.; Richard, N. S. (2001). "Relaxing Music Prevents Stress-Induced Increases in Subjective Anxiety, Systolic Blood Pressure, and

Heart Rate in Healthy Males and Females." *Journal of Music Therapy*, 38(4), 254-272.

[21] *Muscle relaxation techniques are effective in reducing speaking anxiety*: Goldfried, M. R.; Trier, C. S. (1974). "Effectiveness of Relaxation as an Active Coping Skill." *Journal of Abnormal Psychology*, 83(4), 348-355.

[22] *Heart rate biofeedback is effective in reducing speaking anxiety*: Gatchel, R.J.; Hatch, J. P.; Watson, P. J.; Smith, D.; Gaas, E. (1977)."Comparative Effectiveness of Voluntary Heart Rate Control and Muscular Relaxation as Active Coping Skills for Reducing Speech Anxiety." *Journal of Consulting and Clinical Psychology*, 45(6), 1093-1100.

[23] *Self-administered hand massage is effective in reducing speaking anxiety*: Schmidt, N. L. (2006). "Self Administered Tactile Therapy: A Proposed Intervention for the Treatment of Public Speaking Apprehension." Doctoral Dissertation at Washington State University.

[24] *Watching cat videos decreases anxiety and increases relaxation*: Myrick, J. G. (2015). "Emotion Regulation, Procrastination, and Watching Cat Videos Online: Who Watches Internet Cats, Why, and to What Effect?" *Computers in Human Behavior*, 52, 168-176.

[25] For more on the science of meditation, see "Be Here Now" in Powers, R.; Enge, N. (2013). *Waltzing: A Manual for Dancing and Living*. Stanford: Redowa Press.

[26] *One-moment meditation*: Boroson, M. (2009). *One-Moment Meditation: Stillness for People on the Go*. New York: Winter Road.

[27] *Thinking about a time when you felt powerful can have a similar effect*: Lammers, J.; Dubois, D.; Rucker, D. D.; Galinsky, A. D. (2013). "Power Gets the Job: Priming Power Improves Interview Outcomes." *Journal of Experimental Social Psychology*, 49(4), 776-779.

[28] *Dana Carney's critique of power posing*: Singal, J. (2016, September 26). "Power Posing Co-Author: 'I Do Not Believe That Power Pose Effects Are Real.'" *Science of Us (New York Magazine)*. http://nymag.com/scienceofus/2016/09/power-poses-co-author-i-dont-think-power-poses-are-real.html

[29] *Amy Cuddy's response in defense of power posing*: Singal, J.; Dahl, M. (2016, September 30). "Here Is Amy Cuddy's Response to Critiques of Her Power-Posing Research." *Science of Us (New York Magazine)*. http://nymag.com/scienceofus/2016/09/read-amy-cuddys-response-to-power-posing-critiques.html

[30] *The original study found that high power poses increase testosterone and decrease cortisol, and increase feelings of power and risk-tolerance, while low power poses have the opposite effect*: Carney, D. R.; Cuddy, A. J. C.; Yap, A. J. (2010). "Power Posing: Brief Nonverbal Displays Affect Neuroendocrine Levels and Risk Tolerance." *Psychological Science*, 21(10), 1363-1368. / / / / / *But some of these changes have been called into question*: Ranehill, E.; Dreber, A.; Johannesson, M.; Leiberg, S.; Sul, S.; Weber, R. A. (2015). "Assessing the Robustness of Power Posing: No Effect on Hormones and Risk Tolerance in a Large Sample of Men and Women." *Psychological Science*, 26(5), 653-656. / / / / / *Other studies show that power posing can increase pain tolerance*: Bohns, V. K.; Wiltermuth, S. S. (2012). "It Hurts When I Do This (or You Do That):

Posture and Pain Tolerance." *Journal of Experimental Psychology,* 48(1), 341-345. / / / / / / Or that it can increase ratings of performance and hireability in a mock interview: Cuddy, A. J. C.; Wilmuth, C. A.; Yap, A. J.; Carney, D. R. (2015). "Preparatory Power Posing Affects Nonverbal Presence and Job Interview Performance." *Journal of Applied Psychology,* 100(4), 1286-1295. / / / / / / *Additional research on power posing*: Park, L. E.; Streamer, L.; Huang, L.; Galinsky, A. D. (2013). "Stand Tall, but Don't Put Your Feet Up: Universal and Culturally-Specific Effects of Expansive Postures on Power." *Journal of Experimental Social Psychology,* 49(6), 965-971. / / / Yap A. J.; Wazlawek A. S.; Lucas B. J.; Cuddy A. J. C.; Carney D. R. (2013). "The Ergonomics of Dishonesty: The Effect of Incidental Posture on Stealing, Cheating, and Traffic Violations." *Psychological Science,* 24, 2281-2289. / / / Cesario J., McDonald, M. M. (2013). "Bodies in Context: Power Poses as a Computation of Action Possibility." *Social Cognition,* 31, 260-274. / / / Huang, L.; Galinsky, A. D.; Gruenfeld, D. H.; Guillory, L. E. (2011). "Powerful Postures Versus Powerful Roles: Which Is the Proximate Correlate of Thought and Behavior?" *Psychological Science,* 22(1), 95-102.

[31] *Natural gift vs. skill that can be honed*: For more on this general concept, see: Dweck, Carol. (2006). *Mindset: The New Psychology of Success.* New York: Random House Books.

[32] *Martin Luther King, Jr. received a C in Public Speaking*: Batten, C. E. (1950, December 6). "Transcript of Record for Martin Luther King." Chester, PA: Crozer Theological Seminary.

[33] *After receiving public speaking skills training, speakers report lower speaking anxiety*: Fremouw, W.; Zitter, R. (1978). "A Comparison of Skills Training and Cognitive Restructuring-Relaxation for the Treatment of Speech Anxiety." *Behaviour Therapy,* 9, 248-259.

[34] *After receiving public speaking skills training, speakers are perceived as less nervous by an audience*: Merritt, L.; Richards, A.; Davis, P. (2001). "Performance Anxiety: Loss of the Spoken Edge." *Journal of Voice,* 15(2), 257-269.

[35] *Taking a public speaking class helps build your confidence*: Ford, W. S. Z.; Wolvin, A. D. (1993). "The Differential Impact of a Basic Communication Course on Perceived Communication Competencies in Class, Work, and Social Contexts." *Communication Education,* 42(3), 215-223.

[36] *Speakers who have given more speeches in the past report less speaking anxiety in the present*: Ayres, J.; Hopf, T. S. (1985). "Visualization: A Means of Reducing Speech Anxiety." *Communication Education,* 34(4), 318-323. / / / / / / *You're more likely to regret the things you didn't do than to regret the things you did*: Gilovich, T.; Medvec, V. H. (1995). "The Experience of Regret: What, When, Why." *Psychological Review,* 102(2), 379-95. / / / Zaslow, J. (2016, January 25). "What's Your Biggest Regret?" https://www.youtube.com/watch?v=R45HcYA8uRA

[37] *Rational emotive therapy can be an effective treatment for severe public speaking anxiety*: Watson, A. K.; Dodd, C. H. (1984). "Alleviating Communication Apprehension Through Rational Emotive Therapy: A Comparative Evaluation." *Communication Education,* 33(3), 257-266.

[38] *The only thing we have to fear*: Roosevelt, F. D. (1933, March 4). "First Inaugural Address."

[39] *Gregg Allman*: Richardson, J. H. (2013, December 19). "Gregg Allman: What I've Learned." *Esquire*. http://www.esquire.com/entertainment/music/news/a26474/gregg-allman-interview-0114/

[40] *Stevie Nicks*: Koha, N. T. (2004, February 8). "Original Rock Chick." *The Sunday Mail (Australia)*. http://www.fleetwoodmac-uk.com/articles/2004/feb/feb004-001.html

[41] *Positive nervousness*: Snyder, E. (1983). *Speak for Yourself—With Confidence*. New York: New American Library. 113

[42] *Stage excitement, or stage enthusiasm*: Aschaiek, S. (2005, March 16). "Conquer Your Fear of Public Speaking." *Toronto Sun*. http://www.canoe.com/CareerConnectionNews/050316_publicspeak.html

[43] *People who tell themselves they are excited perform better at speaking, math, and karaoke*: Brooks, A. W. (2014). "Get Excited: Reappraising Pre-Performance Anxiety as Excitement." *Journal of Experimental Psychology*, 143(3), 1144-1158.

[44] *People who are told that feeling nervous about a test can be a good thing perform better on that test*: Jamieson, J. P.; Mendes, W. B.; Blackstock, E.; Schmader, T. (2010). "Turning the Knots in Your Stomach into Bows: Reappraising Arousal Improves Performance on the GRE." *Journal of Experimental Social Psychology*, 46, 208-212.

[45] *Dale Carnegie*: Dale Carnegie Training. (2011). *Stand and Deliver: How to Become a Masterful Communicator and Public Speaker*. New York: Simon & Schuster.

[46] *Research has shown that the body language of an audience can have a significant impact on speaking anxiety, with negative body language increasing nervousness, so by being a friendly face, you can have a major positive impact for the speaker*: Pertaub. D.-P.; Slater, M.; Barker, C. (2002). "An Experiment on Public Speaking Anxiety in Response to Three Different Types of Virtual Audience." *Presence*, 11(1), 68-78.

[47] *Faces identified as having "resting bitch face" show physical markers of contempt*: Connaughton, M. (2016, February 9). "Science Finally Explained My Resting Bitch Face to Me." *Vice*. https://www.vice.com/read/finally-my-resting-bitch-face-explained

[48] *The spotlight effect*: Gilovich, T.; Medvec, V. H.; Savitsky, K. (2000). "The Spotlight Effect in Social Judgment: An Egocentric Bias in Estimates of the Salience of One's Own Actions and Appearance." *Journal of Personality and Social Psychology*, 78(2), 211-222.

[49] *The more self-focused we are, the more anxious we feel*: Mor, N.; Winquist, J. (2002). "Self-Focused Attention and Negative Affect: A Meta-Analysis." *Psychological Bulletin*, 128(4), 638-62.

[50] *Anxiety level fluctuates as a function of where you are in the speech-making process*: Behnke, R. R.; Sawyer, C. R. (2004). "Public Speaking Anxiety as a Function of Sensitization and Habituation Processes." *Communication Education*, 53(2), 164-173. / / / Behnke, R. R.; Sawyer, C. R. (1999). "Milestones of Anticipatory Public Speaking Anxiety." *Communication Education*, 48(2), 165-172.

[51] *Rituals reduce anxiety and improve performance*: Brooks, A. W.; Schroeder, J.; Risen, J.; Gino, F.; Galinsky, A. D.; Norton, M. I.; Schweitzer, M. (2016). "Don't Stop

Believing: Rituals Improve Performance by Decreasing Anxiety." *Organizational Behavior and Human Decision Processes*, 137, 71-85.

[52] *Option B*: Sandberg, S.; Grant, A. (2017). *Option B: Facing Adversity, Building Resilience, and Finding Joy*. New York: Knopf. 46-47.

[53] *The button*: Reim, B.; Glass, D. C.; Singer, J. E. (1971). "Behavioral Consequences of Exposure to Uncontrollable and Unpredictable Noise." *Journal of Applied Social Psychology*, 1(1), 44-56.

Part III. Delivery

[1] *Watching videos of yourself speaking can reduce your speaking anxiety*: Leeds, E. M.; Maurer, R. A. (2009). "Using Digital Video Technology to Reduce Communication Apprehension in Business Education." *INFORMS Transactions on Education.*, 9(2), 84-92. / / / Hinton, J. S.; Kramer, M. W. (1998). "The Impact of Self-Directed Videotape Feedback on Students' Self-Reported Levels of Communication Competence and Apprehension." *Communication Education*, 47(2), 151-161.

Chapter 3. The Body

[1] *Locking your knees can cause fainting*: University of Arkansas for Medical Sciences. (2016). "Can Standing Up Straight for a Long Period Cause Fainting?" http://uamshealth.com/healthlibrary2/medicalmyths/standingcausefainting

[2] *An open body position makes you more convincing*: McGinley, H.; LeFevre, R.; McGinley, P. (1975). "The Influence of a Communicator's Body Position on Opinion Change in Others." *Journal of Personality and Social Psychology*, 31(4), 686-690.

[3] *Fidgeting with your hands results in lower ratings of speaker effectiveness*: Ambady, N.; Rosenthal, R. (1993). "Half a Minute: Predicting Teacher Evaluations from Thin Slices of Nonverbal Behavior and Physical Attractiveness." *Journal of Personality and Social Psychology*, 64(3), 431-441.

[4] *All ages and cultures gesture*: Feyereisen, P.; deLannoy, J.-D. (1991). *Gesture and Speech*. New York: Cambridge University Press.

[5] *Babies gesture before they can talk*: Iverson, J. M.; Goldin-Meadow, S. (2005). "Gesture Paves the Way for Language Development." *Gesture and Language Development*, 16(5), 367-371. / / / / / / Even blind people gesture when they speak: Iverson, J. M.; Goldin-Meadow, S. (1998). "Why People Gesture When They Speak." *Nature*, 396(6708), 228.

[6] *Gesturing while speaking decreases demand on working memory and improves speaker recall*: Goldin-Meadow, S.; Nusbaum, H.; Kelly, S. D.; Wagner, S. (2001). "Explaining Math: Gesturing Lightens the Load." *Psychological Science*, 12(6), 516-522. / / / Wagner, S. M.; Nusbaum, H.; Goldin-Meadow, S. (2004). "Probing the Mental Representation of Gesture: Is Handwaving Spatial?" *Journal of Memory &*

Language, 50(4), 395-407. / / / Stevanoni, E.; Salmon, K. (2005). "Giving Memory a Hand: Instructing Children to Gesture Enhances their Event Recall." *Journal of Nonverbal Behavior*, 29(4), 217-233.

[7] *Gestures increase speech comprehension, particularly when the verbal message is complex*: Graham, J. A.; Heywood, S. (1976). "The Effects of Elimination of Hand Gesture and of Verbal Codability on Speech Performance." *European Journal of Social Psychology*, 5, 189-195. / / / McNeil, N. M.; Alibali, M. W.; Evans, J. L. (2000). "The Role of Gesture in Children's Comprehension of Spoken Language: Now They Need it, Now They Don't." *Journal of Nonverbal Behavior*, 24, 131-150. / / / / / Or ambiguous: Thompson, L. A.; Massaro, D. W. (1986). "Evaluation and Integration of Speech and Pointing Gestures During Referential Understanding." *Journal of Experimental Child Psychology*, 42, 144-168. / / / / / Or spoken in a soft voice: Berger, K. W.; Popelka, G. R. (1971). "Extra-Facial Gestures in Relation to Speech Reading." *Journal of Communication Disorders*, 3, 302-308.

[8] *Gestures help capture and maintain your listeners' attention, provide additional support for your verbal message, and ground your words in the physical world*: Valenzeno, L.; Alibali, M. W.; Roberta Klatzky, R. (2003). "Teachers' Gestures Facilitate Students' Learning: A Lesson in Symmetry." *Contemporary Educational Psychology*, 28, 187–204.

[9] *A gesture can make a piece of information five times more memorable*: Woodall, W. G.; Folger, J. P. (1985). "Nonverbal Cue Context and Episodic Memory: On the Availability and Endurance of Nonverbal Behaviors as Retrieval Cues." *Communication Monographs*, 52(4), 319-333. / / / Woodall, W. G.; Folger, J. P. (1981). "Encoding Specificity and Nonverbal Cue Context: An Expansion of Episodic Memory Research." *Communication Monographs*, 48(1), 39-53.

[10] *The popularity of a TED talk is correlated with the number of gestures it contains*: Van Edwards, V. (2015). "5 Secrets of a Successful TED Talk." *The Huffington Post*. http://www.huffingtonpost.com/vanessa-van-edwards/5-secrets-of-a-successful_b_6887472.html / / / / / *Gesturing is correlated with ratings of social skill and hireability in interviews*: Gifford, R.; Ng, C. K.; Wilkinson, M. (1985). "Nonverbal Cues in the Employment Interview: Links Between Applicant Qualities and Interviewer Judgments." *Journal of Applied Psychology*, 70(4), 729-736.

[11] *Ratings of charisma, credibility, and intelligence are the same if a speaker is put on mute*: ibid.

[12] *Nixon Kennedy debate*: Webley, Kayla. (2010, September 23). "How the Nixon-Kennedy Debate Changed the World." *Time*. http://content.time.com/time/nation/article/0,8599,2021078,00.html

[13] *Gestures don't always have the same meaning around the world*: Lefevre, R. (2011). *Rude Hand Gestures of the World: A Guide to Offending without Words*. San Francisco: Chronicle Books.

[14] *Actors recall their lines better while moving*: Noice, H.; Noice, T. (1999). "Long-Term Retention of Theatrical Roles." *Memory*, 7(3), 357-382. / / / / / *Actors learn lines better while moving*: Noice, H.; Noice, T. (2001). "Learning Dialogue With and Without Movement." *Memory and Cognition*, 29(6), 820-827.

[15] *The onset of movement attracts attention*: Abrams, R. A.; Christ, S. E. (2003). "Motion Onset Captures Attention." *Psychological Science*, 14, 427-432.

[16] *Changes in movement attract attention*: Howard, C. J.; Holcombe, A. O. (2010). "Unexpected Changes in Direction of Motion Attract Attention." *Attention, Perception, and Psychophysics*, 72(8), 2087-2095.

[17] *Student presenters dressed in business formal attire are rated as more professional, more confident, more competent, and their presentations are rated as higher quality*: Gurung, R. A. R.; Kempen, L.; Klemm, K.; Senn, R.; Wysocki, R. (2014). "Dressed to Present: Ratings of Classroom Presentations Vary With Attire." *Teaching of Psychology*, 41(4), 349-353.

[18] *People learn more from presenters wearing formal attire*: Roach, K. D. (1997). "Effects of Graduate Teaching Assistant Attire on Student Learning, Misbehaviors, and Ratings of Instruction." *Communication Quarterly*, 45(3), 125-141.

[19] *People are more likely to follow a man across the street when he's wearing a business suit*: Lefkowitz, M.; Blake, R. R.; Mouton, J. S. (1955). "Status Factors in Pedestrian Violations of Traffic Signals." *Journal of Abnormal Psychology*, 51(3), 704-706.

[20] *There are trade-offs to formal attire*: Gurung, R. A. R.; Kempen, L.; Klemm, K.; Senn, R.; Wysocki, R. (2014). "Dressed to Present: Ratings of Classroom Presentations Vary With Attire." *Teaching of Psychology*, 41(4), 349-353. / / / Carr, D.; Davies, T.; Lavin, A. (2010). "The Impact of Instructor Attire on College Student Satisfaction." *College Student Journal*, 44, 101-111.

[21] *People are more likely to help those wearing similar attire and less likely to help those wearing dissimilar attire*: Emswiller, T.; Deaux, K.; Willits, J. E. (1971). "Similarity, Sex, and Requests for Small Favors." *Journal of Applied Social Psychology*, 1(3), 284-291. / / / Suedfeld, P.; Bochner, S.; Matas, C. (1971). "Petitioner's Attire and Petition Signing by Peace Demonstrators: A Field Experiment." *Journal of Applied Social Psychology*, 1(3), 278-283.

[22] *People are more likely to remember a health message when it is presented by someone wearing a stethoscope*: Castledine, G. (1996). "Nursing Image: It Is How You Use Your Stethoscope That Counts!" *British Journal of Nursing*, 5(14), 882.

[23] *People are twice as likely to pick up litter when the requester is dressed as a security guard*: Bickman, L. (1974). "The Social Power of a Uniform." *Journal of Applied Social Psychology*, 4(1), 47-61.

[24] *A first person account of how uniforms influence interactions*: Chiarella, T. (2015, August 24). "What Happened When I Dressed Like A Priest." *Esquire*. http://www.esquire.com/style/mens-fashion/a36947/how-uniform-style-affects-daily-life/

[25] *Wearing a lab coat increases the selective attention of the wearer*: Adam, H.; Galinsky, A. D. (2012). "Enclothed Cognition." *Journal of Experimental Social Psychology*, 48, 918-925.

[26] *Wearing formal clothing increases feelings of power and enhances abstract cognitive processing*: Slepian, M. L.; Ferber, S. N.; Gold, J. M.; Rutchick, A. M. (2015). "The Cognitive Consequences of Formal Clothing." *Social Psychological and Personality Science*, 6(6), 661-668.

[27] *"Hey, I put some new shoes on, and suddenly everything is right"*: Nutini, P. (2007). "New Shoes." New York: Atlantic Records.

[28] *New clothing can put the wearer in a good mood*: Subhani, M. I.; Hasan, S. A.; Osman, A. (2011). "New Article of Clothing Translates the Mood of an Individual." *International Journal of Business and Social Science*, 2(23), 183-185.

Chapter 4. The Voice

[1] *Loudness projects confidence*: Scherer, K. R.; London, H.; Wolf, J. J. (1973). "The Voice of Confidence: Paralinguistic Cues and Audience Evaluation." *Journal of Research in Personality*, 7(1), 31-44. / / / Kimble, C. E.; Seidel, S. D. (1991). "Vocal Signs of Confidence." *Journal of Nonverbal Behavior*, 15(2), 99-105.

[2] *Optimal speech rates of 163 to 225 wpm have been reported*: Hutton, C. L. (1954). "A Psychophysical Study of Speech Rate." Doctoral Dissertation at the University of Illinois Urbana-Champaign. / / / Foulke, E.; Sticht, T. G. (1966). "Listening Rate Preferences of College Students for Literary Material of Moderate Difficulty." *Journal of Auditory Research*, 6, 397-401. / / / Lass, N. J.; Prater, C. E. (1973). "A Comparative Study of Listening Rate Preferences for Oral Reading and Impromptu Speaking Tasks." *Journal of Communication*, 23(1), 95-102. / / / Lass, N. J.; Fultz, V. A. (1976). "A Normative Study of Children's Listening Rate Preferences." *Language and Speech*, 19(2), 144-149. / / / Lass, N. J.; Leeper, H. A. (1977). "Listening Rate Preference: Comparison of Two Time Alteration Techniques." *Perceptual and Motor Skills*, 114, 1163-1168. / / / Leeper, H., Jr.; Thomas, C. L. (1978). "Young Children's Preferences for Listening Rates." *Perceptual and Motor Skills*, 47, 891-898.

[3] *Ratings of competence increase linearly with speaking rate*: Smith, B. L.; Brown, B. L.; Strong, W. J.; Rencher, A. C. (1975). "Effects of Speech Rate on Personality Perception." *Language and Speech*, 18(2), 145-152.

[4] *Fast talkers are more persuasive*: Miller, N.; Maruyama, G.; Beaber, R. J.; Valone, K. (1976). "Speed of Speech and Persuasion." *Journal of Personality and Social Psychology*, 34(4), 615-624.

[5] *There is little to no difference in comprehensibility within a reasonable range of speaking rates*: Foulke, E.; Sticht, T. G. (1969). "Review of Research on the Intelligibility and Comprehension of Accelerated Speech." *Psychological Bulletin*, 72(1), 50-62.

[6] *Non-native speakers sound more accented, and less comprehensible, when asked to slow down*: Munro, M. J. Derwing, T. M. (1998). "The Effects of Speaking Rate on Listener Evaluations of Native and Foreign-Accented Speech." *Language Learning*, 48(2), 159-182. / / / Munro, M. J.; Derwing, T. M. (2001). "What Speaking Rates Do Non-Native Listeners Prefer?" *Applied Linguistics*, 22(3), 324-337.

[7] *Indistinct enunciation can cut comprehension in half*: Glasgow, G. (1943). "The Relative Effects of Distinct and Indistinct Enunciation on Audiences' Comprehension of Prose and Poetry." *The Journal of Educational Research*, 37(4), 263-267.

[8] *American listeners learn more when they are taught by someone with a standard American accent than when they are taught by someone with a foreign accent. In one study, even though 97% of the foreign-accented words were discernible, students who had a teacher with a foreign accent scored 33% worse on a comprehension test compared to those whose teacher had an American accent*: Mayer, R. E.; Sobko, K.; Mautone, P. D.

(2003). "Social Cues in Multimedia Learning: Role of Speaker's Voice." *Journal of Educational Psychology*, 95(2), 419-425. / / / / / *American listeners also rate a voice with an American accent as more credible than a foreign-accented voice*: Lev-Ari, S.; Keysar, B. (2010). "Why Don't We Believe Non-Native Speakers? The Influence of Accent on Credibility." *Journal of Experimental Social Psychology*, 46, 1093-1096.

[9] *Rightly timed pause*: Twain, M.; Paine, A. B. (1923). *Mark Twain's Speeches*. New York: Wells. xv.

[10] *Listeners are more likely to recognize and remember a word when it occurs after a silent pause*: MacGregor, L. J.; Corley, M.; Donaldson, D. I. (2010). "Listening to the Sound of Silence: Disfluent Silent Pauses in Speech Have Consequences for Listeners." *Neuropsychologia*, 48(14), 3982-3992. / / / / / *This is also true after filled pauses, but silent pauses are preferable for other reasons*: Fraundorf, S. H.; Watson, D. G. (2011). "The Disfluent Discourse: Effects of Filled Pauses on Recall." *Journal of Memory and Language*, 65(2), 161-175. / / / Corley, M.; MacGregor, L. J.; Donaldson, D. I. (2007). "It's the Way That You, Er, Say It: Hesitations in Speech Affect Language Comprehension." *Cognition*, 105(3), 658-668.

[11] *Filler words can play a useful role in conversation*: Clark, H. H.; Tree, J. E. F. (2002). "Using Uh and Um in Spontaneous Speaking." *Cognition*, 84(1), 73-111.

[12] *Speakers using a silent pause are perceived as more knowledgeable than speakers using "umm" and "uh"*: Brennan, S. E.; Williams, M. (1995). "The Feeling of Another's Knowing: Prosody and Filled Pauses as Cues to Listeners about the Metacognitive States of Speakers." *Journal of Memory and Language*, 34(3), 383-398.

[13] *Replacing a bad habit with a good habit is more effective than just trying to stop the bad habit*: Duhigg, C. (2012). *The Power of Habit: Why We Do What We Do in Life and Business*. New York: Random House.

[14] *Five days later, listeners remember twice as many details when a reader varies his pitch, time, intensity, and timbre*: Woolbert, C. H. (1920). "Effects of Various Modes of Public Reading." *Journal of Applied Psychology*, 4(2-3), 162-185.

[15] *Vocal variation is correlated with higher views on TED.com, as well as higher ratings of credibility and charisma*: Van Edwards, V. (2015). "5 Secrets of a Successful TED Talk." *The Huffington Post*. http://www.huffingtonpost.com/vanessa-van-edwards/5-secrets-of-a-successful_b_6887472.html

[16] *The Mehrabian statistic was derived from a combination of two different studies*: Mehrabian, A.; Wiener, M. (1967). "Decoding of Inconsistent Communications." *Journal of Personality and Social Psychology*, 6(1), 109-114. / / / Mehrabian, A.; Ferris, S. R. (1967). "Inference of Attitudes from Nonverbal Communication in Two Channels." *Journal of Consulting Psychology*, 31(3), 248-252.

[17] *Surgeons whose tone of voice sounds less empathetic are significantly more likely to be sued for malpractice*: Ambady, N.; Laplante, D.; Nguyen, T.; Rosenthal, R.; Chaumeton, N.; Levinson, W. (2002). "Surgeons' Tone of Voice: A Clue to Malpractice History." *Surgery*, 132(1), 5-9.

Chapter 5. The Face

[1] *Eye contact increases ratings of competence for presenters*: Beebe, S. A. (1974). "Eye Contact: A Nonverbal Determinant of Speaker Credibility." *The Speech Teacher*, 23, 21-25. / / / / / / *Eye contact increases ratings of competence for experimenters*: LeCompte, W. F.; Rosenfeld, H. M. (1971). "Effects of Minimal Eye Contact in the Instruction Period on Impressions of the Experimenter." *Journal of Experimental Social Psychology*, 7, 211-220. / / / / / / *Eye contact increases ratings of competence for interviewers*: Sodikoff, C. L.; Firestone, I. J.; Kaplan, K. J. (1974). "Distance Matching and Distance Equilibrium in the Interview Dyad." *Personality and Social Psychology Bulletin*, 1, 243-245. / / / / / / *Eye contact increases ratings of competence for counselors*: Fretz, B. R.; Cora, R.; Tuemmler, J. M.; Bellet, W. (1979). "Counselor Nonverbal Behaviors and Client Evaluations." *Journal of Counseling Psychology*, 26, 304-311. / / / Haase, R. F.; Tepper, D. T. (1972). "Nonverbal Components of Empathic Communication." *Journal of Counseling Psychology*, 19, 417-424. / / / Kelly, E. W.; True. J. H. (1980). "Eye Contact and Communication of Facilitation Conditions." *Perceptual and Motor Skills*, 51, 815-820. / / / Tipton, R. M.; Rymer, R. A. (1978). "A Laboratory Study of the Effects of Varying Levels of Counselor Eye Contact on Client-Focused and Problem-Focused Counseling Styles." *Journal of Counseling Psychology*, 25, 200-204. / / / / / / *Eye contact increases ratings of speaker credibility*: Hemsley, G. D.; Doob, A. N. (1978). "The Effect of Looking Behavior on Perceptions of a Communicator's Credibility." *Journal of Applied Social Psychology*, 8, 136-144. / / / / / / *Longer durations of eye contact are perceived as more intelligent, and more frequent eye shifts are perceived as less intelligent*: Wheeler, R. W.; Baron, J. C.; Mitchell, S.; Ginsburg, H. J. (1979). "Eye Contact and the Perception of Intelligence." *Bulletin of the Psychonomic Society*, 13(2), 101-102. / / / / / / *Someone making eye contact is perceived as more attractive and more trustworthy*: Kaisler, R. E.; Leder, H. (2016). "Trusting the Looks of Others: Gaze Effects of Faces in Social Settings." *Perception*, 45(8), 875-892. / / / / / / *Frequent eye contact increases people's liking for each other*: Argyle, M.; Lefebvre, L.; Cook, M. (1974). "The Meaning of Five Patterns of Gaze." *European Journal of Social Psychology*, 4, 125-136. / / / Exline, R. (1971). "Visual Interaction: The Glances of Power and Preference." *Nebraska Symposium on Motivation*, 19, 163-206.

[2] *Lack of gaze is perceived as a sign of nervousness and lack of confidence*: Cook, M.; Smith, J. M. C. (1975). "The Role of Gaze in Impression Formation." *British Journal of Social and Clinical Psychology*, 14, 19-25. / / / / / / *Eye contact increases ratings of power and potency*: Argyle, M.; Lefebvre, L.; Cook, M. (1974). "The Meaning of Five Patterns of Gaze." *European Journal of Social Psychology*, 4, 125-136. / / / / / / *Eye contact is particularly effective at intensifying emotional messages*: Kimble, C. E.; Olszewski, D. A. (1980). "Gaze and Emotional Expression: The Effects of Message Positivity-Negativity and Emotional Intensity." *Journal of Research in Personality*, 14, 60-69. / / / Kimble, C. E., Forte, R. A., Yoshikawa, J. C. (1981). "Nonverbal Concomitants of Enacted Emotional Intensity and Positivity: Visual and Vocal Behavior." *Journal of Personality*, 49, 271-283.

[3] *Listeners remember more of what was said when they received frequent eye contact*: Fry, R.; Smith, G. F. (1975). "The Effects of Feedback and Eye Contact on Per-

formance of a Digit-Coding Task." *Journal of Social Psychology*, 96, 145-146. / / / Otteson, J. D.; Otteson, C. R. (1980). "Effect of Teacher's Gaze on Children's Story Recall." *Perceptual and Motor Skills*, 50, 35-42. / / / Sherwood, J. V. (1988). "Facilitative Effects of Gaze Upon Learning." *Perceptual and Motor Skills*, 64 (3 Part 2), 1275-1278. / / / Fullwood, C.; Doherty-Sneddon, G. (2006). "Effect of Gazing at the Camera During a Video Link on Recall." *Applied Ergonomics*, 37(2), 167-175.

[4] *Bystanders are more willing to make change for, and lend change to, gazing experimenters*: Kleinke, C. L. (1977). "Compliance to Requests Made by Gazing and Touching Experimenters in Field Settings." *Journal of Experimental Social Psychology*, 13, 218-223. / / / Kleinke, C. L. (1980). "Interaction Between Gaze and Legitimacy of Request on Compliance in a Field Setting." *Journal of Nonverbal Behavior*, 5, 3-12. / / / Brockner, J.; Pressman, B.; Cabitt, J.; Moran, P. (1982). "Nonverbal Intimacy, Sex, and Compliance: A Field Study." *Journal of Nonverbal Behavior*, 6, 253-258. / / / / / / *Bystanders are more willing to accept leaflets from, and give charitable contributions to, gazing experimenters*: Kleinke, C.L.; Singer, D.A. (1979). "Influence of Gaze on Compliance with Demanding and Conciliatory Requests in a Field Setting." *Personality and Social Psychology Bulletin*, 5, 387-390. / / / Bull, R.; Gibson-Robinson, E. (1981). "The Influence of Eye-Gaze, Style of Dress, and Locality on the Amounts of Money Donated to Charity." *Human Relations*, 34, 895-905. / / / / / / *Bystanders are more likely to help gazing person picked up dropped objects*: Valentine, M. E. (1980). "The Attenuating Influence of Gaze Upon the Bystander Intervention Effect." *The Journal of Social Psychology*, 111, 197-203. / / / Goldman, M.; Fordyce, J. (1983). "Prosocial Behavior as Affected by Eye Contact, Touch, and Voice Expression." *The Journal of Social Psychology*, 121, 125-129. / / / / / / *Drivers are more likely to stop for staring hitchhikers*: Snyder, Mark; Grether, John; Keller, Kristine. (1974). "Staring and Compliance: A Field Experiment on Hitchhiking." *Journal of Applied Social Psychology*, 4(2), 165-170. / / / / / / *Bystanders are more likely to help a gazing injured jogger, or a gazing woman who lost a contact lens*: Shotland, R. Lance; Johnson, Michael P. (1978). "Bystander Behavior and Kinesics: The Interaction Between the Helper and Victim." *Environmental Psychology and Nonverbal Behavior*, 2(3), 181-190. / / / Ellsworth, P. C.; Langer, E.J. (1976). "Staring and Approach. An Interpretation of the Stare as a Nonspecific Activator." *Journal of Personality and Social Psychology*, 33, 117-122. / / / / / / *Eye contact is integral to the process of cooperation*: Jellison, J. M.; Ickes, W. J. (1974). "The Power of the Glance: Desire to See and Be Seen in Cooperative and Competitive Situations." *Journal of Experimental Social Psychology*, 10, 444-450. / / / Foddy, M. (1978). "Patterns of Gaze in Cooperative and Competitive Negotiation." *Human Relations*, 31, 925-938. / / / / / / *Eye contact improves cooperation in the Prisoner's Dilemma*: Gardin, H.; Kaplan, K. J.; Firestone, I.J.; Cowan, G. A. (1973). "Proxemic Effects on Cooperation, Attitude, and Approach-Avoidance in a Prisoner's Dilemma Game." *Journal of Personality and Social Psychology*, 21, 13-18. / / / Wichman, H. (1970). "Effects of Isolation and Communication on Cooperation in a Two-Person Game." *Journal of Personality and Social Psychology*, 16, 114-120. / / / / / / *Negotiators in a position of power more are likely to bargain and compromise when face-to-face*: Morley, I. E.; Stephenson, G. M. (1969). "Interpersonal and Interparty Exchange: A Laboratory Simulation

of an Industrial Negotiation at the Plant Level." *British Journal of Psychology*, 60, 543-545. / / / Morley, I. E.; Stephenson. G. M. (1970). "Formality in Experimental Negotiations: A Validity Study." *British Journal of Psychology*, 61, 383-384. / / / Morley, I. E.; Stephenson. G. M. (1970b). "Strength of Case, Communication Systems and Outcomes of Simulated Negotiations: Some Social Psychological Aspects of Bargaining." *Industrial Relations Journal*, 1, 19-29.

[5] *Eye contact increases participation*: Caproni, V.; Levine, D.; O'Neal. E.; McDonald. R.; Garwood, G. (1977). "Seating Position, Instructor's Eye Contact Availability, and Student Participation in a Small Seminar." *Journal of Social Psychology*, 103, 315-316. / / / Sommer, R. (1967). "Classroom Ecology." *Journal of Applied Behavioral Science*, 3, 489-503. / / / / / *Eye contact improves test scores*: Christiansen, E.; Larson, D. (1972). "The Effect of a Lecturer's Gaze Direction Upon His Teaching Effectiveness." *Journal Supplement Abstract Service*, 2, Ms. No. 226. / / / Breed, G.; Colaiuta, V. (1974). "Looking, Blinking, and Sitting: Non-Verbal Dynamics in the Classroom." *Journal of Communication*, 24, 74-81. / / / / / *Eye contact improves course evaluations*: Pedersen, D. M. (1977). "Relationship of Ratings of Classroom Performance and Enjoyment with Seat Selection." *Perceptual and Motor Skills*, 45, 601-602.

[6] *Humans have white sclera to make it easier to tell what our companions are looking at*: Tomasello, Michael. (2007, January 13). "For Human Eyes Only." *The New York Times*. http://www.nytimes.com/2007/01/13/opinion/13tomasello.html

[7] *Humans reliably look to see where their companions are looking*: Bräuer, J.; Call, J.; Tomasello, M. (2005). "All Great Ape Species Follow Gaze to Distant Locations and Around Barriers." *Journal of Comparative Psychology*, 119(2), 145-154.

[8] *When making eye contact with a listener, a speaker is evaluated more positively by a third party observer*: Shrout, P. E.; Fiske, D. W. (1981). "Nonverbal Behaviors and Social Evaluation." *Journal of Personality*, 49(2), 115-128. / / / Abele, A. (1981). "Acquaintance and Visual Behaviour Between Two Interactants: Their Communicative Function for the Impression Formation of an Observer." *European Journal of Social Psychology*, 11(4), 409-425.

[9] *Preferred gaze duration*: Binetti, N.; Harrison, C.; Coutrot, A.; Johnston, A.; Mareschal, I. (2016). "Pupil Dilation as an Index of Preferred Mutual Gaze Duration." *Royal Society Open Science*.

[10] *Smiling people are perceived as more pleasant, more attractive, more sincere, more sociable, more competent, more likable, and more trustworthy*: LaFrance, M.; Hecht, M. A. (1995). "Why Smiles Generate Leniency." *Personality and Social Psychology Bulletin*, 21(3), 207-214. / / / / / *Smiling people are perceived as more intelligent*: Van Edwards, Vanessa. (2015). "5 Secrets of a Successful TED Talk." *The Huffington Post*. http://www.huffingtonpost.com/vanessa-van-edwards/5-secrets-of-a-successful_b_6887472.html

[11] *Emotions are highly contagious*: Hatfield, E.; Cacioppo, J. T.; Rapson, R. L. (1994). *Emotional Contagion*. New York: Cambridge University Press.

[12] *Emotional contagion is more powerful when the emotion is genuine*: Hennig-Thurau, T.; Groth, M.; Paul, M.; Gremler, D. D. (2006) "Are All Smiles Created Equal? How Emotional Contagion and Emotional Labor Affect Service Relation-

ships." *Journal of Marketing*, 70(3), 58-73. / / / Surakka, V.; Hietanen, J. K. (1998). "Facial and Emotional Reactions to Duchenne and Non-Duchenne Smiles." *International Journal of Psychophysiology*, 29(1), 23-33.

[13] *Unscripted vs. scripted remarks*: Weber, S. (2016, April 12). "Do Prepared Remarks Help or Hurt an Earnings Call? What the Data Says." http://www.quantifiedcommunications.com/blog/financial-communications-earnings-call

[14] *Extemporaneous speaking is more nerve-wracking than scripted speaking*: Witt, P. L.; Behnke, R. R. (2006). "Anticipatory Speech Anxiety as a Function of Public Speaking Assignment Type." *Communication Education*, 55(2), 167-177.

Part IV. Organization

[1] *1, 7, 4, 6, 9, 3, 2, 8, 5, 10*: Beckley, J. L. (1984). *The Power of Little Words*. Fairfield, NJ: The Economics Press. 38.

Chapter 6. The Gift

[1] *Mimi Goss, the iceberg's inventor*: Goss, M. (2012). *What Is Your One Sentence?: How to Be Heard in the Age of Short Attention Spans*. New York: Prentice Hall Press. 54-55.

[2] *Shorter letter*: O'Toole, G. (2012, April 28). "If I Had More Time, I Would Have Written a Shorter Letter." http://quoteinvestigator.com/2012/04/28/shorter-letter

[3] *Woodrow Wilson*: ibid.

[4] *How people become creative geniuses*: Grant, A. (2016). *Originals: How Non-Conformists Move the World*. New York: Penguin Books. 35-36.

[5] *The best performing stock traders are those with the best information, not the most information*: Huber, J.; Kirchler, M.; Sutter, M. (2008). "Is More Information Always Better?: Experimental Financial Markets with Cumulative Information." *Journal of Economic Behavior & Organization*, 65(1), 86-104.

[6] *Blood, sweat, toil, and tears*: Churchill, Winston. (1940, May 13). "Speech to the House of Commons."

[7] *Three claims is more persuasive than four*: Shu, S. B.; Carlson, K. A. (2014). "When Three Charms but Four Alarms: Identifying the Optimal Number of Claims in Persuasion Settings." *Journal of Marketing*, 78(1), 127-139.

Chapter 7. The Box

[1] *The importance of organization*: Thorndyke, P. W. (1977). "Cognitive Structures in Comprehension and Memory of Narrative Discourse." *Cognitive Psychology*, 9(1), 77-110.

[2] *Doing the laundry*: Bransford, J. D.; Johnson, M. K. (1972). "Contextual Prerequisites for Understanding: Some Investigations of Comprehension and Recall." *Journal of Verbal Learning and Verbal Behavior*, 11(6), 717-726.

[3] *"Tell 'em"*: Quote Investigator has traced the origin of this quote back to at least as early as 1908: O'Toole, G. (2017, August 15). "Tell 'Em What You're Going To Tell 'Em; Next, Tell 'Em; Next, Tell 'Em What You Told 'Em." https://quoteinvestigator.com/2017/08/15/tell-em/

[4] *Agreement with a message peaks at three repetitions*: Cacioppo, J. T.; Petty, R. E. (1979). "Effects of Message Repetition and Position on Cognitive Response, Recall, and Persuasion." *Journal of Personality and Social Psychology*, 37(1), 97-109.

Chapter 8. The Bow

[1] *On Twitter, the first thing you see is most memorable*: Ballenger, G. (2017, February 27). "Love at First View: Owning the Timeline and the Moment." https://marketing.twitter.com/na/en/insights/love-at-first-view-owning-the-timeline-and-the-moment.html

[2] *Greetings on OkCupid*: OkCupid. (2009, September 13). "Exactly What to Say in a First Message." https://theblog.okcupid.com/exactly-what-to-say-in-a-first-message-2bf680806c72

[3] *Listeners make reliable judgments about speakers in less than half a second*: McAleer, P.; Todorov, A.; Belin, P. (2014). "How Do You Say 'Hello'? Personality Impressions from Brief Novel Voices." *PLoS ONE*, 9(3), e90779.

[4] *Viewers make reliable judgments about a face in one-tenth of a second*: Willis, J.; Todorov, A. (2006). "First Impressions: Making Up Your Mind After a 100-ms Exposure to a Face." *Psychological Science*, 17(7), 592-598.

[5] *First impressions based on a photograph significantly predict how someone will feel after a live interaction a month later*: Gunaydyn, G.; Selcuk, E.; Zayas, V. (2015). "Impressions Based on a Portrait Predict, One-Month Later, Impressions Following a Live Interaction." Cornell University Working Paper.

[6] *First impressions after a short conversation significantly predict impressions nine weeks later*: Sunnafrank, M.; Ramirez, A. (2004). "At First Sight: Persistent Relational Effects of Get-Acquainted Conversations." *Journal of Social and Personal Relationships*, 21(3), 361-379.

[7] *First impressions based on 6 seconds of a lecture significantly predict end-of-quarter teaching evaluations*: Ambady, N.; Rosenthal, R. (1993). "Half a Minute: Predicting Teacher Evaluations from Thin Slices of Nonverbal Behavior and Physical Attractiveness." *Journal of Personality and Social Psychology*, 64(3), 431-441. / / / / / For more

on first impressions, see: Ambady, N.; Rosenthal, R. (1992). "Thin Slices of Expressive Behavior as Predictors of Interpersonal Consequences: A Meta-Analysis." *Psychological Bulletin*, 111(2), 256-274.

[8] *Curiosity primes memory*: Gruber, M. J.; Gelman, B. D.; Ranganath, C. (2014). "States of Curiosity Modulate Hippocampus-Dependent Learning via the Dopaminergic Circuit." *Neuron*, 84(2), 486-496. / / / Carpenter, S. K.; Toftness, A. R. (2017). "The Effect of Prequestions on Learning from Video Presentations." *Journal of Applied Research in Memory and Cognition*, 6(1), 104-109.

[9] *"God damn"*: Although we don't know the original source of this story, we got it from Ruppanner, Andy. (2001). *"White Knuckle" Speaking: Overcoming the Fear of Public Speaking*. San Jose: Writers Club Press.

[10] *Subverting presentation guidelines can make you seem more competent*: Bellezza, S.; Gino, F.; Keinan, A. (2014). "The Red Sneakers Effect: Inferring Status and Competence from Signals of Nonconformity." *Journal of Consumer Research*, 41, 35-54.

[11] *Show order effect*: Bruine de Bruin, W. (2006). "Save the Last Dance II: Unwanted Serial Position Effects in Figure Skating Judgments." *Acta Psychologica*, 123(3), 299-311.

[12] *Patient ratings of a colonoscopy are primarily based on their evaluation of its peak and end*: Redelmeier, D. A; Kahneman, D. (1996). "Patients' Memories of Painful Medical Treatments: Real-Time and Retrospective Evaluations of Two Minimally Invasive Procedures." *Pain*, 66(1), 3-8.

[13] *When a less unpleasant ending is added to a colonoscopy, patients rate the whole thing as less unpleasant*: Redelmeier, D. A; Katz, J.; Kahneman, D. (2003). "Memories of Colonoscopy: A Randomized Trial." *Pain*, 104(1-2), 187-194. / / / / / / *The same is true for holding a hand in cold water*: Kahneman, D.; Fredrickson, B. L.; Schreiber, C. A.; Redelmeier, D. A. (1993). "When More Pain Is Preferred to Less: Adding a Better End." *Psychological Science*, 4(6), 401-405. / / / / / / *Hearing loud noises*: Schreiber, C. A.; Kahneman, D. (2000). "Determinants of the Remembered Utility of Aversive Sounds." *Journal of Experimental Psychology General*, 129(1), 27-42. / / / / / / *And waiting in line*: Carmon, Z.; Kahneman, D. (1996). "The Experienced Utility of Queuing: Experience Profiles and Retrospective Evaluations of Simulated Queues." Duke University Working Paper. / / / / / / *For a review, see*: Barbara L. Fredrickson, B. L. (2000). "Extracting Meaning From Past Affective Experiences: The Importance of Peaks, Ends, and Specific Emotions." *Cognition and Emotion*, 14(4), 577-606.

[14] *The peak-end rule is also true for positive experiences*: Baumgartner, H.; Sujan, M.; Padgett, D. (1997). "Patterns of Affective Reactions to Advertisements: The Integration of Moment-to-Moment Responses into Overall Judgments." *Journal of Marketing Research*, 34(2), 219-232. / / / / / / *But in that case, it's still important that the end is more positive than everything else, as a less positive ending waters down a more positive overall experience*: Do, A. M.; Rupert, A. V.; Wolford, G. (2008). "Evaluations of Pleasurable Experiences: The Peak-End Rule." *Psychonomic Bulletin and Review*, 15(1), 96-98.

[15] *Alliterative phrases are more likely to be remembered*: Boers, F.; Lindstromberg, S. (2005). "Finding Ways to Make Phrase-Learning Feasible: The Mnemonic Effect

of Alliteration." *System*, 33, 225-238. / / / Lindstromberg, S.; Boers, F. (2008). "The Mnemonic Effect of Noticing Alliteration in Lexical Chunks." *Applied Linguistics*, 29, 200-222. / / / Boers, F.; Lindstromberg, S.; Eyckmans, J. (2012). "Are Alliterative Word Combinations Comparatively Easy to Remember for Adult Learners?" *RELC Journal*, 43(1), 127-135. / / / Boers, F.; Lindstromberg, S.; Eyckmans, J. (2014). "Is Alliteration Mnemonic Without Awareness Raising?" *Language Awareness*, 23, 291-303. / / / Rogers, P. W. (1970). "Effect of Alliteration on Acquisition and Retention of Meaningful Verbal Material." *Perceptual and Motor Skills*, 30, 671-675. / / / / / / *A similar effect has been found with assonance, or the repetition of vowel sounds*: Lindstromberg, S.; Boers, F. (2008). "Phonemic Repetition and the Learning of Lexical Chunks: The Power of Assonance." *System*, 36, 423-436.

[16] *Alliterative product deals are more attractive*: Davis, D.; Bagchi, R.; Block, L. (2012). "Alliteration Alters: Its Influence in Perceptions for Product Promotions and Pricing." *Advances in Consumer Research*, 40, 600-601.

[17] *Teaching with acronyms improves students' final exam scores*: Lakin, J. L.; Giesler, R. B.; Morris, K. A.; Vosmik, J.R. (2007). "HOMER as an Acronym for the Scientific Method." *Teaching of Psychology*, 34(2), 94-96.

[18] *Techniques for better acronyms*: Stalder, D. R. (2005). "Learning and Motivational Benefits of Acronym Use in Introductory Psychology." *Teaching of Psychology*, 32(4), 222-228. / / / / / / *More research on acronyms*: Kibler, J. L., III; Blick, K. A. (1972). "Evaluation of Experimenter-Supplied and Subject-Originated First-Letter Mnemonics in a Free-Recall Task." *Psychological Reports*, 30, 307-313. / / / Nelson, D. L.; Archer, C. S. (1972). "The First Letter Mnemonic." *Journal of Educational Psychology*, 63, 482-486. / / / Morris, P. E.; Cook, N. (1978). "When Do First Letter Mnemonics Aid Recall?" *British Journal of Educational Psychology*, 48, 22-28.

[19] *Rhyming statements are perceived to be more accurate*: McGlone, M. S.; Tofighbakhsh, J. (1999). "The Keats Heuristic: Rhyme as Reason in Aphorism Interpretation." *Poetics*, 26, 235-244. / / / McGlone, M. S.; Tofighbakhsh, J. (2000). "Birds of a Feather Flock Conjointly (?): Rhyme as Reason in Aphorisms." *Psychological Science*, 11(5), 424-428.

[20] *Rhyming statements are more likable, more original, more memorable, more persuasive, and more trustworthy*: Filkukova, P.; Klempe, S. H. (2013). "Rhyme as Reason in Commercial and Social Advertising." *Scandinavian Journal of Psychology*, 54, 423-431.

[21] *Parallel structure makes statements more memorable*: Kamil, M. L. (1970). *Memory of Parallel Structure and Repeated Items in Compound Sentences and Digit, Letter, and Word Strings*. Madison: Wisconsin Research and Development Center for Cognitive Learning. / / / / / / *Parallel structure facilitates sentence comprehension*: Frazier, L.; Taft, L.; Roeper, T.; Clifton, C.; Ehrlich, K. (1984). "Parallel Structure: A Source of Facilitation in Sentence Comprehension." *Memory & Cognition*, 12(5), 421-430.

[22] *For more on memorable phrase-making, see*: Forsyth, M. (2014). *The Elements of Eloquence: Secrets of the Perfect Turn of Phrase*. New York: Penguin Books.

Part V. Visual Aids

[1] *The Boeing slide*: Parker, P.; Chao, D.; Norman, I.; Dunham, M. (2003, January 23). "Orbiter Assessment of STS-107 ET Bipod Insulation Ramp Impact."
[2] *The Columbia example comes from*: Tufte, E. (2006). *The Cognitive Style of PowerPoint: Pitching Out Corrupts Within*. Cheshire, CT: Graphics Press.

Chapter 9. Pick

[1] *30 million presentations*: Estimate from Microsoft, as quoted by Parker, I. (2001, May 28). "Absolute PowerPoint: Can a Software Package Edit Our Thoughts?" *The New Yorker*. http://www.newyorker.com/magazine/2001/05/28/absolute-powerpoint
[2] *People place higher value on objects that are physically present*: Bushong, B.; King, L. M.; Camerer, C. F.; Rangel, A. (2010). " Pavlovian Processes in Consumer Choice: The Physical Presence of a Good Increases Willingness-to-Pay." *American Economic Review*, 100(4), 1556-1571.
[3] *Research has also found benefits to passing around props, namely, that people attribute higher value to products that they have touched compared to products they haven't touched*: Peck, J.; Shu, S. B. (2009). "The Effect of Mere Touch on Perceived Ownership." *Journal of Consumer Research*, 36(3), 434-447.
[4] *Dance vs. PowerPoint*: Bohannon, J. (2011). "Dance vs. PowerPoint: A Modest Proposal." *TED 2011*. https://www.ted.com/talks/john_bohannon_dance_vs_powerpoint_a_modest_proposal
[5] *Dance Your Ph.D.*: http://gonzolabs.org/dance/
[6] *Ekphrasis*: Webb, R. (2016). *Ekphrasis, Imagination and Persuasion in Ancient Rhetorical Theory and Practice*. New York: Routledge. 1.
[7] *Visual imagery engages many of the same processes as visual perception*: Ganis, G.; Thompson, W. L.; Kosslyn, S. M. (2004). "Brain Areas Underlying Visual Mental Imagery and Visual Perception: An fMRI Study." *Brain Research Cognitive Brain Research*. 20(2), 226-241. / / / / / *Smell-related words activate olfactory regions of the brain*: González, J.; Barros-Loscertales, A.; Pulvermüller, F.; Meseguer, V.; Sanjuán, A; Belloch, V.; Avila C. (2006). "Reading Cinnamon Activates Olfactory Brain Regions." *Neuroimage*, 32(2), 906-912. / / / / / *Texture words activate brain regions associated with touch*: Lacey, S.; Stilla, R.; Sathian, K. (2012). "Metaphorically Feeling: Comprehending Textural Metaphors Activates Somatosensory Cortex." *Brain & Language*, 120(3), 416-421. / / / / / *Motion words activate the motor cortex*: Romero Lauro, L. J.; Mattavelli, G.; Papagno, C.; Tettamanti, M. "She Runs, The Road Runs, My Mind Runs, Bad Blood Runs Between Us: Literal and Figurative Motion Verbs: An fMRI Study." *Neuroimage*, 83, 361-371.
[8] *When we imagine something, we're more likely to believe it, e.g., voters who are asked to imagine a particular candidate winning an election become more convinced that that candidate will win it*: Carroll, J. S. (1978). "The Effect of Imagining an Event

on Expectations for the Event: An Interpretation in Terms of the Availability Heuristic." *Journal of Experimental Social Psychology*, 14(1), 88-96. / / / / / *People who are asked to imagine having a disease come to believe that it is more likely they will catch it*: Sherman, S. J.; Cialdini, R. B.; Schwartzman, D. F.; Reynolds, K. D. (1985). "Imagining Can Heighten or Lower the Perceived Likelihood of Contracting a Disease: The Mediating Effect of Ease of Imagery." *Personality and Social Psychology Bulletin*, 11(1), 118-127. / / / / / *This is also true for winning a contest and getting arrested for a crime*: Gregory, W. L.; Cialdini, R. B.; Carpenter, K. M. (1982). "Self-Relevant Scenarios as Mediators of Likelihood Estimates and Competence: Does Imagining Make It So?" *Journal of Personality and Social Pscyhology*, 43(1), 89-99. / / / / / *On the other hand, when an outcome is difficult to imagine, people believe it is less likely to happen*: Sherman, S. J.; Cialdini, R. B.; Schwartzman, D. F.; Reynolds, K. D. (1985). "Imagining Can Heighten or Lower the Perceived Likelihood of Contracting a Disease: The Mediating Effect of Ease of Imagery." *Personality and Social Psychology Bulletin*, 11(1), 118-127. / / / / / *The more image-based language you use, the more charismatic you will seem*: Emrich, C. G.; Brower, H. H.; Feldman, J. M.; Garland, H. (2001). "Images in Words: Presidential Rhetoric, Charisma, and Greatness." *Administrative Science Quaterly*, 46(3), 527-557.

Chapter 10. Optimize

[1] *The redundancy principle states that people learn better from graphics and narration alone than from graphics, narration, and on-screen text*: Sweller, J. (2005). "The Redundancy Principle in Multimedia Learning." *The Cambridge Handbook of Multimedia Learning*. Cambridge: Cambridge University Press. 159-168. / / / Mayer, R. E. (2005). "Principles for Reducing Extraneous Processing in Multimedia Learning: Coherence, Signaling, Redundancy, Spatial Contiguity and Temporal Contiguity Principles." *The Cambridge Handbook of Multimedia Learning*. Cambridge: Cambridge University Press. 183-200.

[2] *The multimedia principle states that people learn better from words and graphics together than from words alone*: Fletcher, J. D.; Tobias, S. (2005). "The Multimedia Principle." *The Cambridge Handbook of Multimedia Learning*. Cambridge: Cambridge University Press. 117.

[3] *We have two channels for processing information: a verbal channel and a visual channel*: Schnotz, W. (2005). "An Integrated Model of Text and Picture Comprehension." *The Cambridge Handbook of Multimedia Learning*. Cambridge: Cambridge University Press. 49-69.

[4] *Pictures make things more believable*: Newman, E. J.; Garry, M.; Unkelbach, C.; Bernstein, D. M.; Lindsay, D. S.; Nash, R. A. (2015). "Truthiness and Falsiness of Trivia Claims Depend on Judgmental Contexts." *Journal of Experimental Psychology: Learning, Memory, and Cognition*, 41(5), 1337-1348.

[5] *In order to improve learning, speech and graphics must be mutually supportive*: Schnotz, W. (2005). "An Integrated Model of Text and Picture Comprehension."

The Cambridge Handbook of Multimedia Learning. Cambridge: Cambridge University Press. 60.

[6] *Irrelevant images distract the audience, reducing learning*: Mayer, R. E. (2005). "Principles for Reducing Extraneous Processing in Multimedia Learning: Coherence, Signaling, Redundancy, Spatial Contiguity and Temporal Contiguity Principles." *The Cambridge Handbook of Multimedia Learning*. Cambridge: Cambridge University Press. 183-200.

[7] *It's better to leave out irrelevant details*: ibid.

[8] *Writing numbers with numerals makes them more salient*: Nielson, J. (2007, April 16). "Show Numbers as Numerals When Writing for Online Readers." https://www.nngroup.com/articles/web-writing-show-numbers-as-numerals/

[9] *Human-scale statistics*: Heath, C.; Heath, D. (2007). *Made to Stick: Why Some Ideas Survive and Others Die*. New York: Random House. 144.

[10] *Irrelevant visual elements distract the audience, reducing learning*: Mayer, R. E. (2005). "Principles for Reducing Extraneous Processing in Multimedia Learning: Coherence, Signaling, Redundancy, Spatial Contiguity and Temporal Contiguity Principles." *The Cambridge Handbook of Multimedia Learning*. Cambridge: Cambridge University Press. 183-200.

[11] *2D charts are preferred to 3D charts*: Mackiewicz, J. (2007). "Perceptions of Clarity and Attractiveness in PowerPoint Graph Slides." *Technical Communication*, 54(2), 145-156.

[12] *It's better to put labels directly on a graph than to rely on a legend*: Ayres, P.; Sweller, J. (2005). "The Split-Attention Principle in Multimedia Learning." *The Cambridge Handbook of Multimedia Learning*. Cambridge: Cambridge University Press. 135-146.

[13] *The signaling principle states that people learn better when they are given visual cues that illustrate the structure of a lesson*: Mayer, R. E. (2005). "Principles for Reducing Extraneous Processing in Multimedia Learning: Coherence, Signaling, Redundancy, Spatial Contiguity and Temporal Contiguity Principles." *The Cambridge Handbook of Multimedia Learning*. Cambridge: Cambridge University Press. 183-200. / / / Rouet, J.-F.; Potelle, H. (2005). "Navigational Principles in Multimedia Learning." *The Cambridge Handbook of Multimedia Learning*. Cambridge: Cambridge University Press. 297-312. / / / Shapiro, A. M. (2005). "The Site Map Principle in Multimedia Learning." *The Cambridge Handbook of Multimedia Learning*. Cambridge: Cambridge University Press. 313-324.

[14] *Different languages have different ways of representing time*: Boroditsky, L. (2011). "How Languages Construct Time." *Space, Time and Number in the Brain: Searching for the Foundations of Mathematical Thought*. London: Academic Press. 333-341. / / / / / / *Kuuk Thaayorre*: Boroditsky, L. (2009, June 11). "How Does Our Language Shape the Way We Think." *The Edge*. https://www.edge.org/conversation/lera_boroditsky-how-does-our-language-shape-the-way-we-think

[15] *People trust based on content but distrust based on design*: Sillence, E.; Briggs, P.; Fishwick, L.; Harris, P. (2004). "Trust and Mistrust of Online Health Sites." *Proceedings of the SIGCHI Conference on Human Factors in Computing Systems*. 663-670.

[16] *There's no clear winner in the battle between serif and sans serif fonts*: Poole, A. (2008, February 17). "Which Are More Legible: Serif or Sans Serif Typefaces?" http://alexpoole.info/blog/which-are-more-legible-serif-or-sans-serif-typefaces/

[17] *Guy Kawasaki on minimum font size*: Kawasaki, G. (2005, December 30). "The 10/20/30 Rule of PowerPoint." http://guykawasaki.com/the_102030_rule

[18] *Easy to read content is more believable*: Reber, R.; Schwarz, N. (1999). "Effects of Perceptual Fluency on Judgments of Truth." *Consciousness and Cognition*, 8(3), 338-342. / / / *Cool colors are preferred to warm colors, and high contrast is preferred to low contrast*: Mackiewicz, J. (2007). "Perceptions of Clarity and Attractiveness in PowerPoint Graph Slides." *Technical Communication*, 54(2), 145-156.

[19] *Different colors mean different things in different cultures*: McCandless, D. (2009). "Colours in Cultures." *Information is Beautiful*. https://informationisbeautiful.net/visualizations/colours-in-cultures/

[20] *85% of science and engineering slides have titles that do not convey the main message of the slide*: Garner, J.; Alley, M. P.; Gaudelli, A.; Zappe, S. (2009). "Common Use of PowerPoint versus Assertion-Evidence Slide Structure: A Cognitive Psychology Perspective." *Technical Communication*, 56(4), 331-345.

[21] *The assertion-evidence approach improves audience understanding*: Garner, J. K.; Alley, M. P. (2013). "How the Design of Presentation Slides Affects Audience Comprehension: A Case for the Assertion-Evidence Approach." *International Journal of Engineering Education*, 29(6), 1564-1579. / / / / / *For more on the assertion-evidence approach, see*: Alley, M. P.; Neeley, K. A. (2005). "Rethinking the Design of Presentation Slides: A Case for Sentence Headlines and Visual Evidence." *Technical Communication*, 52(4), 417-426. / / / Garner, J. K.; Alley, M. P.; Gaudelli, A. F.; Zappe, S. E. (2009). "Common Use of PowerPoint versus the Assertion-Evidence Structure: A Cognitive Psychology Perspective." *Technical Communication*, 56(4), 331-345.

[22] *Student test scores improve after lecture slides are redesigned using the assertion-evidence approach*: Alley, M. P.; Schreiber, M.; Ramsdell, K. Muffo, J. (2005). "How the Design of Headlines in Presentation Slides Affects Audience Retention." *Technical Communication*, 53(2), 225-233.

[23] *The assertion-evidence approach improves presenter understanding*: Aippersbach, S.; Alley, M. P.; Garner, J. (2013). "How Slide Design Affects a Student Presenter's Understanding of the Content." Paper presented at the 2013 ASEE Annual Conference.

[24] *Viewers are more likely to remember points that have been visually differentiated from the rest of the presentation*: Simon, Carmen. (2016). *Impossible to Ignore: Creating Memorable Content to Influence Decisions*. New York: McGraw-Hill Education. 39.

[25] *The coherence principle states that people learn better when extraneous flourishes are excluded*: Mayer, R. E. (2005). "Principles for Reducing Extraneous Processing in Multimedia Learning: Coherence, Signaling, Redundancy, Spatial Contiguity and Temporal Contiguity Principles." *The Cambridge Handbook of Multimedia Learning*. Cambridge: Cambridge University Press. 183-200.

[26] *As simple as possible*: The direct quote is "It can scarcely be denied that the supreme goal of all theory is to make the irreducible basic elements as simple

and as few as possible without having to surrender the adequate representation of a single datum of experience." But you have to admit that the paraphrased version is stickier. The direct quote comes from "On the Method of Theoretical Physics," The Herbert Spencer Lecture delivered at Oxford University on June 10, 1933. For a fascinating look at the evolution of this quote, see: O'Toole, G. (2011, May 13). "Everything Should Be Made as Simple as Possible, But Not Simpler." http://quoteinvestigator.com/2011/05/13/einstein-simple

[27] *People learn better when information is broken up into manageable segments*: Mayer, R. E. (2005). "Principles for Managing Essential Processing in Multimedia Learning: Segmenting, Pretraining, and Modality Principles." *The Cambridge Handbook of Multimedia Learning*. Cambridge: Cambridge University Press. 169-182.

[28] *One idea per slide*: Duarte, N. (2012). *HBR Guide to Persuasive Presentations*. Boston: Harvard Review Press. 123.

Chapter 11. Present

[1] *It's important for the visuals to match the words being spoken*: Mayer, R. E. (2005). "Principles for Reducing Extraneous Processing in Multimedia Learning: Coherence, Signaling, Redundancy, Spatial Contiguity and Temporal Contiguity Principles." *The Cambridge Handbook of Multimedia Learning*. Cambridge: Cambridge University Press. 183-200.

Part VI. Pitching

[1] *We spend 40% of our workday engaged in non-sales selling*: Pink, D. (2012). *To Sell Is Human: The Surprising Truth About Moving Others*. New York: Riverhead Books. 21.

Chapter 12. Ask, Audience, and Angle

[1] *Ideas demand change*: Berkun, S. (2005). "How to Pitch an Idea." http://scottberkun.com/essays/38-how-to-pitch-an-idea/

[2] *Information alone rarely persuades*: McKenzie-Mohr, D.; Smith, W. (1999). *Fostering Sustainable Behavior: An Introduction to Community-Based Social Marketing*. Gabriola Island, BC: New Society Publishers.

[3] *Information alone doesn't change behavior*: Quotes from McKenzie-Mohr, D.; Smith, W. (1999). *Fostering Sustainable Behavior: An Introduction to Community-Based Social Marketing*. Gabriola Island, BC: New Society Publishers. The original study is Geller, E. S. (1981). "Evaluating Energy Conservation Programs: Is Verbal Report Enough?" *Journal of Consumer Research*, 8(3), 331-335.

[4] *Information alone doesn't change behavior (continued)*: Midden, C. J. H.; Meter, J. F.; Weenig, M. H.; Zieverink, H. J. A. (1983). "Using Feedback, Reinforcement and Information to Reduce Energy Consumption in Households: A Field-Experiment." *Journal of Economic Psychology*, 3(1), 65-86. / / / Jordan, J. R.; Hungerford, H. R.; Tomera, A. N. (1986). "Effects of Two Residential Environmental Workshops on High School Students." *The Journal of Environmental Education*, 18(1), 15-22. / / / Geller, E. S.; Erickson, J. B.; Buttram, B. A. (1983). "Attempts to Promote Residential Water Conservation with Educational, Behavioral and Engineering Strategies." *Population and Environment*, 6(2), 96-112.

[5] *Actions are only loosely correlated with beliefs*: Tedeschi, R. G.; Cann, A.; Siegfried, W. D. (1982). "Participation in Voluntary Auto Emissions Inspection." *Journal of Social Psychology*, 117, 309-310. / / / Finger, M. (1994). "From Knowledge to Action? Exploring the Relationships Between Environmental Experiences, Learning, and Behavior." *Journal of Social Issues*, 50, 141-160. / / / Archer, D.; Pettigrew, T.; Costanzo, M.; Iritani, B.; Walker, I.; White, L. (1987). "Energy Conservation and Public Policy: The Mediation of Individual Behavior." *Energy Efficiency: Perspectives on Individual Behavior*, 69-92. / / / De Young, R. (1989). "Exploring the Difference Between Recyclers and Non-Recyclers: The Role of Information." *Journal of Environmental Systems*, 18, 341-351.

[6] *Behavior doesn't necessarily correspond with belief*: Bickman, L. (1972). "Environmental Attitudes and Actions." *Journal of Social Psychology*, 87, 323-324. / / / / / See also: Darley, J. M.; Batson, D. (1973). "From Jerusalem to Jericho: A Study of Situational and Dispositional Variables in Helping Behavior." *Journal of Personality and Social Psychology*, 27(1), 100-108.

[7] *"Saints" and "Jerks"*: This example is cited in both Chip and Dan Heath's *Switch* and Daniel Pink's *To Sell Is Human*. The original source is Ross, L.; Nisbett, R. E. (1991). *The Person and the Situation: Perspectives of Social Psychology*. New York: McGraw Hill. 132-133.

[8] *Flexible goals are more likely to be met than rigid goals*: Scott, M. L.; Nowlis, S. M. (2013). "The Effect of Goal Specificity on Consumer Goal Reengagement." *Journal of Consumer Research*, 40, 444-459.

[9] *A journey of a thousand miles*: Lao-Tzu. (4th Century BC). *Tao Te Ching*. Chapter 64.

[10] *Adding the phrase "even a penny will help" doubles the number of people willing to donate*: Cialdini, R. B.; Schroeder, D. A. (1976). "Increasing Compliance by Legitimizing Paltry Contributions: When Even a Penny Helps." *Journal of Personality and Social Psychology*, 34(4), 599-604.

[11] *Starting with a small ask can increase compliance with a larger ask down the road*: Freedman, J. L.; Fraser, S. C. (1966). "Compliance Without Pressure: The Foot-in-the-Door Technique." *Journal of Personality and Social Psychology*, 4(2), 195-202.

[12] *Our brains process rejection in much the same way as they process physical pain*: Hsu, D. T.; Sanford, B. J.; Meyers, K. K.; Love, T. M.; Hazlett, K. E.; Wang, H.; Ni, L.; Walker, S. J.; Mickey, B. J.; Korycinski, S. T.; Koeppe, R. A.; Crocker, J. K.; Langenecker, S. A.; Zubieta, J.-K. (2013). "Response of the μ-Opioid System to Social Rejection and Acceptance." *Molecular Psychiatry*, 18, 1211-1217. / / / Eisenberger, N.;

Liberman, M. D.; Williams, K. D. (2003). "Does Rejection Hurt? An FMRI Study of Social Exclusion." *Science*, 302(5643), 290-2.

[13] *We underestimate people's willingness to help by a factor of two*: Flynn, F. J.; Lake, V. K. B. (2008). "If You Need Help, Just Ask: Underestimating Compliance With Direct Requests for Help." *Journal of Personality and Social Psychology*, 95(1), 128-143.

[14] *People in a position to help overestimate the likelihood that someone will ask for help if they need it*: Bohns, V. K.; Flynn, F. J. (2010). "'Why Didn't You Just Ask?' Underestimating the Discomfort of Help-Seeking." *Journal of Experimental Social Psychology*, 46(2), 402-409.

[15] *Rejection Proof*: Jiang, J. (2015). *Rejection Proof: How I Beat Fear and Became Invincible Through 100 Days of Rejection*. New York: Harmony Books.

[16] *Don't Mess with Texas*: McClure, T.; Spence, R. (2006). *Don't Mess with Texas: The Story Behind the Legend*. Austin: Idea City Press.

[17] *Tailoring political arguments to the values of the audience*: Feinberg, M. Willer, R. (2015). "From Gulf to Bridge: When Do Moral Arguments Facilitate Political Influence?" *Personality and Social Psychology Bulletin*, 41(12), 1665-1681. / / / / / *This can even affect support for candidates in a presidential election*: Völkel, J. G.; Feinberg, M. (2016, October 20). "Morally Reframed Arguments Can Affect Support for Political Candidates." https://ssrn.com/abstract=2856536

[18] *World's best lawn*: Heath, C.; Heath, D. (2007). *Made to Stick: Why Some Ideas Survive and Others Die*. New York: Random House. 179.

[19] *Quarter-inch holes*: ibid. / / / / / *This is further supported by research that in both hindsight (remembering) and foresight (imagining), experiences make people happier than things*: Van Boven, L.; Gilovich, T. (2003). "To Do or to Have? That Is the Question." *Journal of Personality and Social Psychology*, 85(6), 1193-1202.

[20] *Personalizing a pitch makes it more than twice as effective*: Gregory, W. L.; Cialdini, R.; Carpenter, K. (1982). "Self-Relevant Scenarios as Mediators of Likelihood Estimates and Compliance: Does Imagining Make it So?" *Journal of Personality and Social Psychology*, 43(1), 89-99. / / / Burnkrant, R. E.; Unnava, H. R. (1989). "Self-Referencing: A Strategy for Increasing Processing of Message Content." *Personality and Social Psychology Bulletin*, 15(4). 628-638.

[21] *Using people's first names makes them significantly more likely to comply with your requests*: Martin, S. J.; Goldstein, N. J.; Cialdini, R. B. (2014). "How Could a Small Change in Name Make a Big Difference to Your Game?" *The Small Big: Small Changes That Spark Big Influences*. New York: Grand Central Publishing. 23-26.

[22] *People whose names begin with the letter R are more likely to donate to support relief efforts for Hurricane Rita than people whose names began with other letters*: Chandler, J.; Griffin, T. M.; Sorenson, N. (2008). "In the 'I' of the Storm: Shared Initials Increase Disaster Donations." *Judgment and Decision Making*, 3(5), 404-410.

[23] *Dennis is more likely to be a dentist, etc.*: ibid. / / / Jones, J. T.; Pelham, B. W.; Carvallo, M.; Mirenberg, M. C. (2004). "How Do I Love Thee? Let Me Count the Js: Implicit Egotism and Interpersonal Attraction." *Journal of Personality and Social Psychology*, 87(5), 665-83. / / / Brendl, C. M.; Chattopadhyay, A.; Pelham, B. W.; Carvallo, M. (2005). "Name Letter Branding: Valence Transfers When Product Specific Needs Are Active." *Journal of Consumer Research*, 32, 405-415.

[24] *A handwritten sticky note more than doubles the response rate to a survey*: Garner, R. (2005). "Post-It Note Persuasion: A Sticky Influence." *Journal of Consumer Psychology*, 15, 230-237. / / / / / / *A request made in person is 34 times more effective than a request made by email*: Roghanizad, M. M.; Bohns, V. K. (2017). "Ask in Person: You're Less Persuasive Than You Think Over Email." *Journal of Experimental Social Psychology*, 69, 223-226.

[25] *People are more likely to return a survey from someone with a similar name*: Garner, R. (2005). "What's in a Name? Persuasion Perhaps." *Journal of Consumer Psychology*, 15(2), 108-116.

[26] *The Manchester United jogger study*: Levine, M.; Prosser, A.; Evans, D.; Reicher, S. (2005). "Identity and Emergency Intervention: How Social Group Membership and Inclusiveness of Group Boundaries Shape Helping Behavior." *Personality and Social Psychology Bulletin*, 31(4), 443-453.

Chapter 13. Push and Pull

[1] *Organ donation rates are much higher when donation is the default*: Johnson, E. J.; Goldstein, D. (2003). "Do Defaults Save Lives?" *Science*, 302(5649), 1338-1339.

[2] *Losing $100 hurts more than gaining $100 feels good*: Goldstein, N. J.; Martin, S. J.; Cialdini, R. B. (2008). "What Can You Gain from Loss?" *Yes! 50 Scientifically Proven Ways to Be Persuasive*. New York: Free Press. 144-149.

[3] *The tetanus shot study*: Leventhal, H.; Singer, R.; Jones, S. (1965). "Effects of Fear and Specificity of Recommendation upon Attitudes and Behavior." *Journal of Personality and Social Psychology*, 2(1), 20-29.

[4] *You should present your new idea as consistent with your audience's current beliefs*: Goldstein, N. J.; Martin, S. J.; Cialdini, R. B. (2008). "How Can You Fight Consistency with Consistency?" *Yes! 50 Scientifically Proven Ways to Be Persuasive*. New York: Free Press. 80-82.

[5] *Gun control*: Horowitz, E. (2013, August 23). "Want to Win a Political Debate? Try Making a Weaker Argument." *Pacific Standard*. https://psmag.com/want-to-win-a-political-debate-try-making-a-weaker-argument-446f21de17a1#.w0blkknry

[6] *Arguing with your audience can cause them to become more entrenched in their original view*: Nyhan, B.; Reifler, J. (2010). "When Corrections Fail: The Persistence of Political Misperceptions." *Political Behavior*, 32(2), 303-330.

[7] *Politics makes us stupid*: Klein, Ezra. (2014, April 6). "How Politics Makes Us Stupid." *Vox*. http://www.vox.com/2014/4/6/5556462/brain-dead-how-politics-makes-us-stupid / / / Kahan, D. M.; Cantrell, E.; Peters, E.; Slovic, P. (2013). "Motivated Numeracy and Enlightened Self-Government." The Cultural Cognition Project, Working Paper No. 116.

[8] *The smarter the person is, the dumber politics can make them*: ibid.

[9] *Curiosity can help bridge the partisan divide*: Resnick, B. (2017, February 1). "Yes, Politics Can Make Us Stupid. But There's an Important Exception to That Rule." *Vox*. http://www.vox.com/science-and-health/2017/2/1/14392290/partisan-bias-

dan-kahan-curiosity / / / Kahan, D. M.; Landrum, A.; Carpenter, K.; Helft, L.; Jamieson, K. H. (2017). "Science Curiosity and Political Information Processing." *Advances in Political Psychology*, 38(S1), 179-199.

[10] *Damasio's patient*: Damasio, A. (1994). *Descartes' Error: Emotion, Reason, and the Human Brain*. New York: Penguin Books.

[11] *Emotional tweets are more popular*: Brady, W. J.; Wills, J. A.; Lost, J. T.; Tucker, J. A.; Van Bavel, J. J. (2017). "Emotion Shapes the Diffusion of Moralized Content in Social Networks." *PNAS*, 114(28), 7313-7318.

[12] *Emotional appeals are more effective than logical ones*: Small, D. A.; Loewenstein, G.; Slovic, P. (2007). "Sympathy and Callousness: The Impact of Deliberative Thought on Donations to Identifiable and Statistical Victims." *Organizational Behavior and Human Decision Processes*, 102, 143-153.

[13] *Stories and statistics*: Heath, C.; Heath, D. (2007). *Made to Stick: Why Some Ideas Survive and Others Die*. New York: Random House. 243.

[14] *A positive pitch is more effective than a negative one*: Kopelman, S.; Rosette, A. S.; Thompson, L. (2006). "The Three Faces of Eve: Strategic Displays of Positive, Negative, and Neutral Emotions in Negotiations." *Organizational Behavior and Human Decision Processes*, 99(1), 81-101. / / / / / *In addition, in an analysis of the communications of Fortune's top 50 leaders of 2015, Quantified Communications found that leaders used significantly more optimistic language than the average speaker*: Zandan, N. (2015, May 21). "Lessons in Leadership Communications from Fortune's 50 Greatest Leaders." http://www.quantifiedcommunications.com/blog/lessons-in-leadership-communications-from-fortunes-50-greatest-leaders

[15] *Nick's column in the Stanford Daily*: Enge, N. (2008, April 17). "We Need A Vision." *The Stanford Daily*.

[16] *We think other people are primarily motivated by money*: Heath, C. (1999). "On the Social Psychology of Agency Relationships: Lay Theories of Motivation Overemphasize Extrinsic Incentives." *Organizational Behavior and Human Decision Processes*, 78(1), 25-62.

[17] *Basic human needs*: Maslow, A. (1943). "A Theory of Human Motivation." *Psychological Review*, 50, 370-396.

[18] *Self-transcendence and metamotivation*: Maslow, A. H. (1971). *The Farther Reaches of Human Nature*. New York: The Viking Press.

[19] *In addition to appealing to the best in your audience, you can also bring out the best in them. For example, people who are randomly told they are above-average citizens become 15% more likely to vote*: Tybout, A. M.; Yalch, R. F. (1980). "The Effect of Experience: A Matter of Salience?" *Journal of Consumer Research*, 6(4), 406-413. / / / / / *Similarly, when children are told that they seem to be the kind of person that cares about good handwriting, they spend more of their free time practicing their handwriting*: Cialdini, R. B.; Eisenberg, N.; Green, B. L.; Rhoads, K.; Bator, R. (1998). "Undermining the Undermining Effect of Reward on Sustained Interest." *Journal of Applied Social Psychology*, 28(3), 249-263.

[20] *Social proof for looking up at the sky*: Milgram, S.; Bickman, L.; Berkowitz, L. (1969). "Note on the Drawing Power of Crowds." *Journal of Personality and Social Psychology*, 13(2), 79-82.

[21] *Social proof for reusing towels*: Goldstein, N. J.; Cialdini, R. B.; Griskevicius, V. (2008). "A Room with a Viewpoint: Using Social Norms to Motivate Environmental Conservation in Hotels." *Journal of Consumer Research*, 35(3), 472-482.

[22] *Negative social proof*: Cialdini, R. B. (2003). "Crafting Normative Messages to Protect the Environment." *Current Directions in Psychological Science*, 12(4), 105-109.

Chapter 14. Expertise and Efficiency

[1] *"The Pitch Coach"*: Rose, D. (2007). "How to Pitch to a VC." TED 2007. https://www.ted.com/talks/david_s_rose_on_pitching_to_vcs

[2] *Holes to poke*: Port, M. (2016). "Steal the Show: From Speeches to Job Interviews to Deal-Closing Pitches, How to Guarantee a Standing Ovation for All the Performances in Your Life." Boston: Mariner Books. 35.

[3] *The Sinatra test*: Heath, C.; Heath, D. (2007). *Made to Stick: Why Some Ideas Survive and Others Die*. New York: Random House. 151.

[4] *Potential often matters more than experience*: Tormala, Z. L.; Jia, J. S.; Norton, M. I. (2012). "The Preference for Potential." *Journal of Personality and Social Psychology*, 103(4), 567-583.

[5] *Hedging and stock price*: Abrahams, M. (2016, April 4). "A Big Data Approach to Public Speaking." *Insights by Stanford Business*. https://www.gsb.stanford.edu/insights/big-data-approach-public-speaking

[6] *Hedging leads to negative perceptions*: Durik, A. M.; Britte, M. A.; Reynolds, R.; Storey, J. (2008). "The Effects of Hedges in Persuasive Arguments: A Nuanced Analysis of Language." *Journal of Language and Social Psychology*, 27(3), 217-234.

[7] *When lawyers mention a weakness in their case, it can help their case*: Williams, K. D.; Bourgeois, M. J.; Croyle, R. T. (1993). "The Effects of Stealing Thunder in Criminal and Civil Trials." *Law and Human Behavior*, 17(6), 597-609. / / / / / Similarly, consumers are more likely to buy a product when the seller lists a competitor's prices, even if the seller's prices aren't the lowest: Trifts, V.; Häubl, G. (2003). "Information Availability and Consumer Preference: Can Online Retailers Benefit From Providing Access to Competitor Price Information?" *Journal of Consumer Psychology*, 13(1-2), 149-159.

[8] *When presenting a weakness, it's best to present it with a corresponding strength*: Bohner, G.; Einwiller, S.; Erb, H.-P.; Siebler, F. (2003). "When Small Means Comfortable: Relations Between Product Attributes in Two-Sided Advertising." *Journal of Consumer Psychology*, 13(4), 454-463. / / / Pechmann, C. (1992). "Predicting When Two-Sided Ads Will Be More Effective than One-Sided Ads: The Role of Correlational and Correspondent Inferences." *Journal of Marketing Research*, 29(4), 441-453.

[9] *Self-promotion is viewed negatively*: Wortman, C.; Linsenmeier, J. (1977). "Interpersonal Attraction and Techniques of Ingratiation in Organizational Settings." *New Directions for Organizational Behavior*. Chicago: St. Clair Press. 133-178. / / / / / *Modest people are better liked*: Forsyth, D. R.; Berger, R.; Mitchell, T. (1981). "The Effects of Self-Serving vs. Other-Serving Claims of Responsibility on Attraction

and Attribution in Groups." *Social Psychology Quarterly*, 44, 59-64 / / / Baumeister, R. F.; Ilko, S. A. (1995). "Shallow Gratitude: Public and Private Acknowledgement of External Help in Accounts of Success." *Basic and Applied Social Psychology*, 16, 191-209.

[10] *Presenters who do not make positive assertions about themselves are also viewed negatively*: Kenrick, D. T.; Neuberg, S. L.; Cialdini, R. B. (2002). *Social Psychology: Unraveling the Mystery*. Boston: Allyn & Bacon. 129.

[11] *It's important to strike a balance between sharing our expertise and coming across as boastful*: Wosinska, W.; Dabul, A. J.; Whetstone-Dion, R.; Cialdini, R. B. (1996). "Self-Presentational Responses to Success in the Organization: The Costs and Benefits of Modesty." *Basic and Applied Social Psychology*, 18, 229-242.

[12] *Having someone else present your credentials makes you appear more competent and more likable*: Pfeffer, J.; Fong, C. T.; Cialdini, R. B.; Portnoy, R. R. (2006). "Overcoming the Self-Promotion Dilemma: Interpersonal Attraction and Extra Help as a Consequence of Who Sings One's Praises." *Personality and Social Psychology Bulletin*, 32(10), 1362-1374

[13] *People outsource their decision-making to expert opinions*: Engelmann, J. B.; Capra, C. M.; Noussair, C.; Berns, G. S. (2009). "Expert Financial Advice Neurobiologically 'Offloads' Financial Decision-Making under Risk." *PLoS ONE*, 4(3), e4957.

[14] *Adding investment options for retirement causes employees to become less likely to invest for retirement at all*: Iyengar, S. S.; Huberman, G.; Jiang, W. (2004). "How Much Choice Is Too Much?: Contributions to 401(k) Retirement Plans." *Pension Design and Structure: New Lessons from Behavioral Finance*. Oxford: Oxford University Press. 83-96.

[15] *People are more likely to buy jam when they have fewer options to choose from*: Iyengar, S. S.; Lepper, M. R. (2000). "When Choice Is Demotivating: Can One Desire Too Much of a Good Thing?" *Journal of Personality and Social Psychology*, 79, 996-1006.

[16] *Head & Shoulders shampoo*: Iyengar, S. (2010). *The Art of Choosing*. New York: Twelve.

[17] *People are much more likely to stick with the default*: Thaler, R. H.; Sunstein, C. R. (2008). *Nudge: Improving Decisions About Health, Wealth, and Happiness*. New Haven: Yale University Press.

[18] *An active choice is more effective than opt-in*: Keller, P.; Harlam, B.; Loewenstein, G.; Volpp, K. G. (2011). "Enhanced Active Choice: A New Method to Motivate Behavior Change." *Journal of Consumer Psychology*, 21, 376-383.

[19] *The averaging effect for multiple benefits*: Weaver, K.; Garcia, S. M.; Schwartz, N. (2012). "The Presenter's Paradox." *Journal of Consumer Research*, 39(3), 445-460.

[20] *Mixing intrinsic and extrinsic motivations is ineffective for decreasing energy use*: Dolan, P.; Metcalfe, R. (2013). "Neighbors, Knowledge, and Nuggets: Two Natural Field Experiments on the Role of Incentives on Energy Conservation." CEP Discussion Paper No. 1222, Centre for Economic Performance, London School of Economics.

[21] *When people are given both egoistic and altruistic reasons for charitable giving, they are less likely to give than when they are given only one of these reasons*: Feiler, D.

C.; Tost, L. P.; Grant, A. M. (2012). "Mixed Reasons, Mixed Givings: The Costs of Blending Egoistic and Altruistic Reasons in Donation Requests." *Journal of Experimental Social Psychology,* 48(6), 1322-1328.

[22] *When a fine was added for late pickups, late pickups doubled:* Shirky, C. (2010). "How Cognitive Surplus Will Change the World." *TED@Cannes.* https://www.ted.com/talks/clay_shirky_how_cognitive_surplus_will_change_the_world / / / Gneezy, U.; Rustichini, A. (2000). "A Fine is a Price." *Journal of Legal Studies,* 29, 1-17.

Part VII. Technical Communication

[1] *Thing Explainer:* Munroe, R. (2015). *Thing Explainer: Complicated Stuff in Simple Words.* Boston: Houghton Mifflin Harcourt.

[2] *How many brains?:* Koenig, J. (2016). "Beautiful New Words to Describe Obscure Emotions." *TEDxBerkeley 2016.* https://www.ted.com/talks/john_koenig_beautiful_new_words_to_describe_obscure_emotions

Chapter 15. Excite

[1] *Importance of dance:* Dunbar, R. (1996). *Grooming, Gossip, and the Evolution of Language.* Cambridge: Harvard University Press. 146-148.

[2] *The benefits of social dancing:* Powers, R.; Enge, N. (2013). *Waltzing: A Manual for Dancing and Living.* Stanford: Redowa Press.

[3] *We are more likely to understand and remember things that interest us:* Garner, R.; Alexander, P. A.; Gillingham, M. G.; Kulikowich, J. M.; Brown, R. (1991). "Interest and Learning from Text." *American Educational Research Journal,* 28(3), 643-659.

[4] *Mystery is a powerful way of generating interest:* Cialdini, R. (2005). "What's the Best Secret Device for Engaging Student Interest? The Answer Is in the Title." *Journal of Social and Clinical Psychology,* 24(1), 22-29.

[5] *Gap theory of curiosity:* Loewenstein, G. (1994). "The Psychology of Curiosity: A Review and Reinterpretation." *Psychological Bulletin,* 116(1), 75-98.

[6] *Instructor enthusiasm is the most powerful motivator:* Patrick, B. C.; Hisley, J.; Kempler, T. (2000). "What's Everybody So Excited About?: The Effects of Teacher Enthusiasm on Student Intrinsic Motivation and Vitality." *The Journal of Experimental Education,* 68(3), 217-236.

[7] *Enthusiasm can be conveyed with enthusiastic delivery:* ibid.

[8] *Benjamin Zander at TED:* Zander, B. (2008). "The Transformative Power of Classical Music." *TED 2008.* https://www.ted.com/talks/benjamin_zander_on_music_and_passion

[9] *An enthusiastic version of a class is rated as significantly better on all measures:* Williams, W. M.; Ceci, S. J. (1997). "'How'm I Doing?' Problems with Student

Ratings of Instructors and Courses." *Change: The Magazine of Higher Learning*, 29(5), 12-23.

[10] *Cialdini's trick for enthusiasm*: Cialdini, R. (2005). "What's the Best Secret Device for Engaging Student Interest? The Answer Is in the Title." *Journal of Social and Clinical Psychology*, 24(1), 22-29.

[11] *Bill Gates' mosquito release*: Gates, B. (2009). "Mosquitoes, Malaria, and Education." TED 2009. http://www.ted.com/talks/bill_gates_unplugged

[12] *STAR moments*: Duarte, N. (2010). *Resonate: Present Visual Stories That Transform Audiences.* Hoboken: John Wiley & Sons. 148-149.

[13] *Seductive details decrease comprehension*: Harp, S. F.; Mayer, R. E. (1997). "The Role of Interest in Learning From Scientific Text and Illustrations: On the Distinction Between Emotional Interest and Cognitive Interest." *Journal of Educational Psychology*, 89(1), 92-102. / / / / / *The same is also true of irrelevant audio*: Moreno, R.; Mayer, R. E. (2000). "A Coherence Effect in Multimedia Learning: The Case for Minimizing Irrelevant Sounds in the Design of Multimedia Instructional Messages." *Journal of Educational Psychology*, 92(1), 117-125.

Chapter 16. Enlighten

[1] *The tapping study*: Newton, Elizabeth (1990). *Overconfidence in the Communication of Intent: Heard and Unheard Melodies.* Stanford University Ph.D. dissertation.

[2] *The curse of knowledge*: Heath, C.; Heath, D. (2006, December). "The Curse of Knowledge." *Harvard Business Review.* https://hbr.org/2006/12/the-curse-of-knowledge

[3] *This is a paraphrased description of the earliest description of the waltz, from 200 years ago*: Wilson, T. (1816). *A Description of the Correct Method of Waltzing.* London: Sherwood, Neely, and Jones.

[4] Nath, L. E. (2007). "Expectation States: Are Formal Words a Status Cue for Competence?" *Current Research in Social Psychology*, 13(5), 50-63.

[5] *The amount of background should be inversely proportional to your audience's knowledge*: Kalyuga, S. (2005). "The Prior Knowledge Principle in Multimedia Learning." *The Cambridge Handbook of Multimedia Learning.* Cambridge: Cambridge University Press. 325-338.

[6] *The LifeSaver bottle*: Pritchard, M. (2009). "How to Make Filthy Water Drinkable." TEDGlobal 2009. http://www.ted.com/talks/michael_pritchard_invents_a_water_filter

[7] *Examples can improve technical communication*: Renkl, A. (2005). "The Worked-Out Examples Principle in Multimedia Learning." *The Cambridge Handbook of Multimedia Learning.* Cambridge: Cambridge University Press. 229-245.

[8] *Gillian Lynne*: Robinson, K. (2006). "Do Schools Kill Creativity?" TED 2006. https://www.ted.com/talks/ken_robinson_says_schools_kill_creativity

[9] *Even on a word-for-word basis, concrete words are more memorable than abstract ones*: Walker, I.; Hulme, C. (1999). "Concrete Words Are Easier to Recall than Abstract Words: Evidence for a Semantic Contribution to Short-Term Serial

Recall." *Journal of Experimental Psychology: Learning, Memory, and Cognition,* 25, 1256-1271.

Acknowledgments

Writing this book has been quite a journey—countless iterations spanning multiple years, even multiple states! As such, we're forever grateful to the following people for their teaching, support, and guidance throughout this process:

The past and present staff of the Technical Communication Program (TCP) at Stanford: Claude Reichard, Mary McDevitt, Midge Eisele, Matt Vassar, and all who came before them – This program stands above the rest in its mission to help students deliver impactful presentations through immersive classes and 1:1 tutorials. The program wouldn't be what it is without you, and we're so grateful we got to teach and learn with you.

All the tutors and students we interacted with as part of the E103 teaching team – To our fellow tutors, your energy and dedication always made us excited to teach with you, and your unique teaching styles helped us grow immensely. To our students, your willingness to get up, day after day, and give speech after speech taught us the true meaning of perseverance, and seeing you succeed in delivering the exact talk you hoped for warmed our hearts every time!

All of our other teachers at Stanford – With a few notable exceptions, you showed us what it means to communicate effectively. In particular, thanks to Gil Masters for being an amazing technical communicator (as well as a stickler for well-labeled charts) and to Wendy Goldberg for trusting Nick to bend the rules and allowing him to expand his ideas of what a presentation could be. And to Mehran Sahami for opening Melissa's eyes to computer science, for throwing candy at students to reward questions, and for teaching with a lightsaber, truly embodying the idea that when you're having fun, your audience will too!

Colleen Bennett – As Melissa's 10th grade Honors Chemistry teacher, you pushed her to expand her scientific competition arena and learn how to communicate complex topics in writing. Your support and enthusiasm in the classroom and at competitions encouraged her to strive for excellence in every endeavor.

Jennifer Williams and Keri Bostwick – As Melissa's 11th and 12th grade AP English teachers, you opened her eyes to the wonderful world of writing, including the ironclad rules and those rules meant to be broken. After being in your classes, rather than being a formulaic process, writing became a medium for conveying information and self-expression simultaneously.

Holly Cornelison, Bear Capron, Ron Huizing, Charlie Shoemaker, Kay Kostopoulos, Dan Klein, and all of the other actors and directors that Nick has had the privilege of working with over the years – Thank you for giving him the opportunity to come out of his shell and see that all the world really is a stage. He wouldn't be out there sharing his ideas without you.

All the judges, staff, and volunteers over many, many years at BDSF, OSSEF, OJAS, AJAS, ISEF, and STS – Through science fair, Melissa learned how to communicate technical information to a wide variety of people. The opportunities to compete in and present at these events over the years refined her interests in both technical topics and clear communication. From the first judging day in first grade to the last technical session as a senior in high school, the intellectual challenges brought on by your questions, comments, and insights always sparked curiosity and a fire to learn and teach others. She is eternally grateful for all your hard work to make these events possible for so many kids!

Bill Behrman – Thank you for giving us the opportunity to work with your data science students at Stanford. Having the opportunity to hold both 1:1 sessions and group workshops with students doing work for industry clients helped us reframe our academic knowledge into practical, actionable advice for any environment and led to many of the insights contained in this book.

Mandy Grover – Thank you for giving us the opportunity to teach a workshop series for engineers at Indeed just as we were finishing up this book and allowing us to bring our thoughts and techniques to the tech industry and interact with so many bright individuals. We can't wait to continue our collaboration!

Richard Powers – Thank you for showing us that technical communication extends to every field, not just STEM. In addition, thank you for your lasting impact on our lives - for Melissa, you enabled her to start living out a childhood dream as a dance teacher (and taught her the immense value of nonverbal communication along the way!) and for Nick, your belief in him and collaboration led to publishing his very first book. We are so very grateful to have you in our lives!

Elaine Enge – As an avid lover of reading yourself, you inspired Nick to become one too. Without this love of reading for its own sake, most of the information in this book would still be locked away in the archives of dry, peer-reviewed journals. And without your help in editing his early writing, he never would've learned how to convey his ideas so clearly.

Per Enge – As a naturally great communicator, you gave Nick a model to aspire to. Whether it's watching you lecture, or listening to a story around the dinner table, he learns something about speaking each time he hears you speak. It's been a pleasure to learn from you over the years, and in recent times, to teach with you.

Brenee Carvell – As Melissa's mom, you've read hundreds if not thousands of essays over the years. Your willingness to question their ideas and structure always resulted in an improved rewrite! You were also always a part of science fair preparation, taking on the role of "general audience member" and forcing her to adapt on the fly to communicate with people of different levels of knowledge. And finally, thank you for your love and support throughout her whole life—she's who she is today thanks to you being her mom.

Lee Carvell – As Melissa's dad, you opened her eyes first to magic of science and then to the joys of scientific communication. Your mentorship meant the advanced reference sources became understandable, interesting, and even fun! You taught her to never fear being honest, whether that was admitting something she didn't know or contradicting a judge with something she did. And you even gave her her first presentation advice ever, "Be sincere. Be brief. Be seated." Having you as her dad gifted her endless laughter and love (to this day and beyond!) for which she can never fully thank you enough for!

Index

accents, 45
accessibility, ratings of, 179
acronyms, 81–82
active choices, 164
aggressiveness, ratings of, 32–35
Alley, Michael, 118–119
alliteration, 80–81
Allman, Gregg, 17
An Inconvenient Truth, 94, 121
analogies, 82–83, 105, 154
angle, *see* pitches: angle
animations, 121, 122, 189
anxiety, *see* nervousness
approachability, ratings of, 40
Arabic (language), 37, 112
archery, argumentative, 166
articulation, *see* pronunciation
ask, *see* pitches: ask
assertion-evidence approach, 118–119
attention, 20, 36, 37, 39, 50, 81, 105, 114, 120
attentiveness, ratings of, 40
attire, 20, 30, 39–41
    fidgeting with clothing, 35
    willingness to help and, 144
attractiveness, ratings of, 50, 52, 76, 118
audience
    in pitches, *see* pitches: audience
    involvement, 97–98, 190
audience analysis, 59, 62, 140–141
audio, 77, 96–97, 127, 190
authority, ratings of, 39
averaging arguments, 164–165
Aymara people, 112

Bach, Johann Sebastian, 63

Back of the Napkin, The, 102
backdrops (slides), 121
backfire effect, 149
background color (slides), 118, 120
background information, 178, 187
ballroom dancing, 171–172, 175, 184–185, 190
bandwagon appeal, 156
bar charts, 32–35, 106–108
basic human needs, 155–156
Beethoven, Ludwig van, 63
Berkun, Scott, 135
big picture, 60, 70–71, 187, 188
blackboard, 95
blanking out, 47
blood pressure, 13, 24
BLUF (Bottom Line Up Front), 67
Bocelli, Andrea, 9
body language, *see* delivery
Boeing, 90, 121
Bohannon, John, 98
boredom, 39, 51, 73, 180, 188
Boroditsky, Lera, 112
Boroson, Martin, 13
breathing, 13–14, 46–47
bullet points, 89–91, 101, 113–115, 122
business formal (attire), 39–40

cable television study, 142–143
Caples, John, 141
career success, importance
    of speaking to, 1
Carnegie, Dale, 18
casual (attire), 39–40
casual executive (power pose), 14
cat videos (and relaxation), 13

charisma, ratings of, 36, 47, 99
charts, 93, 106–108, 116
choices, too many, 163–164
Cialdini, Robert, 177–178, 180
Cicero, 9
clarity, ratings of, 52
classical music, 63
cloud-based presentation software, 94–95
colonoscopy study, 78
color (of visual aids), 117–118, 120
color blindness, 118
Columbia space shuttle, 89–91, 121
common ground, finding, 143–144
communication skills, importance of, 1
competence, ratings of, 18, 39, 40, 44, 50, 52, 76, 77, 162, 185
compliance, *see* persuasion
comprehension, 2, 35, 44–46, 67–72, 101, 103, 107, 112, 115, 118–119, 171–192
concept maps, 110–111
concreteness, 191–192
confidence
    expressions of, 32–35, 44, 47, 50
    faking, 21, 113–114
    feelings of, 15
    ratings of, 18, 32–35, 39, 44, 50, 76
conservatives, 149–151
consistency, 40, 47–48, 52, 119–120, 149, 165–166
control, taking (visuals), 124–125
conversations, 45, 46, 181
convincing, *see* persuasion
counting on fingers, 36, 125
creativity, 63
credibility, ratings of, 36, 39, 40, 47, 50, 160–161, *see also* expertise
criticism, avoiding, 148–151
crossed arms, *see* hand positions
Cuddy, Amy, 14–15
curiosity, 77, 150–151, 177–178
curse of knowledge, 183–187

Damasio, Antonio, 151–152
dance, 98, 171–173, 175, 184–185, 189–192

Dance Your Ph.D., 98
data labels, 106–108
daycare pickup study, 166
defaults, 147, 164
defensiveness, ratings of, 32–35
delivery, 29–54
    enthusiasm and, 179
    nervousness and, 15, 21
    whiteboards and, 95
    with visual aids, 123–127
demonstrations, 96–97, 181, 185, 190
Descartes' Error, 151–152
design, *see* visual aids
diagrams, 108–115
differentiating ideas, 118, 120
distractions, 31, 103, 104, 106, 115, 125, 182
Don't Mess with Texas, 140–141
donations, 137–138, 143, 152, 165
door-to-door solicitation, 138
drawings, 95–96, 103, 126, 189
dual-channel processing, 101
Duarte, Nancy, 121, 181
Dunbar, Robin, 175
dynamism, 36, 39, 51, 52, 95

editing, 97, 120
Einstein, Albert, 121
ekphrasis (imagination), 98
elections, 36
emotion
    expressing, 51–52, 179, 181
    pitches and, 151–154
    ratings of, 75
    uncertainty and, 10
emotional contagion, 52
energy use study, 135, 165
engagement, ratings of, 52
enlightening an audience, *see* technical communication: enlightening an audience
enthusiasm, 17, 40, 51, 178–180
enunciation, *see* pronunciation
environmentalism, 135–141, 150–151, 154–156, 165
equations, 116

"even a penny will help", 138
examples, 180, 191–192
excitement, reappraising
 nervousness as, 17–18
exciting an audience, see
 technical communication:
 exciting an audience
expertise, see pitches: expertise
experts, citing, 162–163
extended metaphor, 82–83, 184–192
extrinsic motivation, 155–156, 165–166
eye contact, 19, 30, 49–51, 123, 179
eyes
 directing eyes, 50–51, 123
 tracking movement, 39

FaceTime, 141–142
facial expressions, 30, 48–49, 51–52, 179
 of audience, 19
fainting, 32
fairness, ratings of, 40, 180
Ferris Bueller's Day Off, 47
fidgeting, 35, 37, 191
fig leaf, see hand positions
filler words, 46–47, 77, 156
finale, see organization: finale
first impressions, 75–77
flexibility
 of ask, 137–138
 ratings of, 40
flowcharts, 112–115
flu shot study, 164
font, 117
 readability, 117
 size, 117
foot-in-the-door technique, 138
football fan study, 144
foreign land metaphor, 82–83, 184–192
formatting, 117–122
friendliness, ratings of, 32–35, 40, 153

Game of Thrones, 57
gaps (and curiosity), 178
Gates, Bill, 181
genuineness, 52
geographic maps, 109

gestures, 30, 35–38, 98, 125, 126, 179
 benefits of, 35–36
 offensive gestures, 37–38
 sequential gestures, 37
 types of, 37
Gettysburg Address, 65, 82, 93
global warming, 150–151
Google Slides, 94–95, 125
Gore, Al, 94, 121
Goss, Mimi, 62
Graduate Record Exam (GRE), 18
Grant, Adam, 24, 63
graphs, 67–71, 93, 106–108, 115–116,
 118–119, 122, 126
growth mindset, 15
gun control study, 149–150

habits, breaking, 46–47
hand positions, 32–35
hands at sides, see hand positions
hands on hips, see hand positions
heart rate, 9, 13, 23, 24
 biofeedback, 13
Heath, Chip and Dan, 141, 183
hedging, 161
help, willingness to, 40, 139, 144
hireability, ratings of, 36
hook, see organization: hook
humor, 180

"I am excited", 18
"I Have A Dream" speech, 15
iceberg model, 60–66, 188–189
illustrating
 how much?, 105–108
 how?, 112–115
 what's the point?, 116
 what?, 102–105
 when?, 111–112
 where?, 108–111
 who?, 102–105
 why?, 115–116
imagination, 77, 98–99, 142–143,
 190–191
impromptu speaking, 9, 13, 20, 29
 nervousness in, 9, 13, 20

improv, 37, 62
influence, *see* persuasion
inhibition, ratings of, 12
intelligence, 150, 175
    ratings of, 36, 40, 44, 50, 52
interactive whiteboard, 96
internationalization, 37–38, 112, 118
intrinsic motivation, 155–156, 165–166
introductions (of speaker), 162
introversion, 46
iOS, 94
iPhone, 141–142, 190
iPod, 164–165
irrational thoughts, 16–21
irrelevance, *see* relevance
issues, *see* pitches: push

jam study, 164
jargon, *see* technical language
Jiang, Jia, 139
Jobs, Steve, 94, 190
jogger study, 144
"journey of a thousand miles", 138

Kawasaki, Guy, 117
Kennedy, John F., 36
Keynote, 94–95
King, Martin Luther, Jr., 15
knowledge
    curse of, *see*
        curse of knowledge
    gaps in, 178
    gift of, 59–66
    ratings of, 40, 44, 46, 179
    technical, *see*
        technical knowledge
Koenig, John, 172
Kuuk Thaayorre, 112

Lao-Tzu, 138
large auditoriums, 36, 51
lawyers (admitting weakness), 161–162
Leadership Potential,
    Assessment of, 161
legends, 106–108
liberals, 149–151

lightning formation study, 182
likability, ratings of, 40, 50, 52, 76, 82, 162
Lincoln, Abraham, 65, 82, 93
linguistic relativity, 112
littering, 40, 140–141, 165
locked knees, 32
Loewenstein, George, 178
loss aversion, 148
Lynne, Gillian, 191–192

MacOS, 94
maps, 108–111, 186–188
Maslow, Abraham, 155
massage, 11, 13
Master Slide, 120
McCaffrey, Christian, 190
McClure, Tim, 140–141
meditation, 13–14
Mehrabian, Albert, 48, 52
memorability, ratings of, 75, 82
memory
    audience's, 2, 35–36, 40, 46, 47, 50, 64, 65, 67–73, 75, 77–83, 119–120, 126, 152–153, 163, 175, 180–182, 185, 187, 189, 192
    speaker's, 35, 38, 80, 101, 126
memory tricks, 79–83
Mendes, Sam, 141–142
metamotivation, 155
mistaken beliefs, 16–21
mistakes, apologizing for, 47
mixed motivations, 165–166
monotone, 47, 51
mosquitoes, 180–181
movement, 30, 38–39, 98, 124, 179
    benefits of, 38–39
    visual aids and, 123–124
Mozart, Wolfgang Amadeus, 63–64
Mr. Wonderful, 155
multimedia learning principles, 101–122
mumbling, 45–46
Munroe, Randall, 172
muscle relaxation, 13

music (and relaxation), 12–13
mysteries, 177–178
myth-busting, 16–21

names, power of, 143
NASA, 90, 91, 172
naturalness, ratings of, 12
navigational aids, 111–112
negative emotions, 153, 154
negative thoughts, 12
nervousness, 9–26
    methods for overcoming, 10–21
    myths about, 16–21
    prevalence of, 9–10, 23
    ratings of, 12, 32–35, 50
    signs of, 31–32, 35, 37, 43
Newton, Elizabeth, 183
Nicks, Stevie, 17
nitty-gritty details, 60, 70–71, 104, 187–189
Nixon, Richard, 36
non-native speakers, 45
non-sales selling, 133
Norvig, Peter, 93
numbers, 105–108
Nutini, Paolo, 41

O'Leary, Kevin, 155
objectivity, ratings of, 44
one idea per slide, 122
one-moment meditation, 13–14, 47
open body position, 14, 32
opt-in vs. opt-out, 147, 164
organ donation, 147
organization, 57–85
    finale, 77–79
    gestures and, 37
    hook, 75–77
    importance of, 57
    in technical speaking, 186–188
    nervousness and, 15
    ratings of, 40, 180
    roadmap, 72–73, 80, 111–112, 166
    scrapbook, 74, 111, 166
    the bow, 75–83
    the box, 67–74
    the gift, 59–66
    thesis, 64–65, 69, 166, 187
    transitions, 95, 111–112, 121, 124
    visual representation of, 111–112
originality, ratings of, 82
overconfidence, 17, 183
overselling, *see* efficiency

Pachelbel's *Canon*, 13
pacing (movement), 39
paradox of choice, 163–164
parallelism, 82
partisan bias, 149
Pascal, Blaise, 62
patterns, breaking, 120
pauses, 14, 46–47, 156
peace offering, *see* hand positions
peak-end rule, 78–79
pen exercise, 47
penguin gestures, 37
perfectionism, 18–19
personalization, 59–62, 142–143
persuasion, 32, 39, 40, 44, 50, 65, 73, 133–167
persuasive speaking, *see* pitches
persuasiveness, ratings of, 18, 82
Petrified Wood National Park, 156
pictures, 102–105, 181
pie charts, 108
Pink, Daniel, 133
pitches, 133–167
    angle, 144–166
    ask, 135–141
    audience, 139–144, 148–151, 155–156
    efficiency, 163–166
    expertise, 159–163
    pull, 153–157
    push, 147–153
politics, 141, 149–151
polka mazurka, 171–172, 175, 189
popularity, ratings of, 36
positive emotions, 153, 154
positive nervousness, 17
Positive Sustainability, 154–155
positive thoughts, 12

power
    feelings of, 14–15, 40
    ratings of, 50
power posing, 14–15, 32
PowerPoint, 89–91, 93, 95, 98, 106, 108, 109, 111, 118, 189
    alternatives to, 94–99
Powerpoint, 94–116
preparation, 10–11, 13, 21–22, 46, 52, 62, 97, 125–127, 159–160, 185
    ratings of, 40
Presenter View, 124
Prezi, 94
Pritchard, Michael, 190
professionalism, ratings of, 39
pronunciation, 45–46
props, 96, 181, 190
public speaking anxiety, *see* nervousness
public speaking classes, 15
push, *see* pitches: push

qualifying language, *see* hedging
qualitative information, 102–105
Quantified Communications, 161
quantitative information, 105–108
questions, 59, 77, 186
quotations, 76

rational emotive therapy, 16
recall, *see* memory
reframing, 16, 19, 141, 151
rejection, 139
relatability, ratings of, 40
relaxation
    ratings of, 32–35
    techniques, 12–14
relevance, 103–104, 117, 125, 140–141, 176–178, 182
    ratings of, 75
remote control, 124–125, 127
repetition, 72–73, 80, 82, 163
respect, ratings of, 40
resting bitch face, 20
retirement fund study, 164
rhyming, 82

right-to-left languages, 37, 112
rigidity, ratings of, 12
rings of Saturn, 177–178
rituals, 23
roadmap, *see* organization: roadmap
Roam, Dan, 102
Robinson, Ken, 191–192
Rokia (one little girl), 152, 191
Roosevelt, Franklin Delano, 16
Rose, David, 160
rule of three, 65, 163

safe driving study, 138
Sandberg, Sheryl, 24
Saturn, 177–178
scatter plots, 115–116
schematics, 110
science curiosity, 150–151
science intelligence, 150
scienceofspeaking.com, 2, 12, 46, 141, 172, 185
scrapbook, *see* organization: scrapbook
seductive details, 182
self-actualization, 155
self-focus, 20–21
self-transcendence, 155
sequential gestures, *see* gestures: sequential gestures
shampoo, 164
Shark Tank, 155, 159–160
shifting weight, 31
signposting, 72
similarities, 40, 143–144
Simon, Carmen, 120
Simonton, Dean, 63
simplicity
    as memory trick, 80
    of visual aids, 120–122
Sinatra test, 160
Sinatra, Frank, 160
sincerity, ratings of, 52
skills training, 15–16
skygazing study, 156
slides, 89–91, 93–95, 111–115, 117–127, 189
SmartArt, 94, 109, 111, 114

smiling, 19, 49, 52, 153
snap judgements, *see* first impressions
Snyder, Elayne, 17
social dancing, 171–172, 175, 184–185, 190
social networks, 109
social obligation, 165–166
social proof, 156
social support, 10–11
solutions, *see* pitches: pull
sound bites, 181
specialized vocabulary, *see* technical language
specificity, 137–138
speech anxiety, *see* nervousness
spotlight effect, 20–21
sprinkler eyes, 51
stage enthusiasm, 17
stage excitement, 17
stage fright, *see* nervousness
stance, 30–35, 106–108
standing still, 31
Stanford Daily, The, 154
Stanford University, 18, 20, 31, 32, 38, 49, 67, 144, 154, 173, 176, 183, 188–190
STAR (Something They'll Always Remember), 180–182, 191–192
starting small, 138
statistics, 76, 152–153, 181
status quo bias, 147, 164
Stein, Ben, 47
stock images, 104
stock price movement, 161
stock traders, 64
stories, 47, 67–73, 76, 152–153, 177–178, 181, 192
Streep, Meryl, 106
strengths, counteracting weaknesses with, 162
stress, 9–11, 13–14, 24, 32, 175
surgeons (and vocal tone), 48
surprise, 52, 69, 77, 151
swaying, 32

sympathy, ratings of, 40

T-rex arms, 37
tapping study, 183
technical communication, 171–194
    curiosity in, 177–178
    drawing a map, 186–188
    enlightening an audience, 183–192
    enthusiasm in, 178–180
    exciting an audience, 175–182
    making it an experience, 189–192
    relevance in, 176–177
    showing the highlights, 188–189
    translating the language, 171–173, 184–186
technical difficulties, 118, 125–127
technical knowledge, 172–173
technical language, 171–173, 184–186
TED, 36, 45, 47, 97, 136, 172, 179, 181, 190, 191
testimonials, 162
tetanus shot study, 148
Texas Department of Transportation, 140–141
"Theory of Human Motivation", 155
thesis, *see* organization: thesis
Thing Explainer, 172
three-peat structure, 73, 163
time, representations of, 112
timelines, 111–112
tip of the iceberg, *see* iceberg model
titles, 69–70, 118–119
tl;dr (too long; didn't read), 67
To Sell Is Human, 133
tolerance, ratings of, 179
tongue twisters, 45–46
topic vs. thesis, 64
tour guide metaphor, 82–83, 184–192
towel reuse study, 156
transitions, 71–72
transparencies, 96
trustworthiness, ratings of, 50, 52, 76, 82, 117, 161
typos, 120

U.S. Army, 67
UC Berkeley, pitching to, 144
uncertainty, effect on emotions, 10
understanding
    audience's, *see* comprehension
    ratings of, 40

VC pitches, 140–141, 155–156, 159–160
Venn diagrams, 110
video, 77, 96–97, 190
videotaping self, 29–30
Vischeck, 118
visual aids, 77, 89–129, 189–191
    in technical presentations,
        189–191
    optimizing, 101–122
    picking types of, 94–99
    presenting with, 123–127
visualization, 12
vocal variation, *see* voice: variation
voice, 30, 43–48, 76, 98, 153
    variation, 47–48, 179
    velocity, 44–47, 179
    volume, 43–44, 179
volume (audio), 97
volunteers, audience, 97

waltz, 171–172, 175, 184–185
Waltzing, 175, 190
weak language, *see* hedging
weaknesses, admitting, 161–162
whiteboard, 95–96, 126, 189
Wilson, Woodrow, 62
Wonder Woman (power pose), 14–15
words per minute (wpm), 44–45
work ethic, 1

xkcd, 172

Zander, Benjamin, 97, 179

This book is set primarily in Alegreya,
drawn by Juan Pablo del Peral for Huerta Tipográfica.
It was designed in LaTeX on a MacBook Pro.
It is published by Cioppino Press in Austin, Texas,
and printed on-demand by CreateSpace.

The cover image is from Adobe Stock.
Many illustrations are adapted from Flaticon.
Author pictures are by Urvi Nagrani.

www.ingramcontent.com/pod-product-compliance
Lightning Source LLC
Chambersburg PA
CBHW071707160426
43195CB00012B/1611